Evelyn Glennie: Sound Creator

Evelyn Glennie:
Sound Creator

Georgina Hughes

THE BOYDELL PRESS

© Georgina Hughes 2024

All Rights Reserved. Except as permitted under current legislation
no part of this work may be photocopied, stored in a retrieval system,
published, performed in public, adapted, broadcast,
transmitted, recorded or reproduced in any form or by any means,
without the prior permission of the copyright owner

The right of Georgina Hughes to be identified as
the author of this work has been asserted in accordance with
sections 77 and 78 of the Copyright, Designs and Patents Act 1988

First published 2024
The Boydell Press, Woodbridge

ISBN 978 1 83765 067 5

The Boydell Press is an imprint of Boydell & Brewer Ltd
PO Box 9, Woodbridge, Suffolk IP12 3DF, UK
and of Boydell & Brewer Inc.
668 Mt Hope Avenue, Rochester, NY 14620–2731, USA
website: www.boydellandbrewer.com

A CIP catalogue record for this book is available
from the British Library

The publisher has no responsibility for the continued existence or accuracy of URLs for
external or third-party internet websites referred to in this book, and does not guaran-
tee that any content on such websites is, or will remain, accurate or appropriate

Contents

List of Figures	vi
List of Music Examples	vii
List of Tables	viii
Acknowledgements	ix

Introduction
"I shall just have to try harder to convince you."
Glennie's Early Career — 1

Chapter 1
"Of course, I just assumed that the world was full of solo percussionists."
The Ascendance of Solo Multi-Percussion Performance — 12

Chapter 2
"I just basically followed my own instincts."
Diversification, Improvisation and Collaboration — 61

Chapter 3
"I'm simply a person who wants to encourage females to do whatever they want to do."
The Issue of Gender — 101

Chapter 4
"I'm not a deaf musician. I'm a musician who happens to be deaf."
Inclusion — 146

Chapter 5
"I hope the seeds I have sown will be taken up by those who follow me."
Legacy: A Series of New Beginnings — 193

Conclusion
"To Teach the World to Listen" — 231

Appendix 1: Concerto Commissions	234
Appendix 2: Solo Commissions	247
Bibliography	256
Videography and Audio Resources	266
Index	269

Figures

Unless otherwise specified, images and permissions are kindly granted by The Evelyn Glennie Collection.

1	Glennie as a student at the Royal Academy of Music (1985)	6
2	Glennie at the Batonka (October 2000). Permission kindly granted by The Evelyn Glennie Collection and Will Embliss	32
3	The Glennie Concert Aluphone	34
4	Glennie rehearsing *Veni, Veni Emmanuel* in Beijing (1997) using instruments from her own collection	41
5	Instrument configuration for *Sounds of Science* world premiere	51
6	Poster for Animotion residency at Edinburgh Fringe Festival	83
7	Trio HLK(G)	92
8	*Light in Darkness* (1991)	108
9	Glennie in rehearsals for *My Dream Kitchen*	111
10	Percussion station for first movement of *Conjurer.* Permission kindly granted by Wise Music Group	124
11	Prototype sketch for pendant (in collaboration with Ortak)	142
12	The Evelyn Glennie Foundation (established 2023)	193
13	Awards received from Her Majesty Queen Elizabeth II	208
14	A selection of instruments from The Evelyn Glennie Collection	215
15	Glennie's first snare drum	228

Musical Examples

1 Aluphone solo in *Heartland Concerto* (© Mark Bowden/ Composers Edition) — 36

2 Scoring for voice in *Sounds of Science* (© Jill Jarman) — 53

3 Percussionist as pianist in *Sounds of Science* (© Jill Jarman) — 54

4 Opening of *Whisper*, using a range of effects on cymbals (Music by Sally Beamish, © 2015 Peters Edition Limited) — 57

5 Opening of "Extra Sensory Perception Part I" (© Richard Harrold/Trio HLK) — 89

6 Opening marimba line for *"The Jig"* (© Richard Harrold/Trio HLK) — 91

7 *My Dream Kitchen* saucepan motif (© Django Bates) — 113

8 *My Dream Kitchen* marimba melody (© Django Bates) — 114

9 Opening of "Wood" cadenza in *Conjurer* (John Corigliano, © Chester Music Limited t/a G. Schirmer Inc.) — 125

10 Balance between specificity and freedom in *Drum of Orfeo* (Marta Ptaszyńska, © Polskie Wydawnictwo Muzyczne, Kraków, Poland) — 131

11 "And I Will Kiss" ostinato figurations. Transcription based on recording of the Olympics Opening Ceremony. Original scoring by Rick Smith — 181

12 Vibraphone in "Awakening Part I" from *The Language of Bells* (© Jill Jarman) — 191

13 "Cressida's Theme" from *Troilus and Cressida* (© Evelyn Glennie and Dave Price) — 199

14 Marimba opening of "Da Vinci's Wings" from *Dreamachine* (Michael Daugherty Music, © 2014 Michael Daugherty) — 223

Tables

1	1989 programme for Glennie's BBC Proms recital	25
2	Structure and instrumentation, *UFO* (Michael Daugherty)	43
3	Instrumentation for YouTube series *Playing Around the Office*	59
4	Speakers at the "Women in Power" fashion show	137
5	Headlines referencing deafness	157
6	Programme for *The Language of Bells* world premiere	190

Acknowledgements

Though the genesis of this book is relatively recent, it is fair to state that its foundations date to my childhood. At the age of eight, I started percussion lessons and quickly became immersed in the joy of making music in an infinite number of ways. Seguing from performance to academia, my role as advocate for the discipline is now primarily in the context of research, sharing my own passion for percussion with others. *Evelyn Glennie: Sound Creator* is a reflection of this vocation.

The opportunity to write a book about Glennie was supported at every stage by Boydell & Brewer. Michael Midekke, in particular, has been a positive and motivating presence from our earliest interactions. I thank him sincerely for sharing my vision for the publication.

No author can reach this point without the advice and guidance of inspiring mentors at all stages of their professional development. To my percussion tutors Tommy Thomas and Monica Bonnie, I thank you for sharing your love of performance with me. Your legacies live on in the many successes of your students. To my PhD supervisor Professor Wolfgang Marx, I am forever grateful for your belief in my potential.

In relation to the book specifically, I have been fortunate to benefit from interactions with composers, performers and innovators who gave so willingly of their time and expertise. Particular gratitude is extended to Michael Daugherty, Jill Jarman, Rich Harrold, Marta Ptaszyńska, Will Embliss, Dave Price, Mark Bowden and Django Bates for your invaluable insights into the creative process.

Special thanks must go to all staff at The Evelyn Glennie Office, especially Emma and Rae, who have always graciously responded to my many requests. Caroline Thompson, head archivist of The Evelyn Glennie Collection, has been essential to my research journey. She embodies the spirit of volunteerism and collaboration to which we should all aspire.

Though everyone named above has been invaluable, the book would simply not have been possible without the limitless patience of Evelyn Glennie. She has given her time, insights, resources and memories to this research. Over the course of multiple interviews, queries and requests, she has provided unrestricted access. I thank her sincerely for trusting me with her history.

My last words of acknowledgement are reserved for my family and friends, who have never doubted that this publication would come to fruition. To my sister Amy, for being a source of both musical and personal assistance, I appreciate everything. To my parents, Brigina and George, who have unflinchingly supported every new adventure. Finally, to my husband Fergal and my two glorious children, Clara and Imogen. Thank you for giving me the time, space and support to make this dream a reality.

Introduction

"I shall just have to try harder to convince you."

Glennie's Early Career

Percussion instruments are defined as those which are struck, shaken or scraped. This broad description is at once extraordinarily simple and immensely complex. Theoretically, any object can become an instrument and anyone can produce sound using these three fundamental techniques. How does one define the identity of the percussionist when sound is everywhere and when everything is percussion? History does not enjoy chaos; the anachronistic nature of a discipline which is both immediately accessible and forebodingly confusing is problematic. Art music determined that the first solution was to divide the instruments of percussion into two categories as they made their way tentatively into the language of Classical and Romantic repertoire. Tuned percussion was separated from untuned (unpitched, auxiliary) in this initial semblance of order, immediately establishing a hierarchy where the latter was deemed inferior. As auxiliary percussion became a presence in the orchestra, it was burdened with a number of negative assumptions connected to this dichotomy. These instruments were categorized as noise-makers and sound effects relegated to the periphery of art music, misunderstood and undervalued addendums to instrumental repertoire. Perceptions of percussion instruments as colouristic, exotic novelties pervaded discourse in orchestration manuals well into the twentieth century. Percussionists were similarly subsumed into reductive tropes whereby their art was misjudged and dismissed as less important or difficult than that of their peers.

As rhythm and timbre assumed new levels of significance in avant-garde composition, this narrative began to gradually shift. The immediacy of auxiliary percussion in particular – its primal and instinctive connections to sound creation – became for some composers a unique attribute. In the second half of the twentieth century, percussion was emancipated from ensemble repertoire, and solo performers were immediately keen to embrace the opportunity. Figures such as Max Neuhaus (1939–2009), Christoph Caskel (1932–2023) and Sylvio Gualda (1939–) instigated new trajectories for the discipline, and the concept of the virtuosic solo multi-percussionist was born. From its inception, the enigmatic and highly subjective nature of interpreting solo percussion repertoire has remained inextricably connected to skilled and charismatic performers with the capacity to create musical meaning from a disparate range of sounding objects. The percussionist is the instrument; in no other discipline is the experience of live performance more important.

When one witnesses a virtuosic percussionist perform, it is easy to forget the othering of percussion in the history of Western art music. This limitless medium of musical communication confounds and enthrals in equal measure; it retains a sense of instinctive connection whilst also offering the listener entirely unanticipated sensory experiences. Percussion offers creative freedom, beholden to no single culture, musical genre, social class or historical period. Solo multi-percussion is a language of extremes, a blurring of dichotomies, a revocation of dated ideologies, and an enticing invitation to engage with the myriad potentialities of sound. The ongoing emergence of new instruments, techniques and repertoire means that the oldest instrumental discipline known to man is somehow still the most vibrant and innovative. For the solo percussionist, ambiguity, upheaval and metamorphosis are embraced in a world of sound which wilfully eludes categorization; they are part of a creative journey with infinite potential.

The work of Dame Evelyn Glennie exemplifies the unique and unpredictable nature of percussion performance. For over five decades she has promoted, sustained and diversified the remit of the solo multi-percussionist, achieving recognition as both a respected musical role model and a popular public figure. Her broad appeal has meant that the fascinations of percussion have at times merged with other equally intriguing narratives, most notably in relation to the fact that Glennie is a deaf musician and a female pioneer working in a traditionally male instrumental discipline. Any comprehensive study of Glennie must therefore address the fact that her significance is intersectional; musical innovations are connected to larger social and cultural issues pertaining particularly (though not exclusively) to gender and disability; as sound creator and expert listener, she has challenged othering both within and beyond the sphere of performance.

Glennie's definitive arrival into the cultural zeitgeist dates to the first solo multi-percussion recital in the history of the BBC Proms. On the stage of Kensington Town Hall (London) in July 1989, Glennie generated palpable excitement for the potentialities of the discipline. The challenges, efforts, rejections and decisive moments which predate this seminal performance are addressed in Glennie's early autobiography *Good Vibrations* (1990). This publication will appraise Glennie's career largely from the point at which *Good Vibrations* concludes, but it is useful to provide a brief account of the experiences which Glennie chose to discuss therein as a prelude to the creative trajectory which follows.

Glennie describes her childhood in a rural Aberdeenshire community under the chapter title "Halcyon Days", idyllic formative years filled with exploration, freedom, cultural richness, national pride and access to an impressive range of music-making activities. Her interest in music and aptitude for performance began at an early age, with lessons on recorder, piano and clarinet seguing to percussion at the age of twelve. This coincided almost directly with the diagnosis of profound deafness in the same year, though the two are not connected. Whilst the multi-sensory nature of percussion is unquestionably suited to diverse modes of listening and engagement, Glennie's choice of instrumental discipline was not born of necessity. As she notes:

> People often ask me why I decided to take up percussion ... I was quite sure that it was what I wanted to do, and my enthusiasm may have dated back to the time a little earlier when I went to a local talent show and saw a young girl playing the xylophone. She was brilliant, just amazing.[1]

Glennie received peripatetic percussion tuition from Ron Forbes, the oft-cited mentor who encouraged her to experience sounds through the body, accessing vibrations and resonance as a supplement to auditory perception. Forbes recognized both the musical potential and ambition of his young student from their first encounter: "She had all the ingredients for becoming a good player. But she didn't want to be good; she wanted to be better than good."[2]

Membership of the Cults Percussion Ensemble (named after the Aberdeen suburb where they rehearsed), a group of accomplished school-aged performers led by Forbes, was a key rite of passage in these early stages. The percussion ensemble articulates the beauty and range of the discipline whilst also offering performers greater challenges than can typically be found in orchestral repertoire. Though preceded by several earlier experimental works by George Antheil (*Ballet Mécanique*, 1924) and Amadeo

---

[1] Evelyn Glennie (1990) *Good Vibrations: My Autobiography*. London: Hutchinson, pp. 42–43.

[2] Ron Forbes in Polar Music Prize (2015) *Polar Music Prize Laureate Dame Evelyn Glennie Meets Her First Percussion Tutor Ron Forbes* (video online), 13 June 2015. Available from: https://www.youtube.com/watch?v=1ZNcMMx_J2I&t=52s (accessed 13 June 2023).

Roldán (*Ritmicas Nos 5 and 6*, 1930), the percussion ensemble in Western art music definitively begins with Edgard Varèse's *Ionisation* (1931). Despite its relative brevity (averaging five minutes in performance), *Ionisation* is a complex work scored for thirteen performers playing thirty-nine instruments. Varèse emancipated percussion from the orchestra in an emphatic manner, focusing on the sound colours of auxiliary instruments. *Ionisation* premiered in New York on 6 March 1933, and the US remained the locus of percussion ensemble creativity in the decades which followed. In 1938, John Cage formed The Cage Percussion Ensemble, and subsequently established percussion ensembles in Seattle, San Francisco, Chicago and New York; he composed fifteen works for percussion between 1935 and 1943, and his fascination with the prepared piano (from 1938) is also connected, given that this instrument is effectively a self-contained percussion ensemble. For experimental composers, percussion offered freedom from ideological confines. As stated by Cage: "Percussion music is revolution."[3]

The birth of the percussion ensemble in Western music was fundamentally aligned with American experimentalism, but in order to establish the concept as an enduring presence in chamber music, pedagogical advancements were required. Paul Price is synonymous with the emergence of the college percussion ensemble in the US, establishing the first at the University of Illinois in 1950; by the end of the decade many music departments in the country had followed his lead. The UK higher education system was slower to respond, and the Cults Percussion Ensemble represented a pioneering early effort to introduce this medium to British audiences and composers. Though the repertoire for the group reflected the young, amateur demographic of its members, the experience proved important for Glennie for two reasons: it allowed her to play more difficult repertoire in various concert contexts and it consolidated her vision of a career as a solo performer.

Forbes proved to be an important mentor to Glennie, and her time in Cults a formative period which had a lasting impact on her understanding of the role of the percussionist: "He felt that all his pupils were first and foremost sound creators, then musicians, and then percussion players, as opposed to percussion players, then musicians who happen to create sound."[4] *Good Vibrations* addresses both the positive and negative experiences of participating in the ensemble, reflecting enjoyment of the

---

[3]   John Cage (1961) *Silence*. Middleton: Wesleyan, p. 87.
[4]   Evelyn Glennie in David Childs (2015) The Dame of Percussion, *Brass Band World* (online). Available from: https://www.brassbandworld.co.uk/features/705/the-dame-of-percussion (accessed 10 May 2017).

performance experiences but also being honest about the jealousy, exclusion and lack of sufficient challenge which further contributed to Glennie's desire to work as a soloist.

A 1979 album titled *The Cults Percussion Ensemble* was re-released in 2012, due in no small part to Glennie's presence on the recording at a time when her public profile was particularly high (as a leading performer at the Opening Ceremony of the London 2012 Olympic Games). Focused on the calming and ethereal sonorities of tuned percussion (marimba and vibraphone in particular), the recording relies largely on steady, repetitive rhythmic figurations and tonal melodies. Auxiliary percussion provides timbral interest and articulates standard rhythmic patterns intended to denote Latin American references (as in "Baia") or to complement folk tunes (including "My Love, She's But a Lassie Yet" and "Irish Washerwoman"). Glennie aspired to further opportunities in her later teens (particularly in relation to sourcing more diverse and experimental repertoire), but the Cults Ensemble unquestionably contributed to her musical evolution: "Although time-wise it was a brief moment I do wonder if my development may have been different if I had not had that experience. Every aspect of being a future touring solo musician was addressed in the ensemble days."[5]

Glennie auditioned for both the Royal College of Music and Royal Academy of Music in London at the age of sixteen. Despite meeting all criteria for the academy (her preferred institution), Glennie was initially refused admission. Glennie discusses the process in her 2003 TED Talk ("How to Truly Listen") and in the Riedelsheimer documentary *Touch the Sound* (2004); her refusal to accept discriminatory judgements on the basis of disability changed the admissions system for all subsequent applicants:

> I then auditioned for the Royal Academy of Music in London and they said, "Well, no. We won't accept you because we haven't a clue of the future of a so-called deaf musician." And I just couldn't quite accept that. So therefore I said to them, "Well look; if you refuse me through those reasons, as opposed to the ability to perform and to understand and love the art of creating sound, then we have to think very hard about the people you do actually accept."[6]

During the course of her undergraduate studies, the foundations of Glennie's future career were established in terms of both professional accomplishment and media interest. Awards for musicianship (including the Gold Medal from the Shell/London Symphony Orchestra Scholarship

---

[5] Interview with Glennie, 4 May 2017.

[6] Evelyn Glennie in Thomas Riedelsheimer (2004) *Touch the Sound: A Sound Journey with Evelyn Glennie* (DVD) Docurama.

Fig. 1: Glennie as a student at the Royal Academy of Music (1985).

in 1984, the Hilda Deane Anderson Prize for Orchestral Playing in 1985 and the Queen's Commendation for All-Round Excellence in the same year) were juxtaposed with increased interest from the general public, which commonly conflated the intrigues of percussion with the equally fascinating narrative of a deaf virtuosic performer. Glennie's first television appearance in 1985, a documentary titled *A Will to Win* (BBC) offers an indicative example, followed shortly thereafter with Yorkshire Television's *Good Vibrations* (which followed a similarly triumphant trajectory). Whilst Glennie's intention to pursue a career as a solo multi-percussionist was not necessarily an ambition shared by all of her lecturers, she benefitted greatly from the enduring support of one mentor at the academy. James Blades, a predecessor who had already made significant contributions to the development of new creative paths for percussion in the UK, notes succinctly that "in 1982, she became my student – or I hers".[7] An experienced and respected performer and pedagogue, Blades instilled in Glennie a lifelong awareness of the multi-faceted nature of the contemporary percussionist's role. In musical terms, this meant a willingness to embrace an eclectic range of musical genres and performance contexts. For Blades, the experience of employment in a circus band was as valid and important as engagements with some of the most prestigious ensembles in the UK (including the London Symphony Orchestra, Melos Ensemble and the English Opera Group). On a larger scale, Blades demonstrated that the work of any percussionist must extend beyond performance into teaching, advocacy and promotion of the discipline. In a 1997 interview, Glennie acknowledged the ways in which Blades continued to influence her work ethic many years after their formal student–teacher relationship had ended: "I don't think a day goes past when I don't think about him at some stage – that's pretty incredible. I'll be at a particular point and think, 'What would you do James?' Every time we meet is a moment to treasure."[8] In the lineage of UK percussionists, Glennie is directly descended from Blades' pioneering efforts to demonstrate and advance the evolution of percussion. Blades encouraged wider engagement and interaction (as a teacher, writer, academic and performer); Glennie brought it to virtuosic heights and the public consciousness. Blades was interested in seeking out new repertoire; Glennie actively commissioned it. Blades invented and promoted new instrumental sonorities (often in collaboration with Benjamin Britten); Glennie extended the remit of solo multi-percussionist to that of sound creator.

The timeline of Glennie's evolution oftentimes omits the transitional period between graduation in 1985 and her Proms performance in 1989. However, many of the defining features of her professional identity were consolidated during this time. Entrepreneurship, exhaustive touring, engaging with a diverse range of repertoire and serving as a representative

---

[7] Hester Lacey (1994) How We Met: James Blades and Evelyn Glennie, *Independent* (online), 21 May 1994. Available from: https://www.independent.co.uk.arts-entertainment/how-we-met-james-blades-and-evelyn-glennie-1437629.html (accessed 10 July 2017).

[8] Emily Moore (1997) My Inspiration: Evelyn Glennie and Her Favourite Teacher Spill the Beans About Each Other, *Guardian*, Education Supplement, 2 December 1997.

for solo percussion contributed to the successes which followed the Proms recital. In 1986, Glennie received a bursary from the Arts Council (the Henry and Lily Davis Fund) to study with marimba virtuoso, composer and improviser Keiko Abe in Japan, whom she previously met at a Royal College of Music masterclass. Abe is a seminal figure in the development of marimba repertoire (particularly in the context of art music). She began her career in 1962 as a founding member of the Xebec Marimba Trio, a commercially successful ensemble which performed transcriptions of Latin American, folk, ragtime and jazz standards. Abe was keen to advance further as a performer, and assumed the role of composer and commissioner in order to create works which offered new directions for the instrument. Her first US performance at the 1977 Percussive Arts Society International Convention (Knoxville, Tennessee), where she presented works by a range of Japanese composers (including Akira Miyoshi, Minoru Miki and Toshimitsu Tanaka), redefined the nature of tuned percussion:

> People were absolutely stunned by her artistry. Abe played at the highest artistic level – a level that musicians in the United States had no concept of – and there was general agreement that she had brought art music to the world of percussion.[9]

Glennie's lessons with Abe allowed her to explore the creative freedom of improvisation, and to engage with works reflective of Japanese practices and philosophies. In three weeks, Glennie studied the communicative power of percussion, with Abe choosing to focus less on technique than on the performer's capacity to establish holistic connections between instrument, repertoire and listener. Music from Japan has remained an abiding feature of Glennie's output, as has interest in improvising on both tuned and untuned instruments. Indicative examples include Abe's *Michi* on Glennie's second CD release *Rhythm Song* (1990), *Wind in the Bamboo Grove* (1995), an album dedicated entirely to works by Japanese composers, and the later *Ecstatic Drumbeat* (2012). As Glennie notes: "Keiko's music has influenced me because they are written-down improvisations ... That freedom really is fitting to how I am as a performer."[10]

Before becoming synonymous with the commissioning and premiering of new repertoire for multi-percussion, Glennie emulated many of her predecessors in interpreting extant works including Bartók's *Sonata for Two Pianos and Percussion* in the years following graduation. Since its composition in 1937, the Bartók sonata has become a rite of passage

---

[9] Tom Siwe in Rebecca Kite (2007) *Keiko Abe: A Virtuosic Life.* Leesburg: GP Percussion, p. 86.

[10] Interview with Glennie, 14 September 2017.

for percussionists, with numerous performances and recordings demonstrating its enduring appeal. Premiered in 1938 (with Bartók and his wife Ditta on piano), percussionists Fritz Schiesser and Philipp Rühig were the first to realize a soundscape which creates the aural effect of an extended piano. An innovative chamber configuration featuring nine sonorities (piano, timpani, bass drum, cymbals, snare drum, triangle, tam-tam and xylophone) the work is a study in balance, nuance, timbre and synergy. In a folder of collated research and reflections on the sonata written during her studies at the Royal Academy, Glennie notes that her first experience of the work dates to 1984, in a collaboration with Canadian pianists Ralph Markham and Kenneth Broadway and fellow Royal Academy percussionist Chris Thomas; two performances followed in 1985, preceded by considerable obstacles in terms of accessing equipment, rehearsal space and time needed to practice as an ensemble: "We eventually got our way (Chris and I threatened to leave the RAM if we were deprived the chance of playing the sonata) ... Finding people enthusiastic enough to discuss and advise me on my part for the work was also difficult. Now I admire how I handled it myself." Glennie's next three performances of the Bartók sonata in 1986 were well received in an ensemble featuring pianists Bracha Eden and Alexander Tamir and percussionist Nigel Thomas. At the venerable Aldeburgh Festival one year later (a seminal site of musical innovation and collaboration initiated by Britten in 1948), Glennie again undertook Bartók's work, in this instance aligned with George Solti and Murray Perahia (pianists) and David Corkhill (percussion). This culminated in a 1988 Grammy Award (for best chamber music performance). At the age of twenty-two, Glennie was a Grammy winner.

A documentary chronicling the creative process of recording the work remains on YouTube as an evocative insight into the collaborative experience.[11] The original programme title, *Solti and Perahia play Bartok*, articulates the power balance in the ensemble (both in terms of the remit of the composition and the public profile of the performers involved). Glennie is introduced as "a young soloist of outstanding talent", juxtaposed with Corkhill's status as "first percussionist of the Philharmonia Orchestra", also an indication of the hierarchy within the percussion pairing. As a section leader, it is unsurprising to see Corkhill assume the role of timpanist (Percussion I), a position invariably occupied by male performers. Assigned

---

[11] Evelyn Glennie (2012) *A rare interesting documentary 1988 Grammy winner recording of Bartok's sonata* (videos online). Available from: https://www.youtube.com/watch?v=A6fyDv-Q3v4, https://www.youtube.com/watch?v=qjorUBaLc2c, and https://www.youtube.com/watch?v=A6MQHFe8loo (accessed 18 November 2022).

Percussion II, the xylophone is the most prominent feature of Glennie's part, supported by bass drum, two snare drums, triangle, tam-tam and cymbals. Interactions are largely centred on decisions made by Solti, in discourse with Perahia; Glennie and Corkhill oftentimes await direction from their peers. Though percussion is important, in Bartók's composition it remains subservient to the primacy of the pianists; the same chain of command is evident in the collaboration. The profession of solo multi-percussionist was subsequently liberated from such conventions and precedents, though it remains intrinsically connected to the larger ecosystem of the music industry. Though Glennie has moved from the ensemble to centre-stage, her success is connected to the support of mentors, the inspiration of peers, the shared creativity of collaborators and the energy of live performance received and reciprocated by her audience. She is a soloist, but she is also keenly aware of the fact that music-making is an inherently social activity; the art of the performer is one which only becomes meaningful when it is shared in a manner that persuades people to listen. Glennie's timeline can be mapped according to the most notable awards, prestigious events, critically acclaimed recordings and prominent "firsts", but as *Good Vibrations* attests, each seminal moment is preceded by considerable effort, hard work, experimentation and risk-taking. The case studies in this publication will often highlight career-defining innovations, but they are also invested in appraising the spaces in between – the unheard and unseen realities of a career in the creative industries. The business of music, the importance of self-promotion and marketing, the scrutiny of the media, active engagement with potential collaborators, the necessity of developing a diverse portfolio and awareness of the social responsibility of the artist are all pertinent to the success of what has become the Evelyn Glennie brand.

The ascendance of the solo multi-percussionist in the late twentieth century, a largely unanticipated phenomenon in the evolution of art music, has escaped the limitations of ensemble repertoire in both practical and philosophical terms. Early divisions between tuned and untuned have been subsumed into a musical language which embraces all sounds; questions concerning the percussionist's skills are answered in a discipline modelling embodied, holistic and experimental performance practice. Sometimes, it is good to be an outsider; the trajectory of solo multi-percussion has been a blank canvas open to new creative paths without convention or precedent. Percussion is indeed everywhere and in everything; the percussionist finds ways to embrace and celebrate this limitless potential.

In order to summarize Glennie's professional evolution, it is perhaps pertinent to employ a metaphor. The germination of solo percussion started before Glennie, in the tumultuous and divergent music of experimental composers and pioneering performers; the emergence of a globally recognized virtuosic solo multi-percussionist is the flowering of that seed. Commissions and collaborations are the pollination of diverse and distant fields and meadows. Expansion into activism and philanthropy is the blossoming of the discipline in new soils. Glennie's work matters beyond the realm of solo percussion; solo percussion matters beyond the world of music; music matters beyond the domain of art; artistic creativity matters to all. This publication is a case study on the contributions of one performer, but ultimately, it is an ode to the power and beauty of percussion. It is an invocation for us all to respond to our own potential to become sound creators and expert listeners both within and beyond the domain of music.

1

"Of course, I just assumed that the world was full of solo percussionists."
The Ascendance of Solo Multi-Percussion Performance

The optimistic Glennie quotation which serves as a title for this chapter offers an appealing disregard for the many ideological obstacles faced by percussion in the timeline of Western art music. The timpani entered the Baroque orchestra directly from the battlefield, and the tentative integration of new sonorities during the course of the Classical and Romantic eras offered few challenges for the performer. With limited repertoire, and a role confined largely to colouristic effect, percussionists and their instruments were assumed to be devoid of potential. As summarized unequivocally in Fidler's 1921 *Handbook of Orchestration*: "The percussion instruments are the least important, the most conspicuous, the most rhythmical, the easiest to write for and the easiest to play."[1]

Though the diversity and experimentation of the twentieth century facilitated further opportunities, the emancipation of solo multi-percussion has been tentative and gradual. Writing in a language of rhythm and timbre for an unlimited range of diverse instruments means that it remains a challenge to compose for multi-percussion. As Glennie's commissioning began in the mid-1980s, there was further advocacy and collaboration required to fully realize the potential of the discipline for virtuosic performers: "There were no real rejections, actually, no 'I don't want to do this'. It was more a

---

[1]   Florence G. Fidler (1921) *A Handbook of Orchestration*. London: Kegan Paul, Trench, Trubner and Co., p. 101.

case of 'Oh crumbs, that's interesting. I'm not quite sure how to write for solo percussion' and so it was a case of nurturing that conversation."[2]

Multi-percussion comes to life when rules and conventions are disregarded, when innovation and experimentation are elevated, and when performers are willing to embrace the challenge of the new. The history of multi-percussion is ultimately a history of performance. As is always the case in Western art music, composers are associated with seminal works and transitions, but it is in the hands of the percussionist where progress is fully realized. This chapter will provide historical context for the evolution of solo multi-percussion, referencing the performers who presented this emerging discipline to the public. This is followed with examination of Glennie's role as commissioner and advocate for the creative potential of the contemporary percussionist.

Historical Context

Multi-percussion describes any composition whereby a single performer is scored to play two or more instruments during the course of a single work. First employed in ensemble repertoire, the multi-percussionist evolved as the consequence of several pragmatic and aesthetic factors in the early decades of the twentieth century. Difficult economic times in the post-war years meant that orchestral percussionists were often asked to play multiple parts in a labour-saving effort; percussive sonorities reflected the emancipation of noise and the growing significance of timbre in avant-garde and experimental music; greater interest in non-Western practices and instruments extended the vocabulary of the percussionist; the influence of popular music – particularly the jazz drum kit – was drawn into art music.

The impact of the latter can be discerned in the earliest scoring for multi-percussion, Igor Stravinsky's *L'Histoire du Soldat* (1918). Written for a chamber ensemble of seven performers, this serves as an important ancestor of solo repertoire. A theatrical work integrating text, dance and music, it also intimates the subsequent direction of solo multi-percussion wherein the soloist functions as dramatist, storyteller and musician. Stravinsky scored for standard auxiliary instruments, creating in effect an expanded drum kit (two snare drums without snares, field drum with and without snares, bass drum, suspended cymbal, tambourine and triangle). Whilst percussive sonorities are an exposed presence in several movements of the septet, the scoring is not difficult for the performer. Stravinsky

---

[2] Interview with Glennie, 27 June 2023.

himself purchased the percussion instruments to learn how to play the part, channelling practical knowledge into the compositional process, but also likely contributing to the relative lack of challenge in the writing. Later composers for multi-percussion would extend Stravinsky's approach, often working directly with percussionists and their instruments in order to gain a more holistic understanding of timbres, techniques and practicalities. In *L'Histoire*, percussion remains colouristic, used to heighten the militaristic tone of the march movements and to allude to popular genres in the "Tango" and "Ragtime" sections; the percussionist had been given more to do, but they had not yet eschewed the confines of ensemble performance.

Darius Milhaud's *Concerto for Percussion and Small Orchestra* (1930) represents the first definitive effort to establish multi-percussion as a solo entity. The rationale for composing this percussion concerto initiated an important precedent witnessed in much of the repertoire which follows: Milhaud was commissioned by a particular performer seeking stimulating repertoire. In this instance, the work was created in collaboration with timpanist Theo Coutelier.[3] The work is scored for an impressive array of primarily untuned percussion instruments (four timpani, three drums, bass drum with foot pedal and cymbal, suspended cymbal, crash cymbal, tam-tam, triangle, wood block, metal block, castanets, tambourine, ratchet and whip). The effect of watching the performer create unity from these disparate elements is unquestionably an important feature and one which Milhaud was cognizant of; the fact that he included a diagram for instrument placement in the score creates an imposing configuration whereby the percussionist is encircled by their instruments. Milhaud's concerto consists of a single two-part movement (generally performed in around seven minutes), and is accompanied by chamber ensemble, offering a somewhat muted interpretation of the dramatic potential of juxtaposing soloist and orchestra. The greatest technical challenge lies in the frequent alternations of time signature and more practically in transitioning between instruments and stick types. The primary focus is on creating musical meaning through the language of auxiliary percussion, using gesture to shape phrases, moving around the set-up with fluency, and exploring nuances of tone colour and dynamics. Glennie first performed the concerto in 1988, and it remained part of her programming until 1997. Her interpretation

---

[3]   "[Theo Coutelier] asked me if I would like to write a concerto for only one percussion performer. He wished to use his piece for his examinations. The idea appealed to me, and this is how I came to compose the concerto." Darius Milhaud (1930) Work Introduction, from *Concerto Pour Batterie et Petit Orchestre*. Vienna: Universal Edition.

features on the 1992 CD release *Rebounds* (a selection of percussion concertos composed between 1930 and 1990).

By the middle of the twentieth century, percussionists were tasked with increasingly diverse modes of scoring, instrumentation and technical demands. Their role in chamber and orchestral repertoire was now consolidated with access to works written specifically for percussion ensemble. The next stage was complete liberation into the uncharted domain of solo repertoire. Cage's *27' 10.554"* (1956) signifies the first effort to fully realize the potential of multi-percussion as a solo entity, followed relatively closely by Karlheinz Stockhausen's *Zyklus* (1959: the first solo multi-percussion work with specified instrumentation), Morton Feldman's *The King of Denmark* (1964) and Iannis Xenakis' *Psappha* (1975). Each of the four compositions, although extremely divergent in many ways, share several common features which informed subsequent writing for solo percussion.

All four use graphic notation, indicative of an interest in exploring the ways in which timbral changes could be scored for auxiliary instruments whilst also providing the performer with greater interpretative autonomy. To define the use of graphic scores as a commonality is somewhat anachronistic given that this form of notation is defined by the very fact that standardization is inconceivable; approaches to scoring are often unique to a particular work or to the opus of an individual composer. *27'10.554"* is a montage of lines, dots and various shapes to be constructed into a performance centred on "an exhaustive rather than conventional use of the instruments".[4] *Zyklus* combines conventional and graphic notation to create a work of considerable intellectual, technical and interpretative challenge. Stockhausen directs the soloist to begin the performance on any page of the score and then move either forwards or backwards through it, coinciding with cyclic movement around the percussion set-up. Clockwise motion informs the audience that the performer has chosen to move towards increasing ambiguity and improvisation whilst anticlockwise motion leads the player towards greater certainty and notational specificity. *The King of Denmark* forms part of a series of works whereby Feldman composed onto graph paper, rejecting traditional scoring methods in order to reflect the fluidity of the medium: "Because this music was not 'fixed', it could not be notated in the old way. Each new thought, each new idea within this thought, suggested its own notation."[5] The score for *Psappha* places performance directives on a grid

---

[4] John Cage (1960) *27'10.554" For a Percussionist*. New York: Henmar Press Inc./C.F Peters Corporation.

[5] Morton Feldman in Walter Zimmerman (1985) *Morton Feldman Essays*. Kerpen: Beginner Press, p. 48.

with symbols, bar numbers, and very little else. Meticulous guidelines on interpreting the score were provided in a preface by Xenakis, and effective realization of the work is inconceivable without comprehensive study of these directives. Well suited to the exploratory and experimental ethos of the composers who initiated the evolution of solo multi-percussion, graphic scoring has not remained a consistent feature of repertoire for the discipline. A solution to the challenge of harnessing the language of timbre in the developmental stages, staff notation returned in subsequent years, albeit with considerable amendments, extensions and directives.

The use of graphic scoring denotes a heightened degree of performer-determination which was further consolidated in other ways. In *27'10.554"*, *The King of Denmark* and *Psappha* the performer is permitted, within certain parameters, to create their own instrumental configuration. All four also elevate the status of silence, allowing the player to make subjective decisions on duration at such points. As repertoire has evolved, this dramatic juxtaposition aligning the cacophony and occasional brutality of multi-percussion with oppositional moments of rest has remained a recurrent feature. Silence is itself a challenge to the multi-percussionist, who must ensure that the continuity and organicism of the work as a whole is not diminished by pauses; this is where gesture becomes intrinsic to effective execution of the score. In many interpretations of *27'10.554"*, periods of silence are elongated to allow the listener to interact with incidental ambient sounds; the world of the performance becomes a living percussion instrument. Silence in *Zyklus* is most tangible during the least dense parts of the cycle, where the player is directed more specifically in the score. In this instance, rests are utilized to create a sense of calm before chaos or (if played in the opposite direction) of clarity following ambiguity. Either way, silence assumes both structural and aesthetic significance, an ever-fluid means of transitioning between action and stillness. The intention is that the work evolves in an instinctive manner, though the audience will be unaware if interpretative decisions are made in advance or in real time. Christoph Caskel, who premiered the work in 1959, admitted that in rehearsing *Zyklus* he had made definitive determinations about the order of events:

> Christoph Caskel, brilliant young percussionist who performed *Zyklus*, upset the composer somewhat at a preconcert enthusiasts' rally by saying he had found the work quite a chore and had simplified his task by always playing the bits in the same order, which, apparently, wasn't quite the intended idea.[6]

---

[6] Ken Winters (1960) Perspectives: The Paris Music Season 1959–60, *Canadian Music Journal*, 4 (4), p. 43.

In the early stages of her career, Glennie performed *Zyklus* six times between 1987 and 1993. Unable to access extant recordings of earlier interpretations, there was freedom by default in her performances. Glennie did not play *Zyklus* in the same direction every time; having studied the score she wanted to respond as fully as possible to Stockhausen's vision of a gradually unfolding live experience for both performer and listener:

> It just made me realize that I had to believe in my own kind of direction with the piece, my own decision-making, and just go with that really. I think after that [first] performance I gained a lot of confidence because I felt that I had created some sort of structure that the audience could feel and get emotion from. I remember the reaction being really positive. Basically, I did change direction. There were passages that were improvised: some of them were spontaneous, some of them were planned.[7]

The King of Denmark is a study of the fine balance between sound and silence. Instruments are struck only with the fingers, fingernails, hands and elbows, with gesture and anticipation as significant as the auditory experience. A *New York Times* review of the premiere performance (by percussionist Max Neuhaus) was confused by the delicate soundscape, describing the work as "an inaudible satire".[8] Alex Ross, and many subsequent listeners, were entirely more receptive to Feldman's interest in softer dynamics and sounds: "In the noisiest century in history, Feldman chose to be glacially slow and snowily soft."[9] In the first third of *Psappha*, rests are brief and infrequent, presenting as breathless moments between frenzied polyrhythmic and accented attacks. The middle section explores in greater depth the powerful apposition of violent, loud aggression and more elongated silences; in both live and recorded performances they serve to create an electrifying sense of anticipation.

These four seminal works initiated the subsequent trajectory of solo multi-percussion as a versatile and diverse medium. For Cage, percussion was the link between music and the world of sound which accompanies everyday life. Stockhausen applied more specific parameters, exploring in detail the range of relative pitches found in auxiliary percussion and using timbre as a structural device. Feldman's study of less obvious performance

---

[7] Interview with Glennie, 10 March 2023.

[8] Howard Klein (1964) Music: Avant-Garde Festival Closes, *New York Times*, September 1964. Cited in David Cline (2016) *The Graph Music of Morton Feldman.* Cambridge: Cambridge University Press, p. 69.

[9] Alex Ross (2006) American Sublime, *The New Yorker*, 19 June 2006 (online). Available from: www.therestisnoise.com/2006/06/morton_feldman_.html (accessed 18 April 2018).

techniques was a direct reaction to the complexity and force of *Zyklus*, amplifying instead the concept of solo percussion as performance art. Xenakis tested the technical and musical skills of the percussionist, exploring what virtuosity might mean in this new discipline.

The sense of freedom embedded in these early works is retained later in cadenzas, sections for improvisation, options for instrumentation and ultimately in the ways by which the soloist chooses to unify gesture, sound and spectacle in the moment of performance. As is so often the case in Western art music, history remembers the composers who changed the path of percussion. In reality, the acceptance and dissemination of such innovative repertoire was entirely dependent on performers willing to embrace the ambiguities and challenges of the unknown. As noted by Small in his articulation of musicking: "Performance does not exist in order to present musical works, but rather, musical works exist in order to give performers something to perform."[10] Percussionists were familiar with extended techniques, graphic scores and heightened interpretative autonomy long before many of their peers in the domain of art music. Those who premiered the first solo multi-percussion works (*Zyklus* premiered by Christoph Caskel; *The King of Denmark* and first full performance of *27' 10.554"* by Max Neuhaus; *Psappha* by Sylvio Gualda) instigated an exciting and eclectic creative sphere intrinsically connected to the multi-sensory nature of the live musical experience. In many ways, the Romantic virtuoso, whose charisma and energy filled concert halls and enthralled audiences, was reborn in the spectacle and dynamism of solo multi-percussion performance.

Multi-Percussion: The Role of the Performer

With Glennie's admission to the Royal Academy of Music in 1982, garnering institutional support for her intended career path as a solo multi-percussionist remained a challenge:

> They just had to take a cool view of it all and see how I got on, but the problems with the percussion repertoire and the sheer cost of ferrying the range of instruments around the country and abroad for solo recitals seemed serious deterrents to my crusade. It would be irresponsible to encourage me to look for a professional career outside the two outlets conventionally available: orchestral performance and teaching.[11]

[10] Christopher Small (1998) *Musicking: The Meanings of Performing and Listening.* Connecticut: Wesleyan University Press, p. 8.
[11] Glennie (1990) *Good Vibrations*, pp. 82–83.

The Ascendance of Solo Multi-Percussion Performance   19

Sourcing sufficient repertoire, accessing instruments and identifying suitable performance spaces are not the only difficulties faced by the aspiring solo multi-percussionist; they must navigate a profession which is never static. There is no specification as to the number, range or type of instruments employed by the composer, nor is there a definitive means of scoring for the soloist. The performer must contend with the demands of selecting and even inventing suitable instruments and then negotiate the practicalities of moving around the set-up. Competence in tuned percussion is aligned with a willingness to experiment on auxiliary instruments. Rhythmic and technical precision must be combined with ancillary gesture and theatricality. All of these fundamental skills must then be brought to fruition in the moment of performance. Multi-percussion offers a primal connection to rhythm and sound which feels instinctive and accessible even at its most complex, forging a symbiotic relationship between musician and listener. It is an exciting language of contrasts: the performer can be housed in a construction of huge proportions, or they can hover delicately over the smallest auxiliary instruments; loud sounds that manifest as tangible vibrations can be juxtaposed with almost inaudible touches of delicacy; intimidating and vicious attack can be aligned with electrifying silence; physical prowess and athleticism akin to a form of choreography can be equalled by the deliberate raising of a single stick. It is aural, visual and tangible, a form of performance art intended to stimulate multi-sensory responses. It belongs to everyone and everything, possessing an inter-genre and inter-cultural identity; erudition is not a prerequisite for understanding and engagement.

One of the greatest challenges facing art music of the later twentieth century has been finding ways to reconnect with the listener. As hyperbolically noted by Young in 2010: "You could set off a bomb at most performances of new music and not kill enough people to make a CNN broadcast."[12] Virtuosic solo multi-percussionists have served an important function in renewing and reinvigorating interest in art music in an age where ticket sales are a constant source of concern. The reasons for this are manifold and pertain both to the intriguingly unpredictable nature of the discipline itself and, most importantly, the performers who promote it. Virtuosity in percussion is different from that of other instruments, since proficiency demands specific and specialized training, culminating in the performance of repertoire which deviates considerably from that scored for tuned and/or single instruments. There is no end to what the percussionist may be asked

---

[12]   James O. Young (2010) Art and the Educated Audience, *The Journal of Aesthetic Education,* 44 (3), p. 33.

to achieve on conceptual, timbral or technical levels, since the number and range of instruments, techniques and styles constantly evolves.

The solo multi-percussionist has emerged as a rebel against the derogatory stereotypes which have been perpetuated in centuries of Western thought, challenging the overly simplistic premise that the striking, shaking or scraping of an object to produce sound is entirely straightforward. From the beginning, the multi-percussionist has been tasked with serving as an advocate for their discipline; virtuosic performances and the commissioning of suitably challenging repertoire are two key facets of this role. Their profession is an ode to multi-tasking in pragmatic, intellectual and artistic terms. The multi-percussionist is the wandering minstrel of contemporary art music, a performer who has embraced and claimed otherness as an attribute. Their art is physical, visual and aural, with a synergy of senses required in order to create meaning for the audience. In a history entirely dependent upon the visceral live experience, it is perhaps more fitting to revise Cage's assertion: "Percussion*ists* are revolution."

Glennie has become the figurehead of this tumultuous and extraordinary profession; her own personal rebellion against conventional career paths is emblematic of a discipline which revels in ambiguity and upheaval. The name Evelyn Glennie is synonymous with the title of the world's first solo percussionist, but it is more accurate to describe her as the world's first *full-time* solo *multi*-percussionist. As a prominent figure in the cultural zeitgeist, Glennie is the most famous solo multi-percussionist in history, but her emergence is the fruition of the gradual emancipation of the percussionist from the rear of the orchestra. Similarly, the concept of a fluid professional identity – so notable in Glennie's output – also has precedents in the evolution of percussion performance. Percussionists have always sought challenges and opportunities which transect genres, ensemble configurations and instrumental specifications. None of these observations undermine Glennie's contribution; in many ways, they serve to highlight Glennie as a defining case study on what it means to be a solo multi-percussionist in the contemporary creative industries.

The rapturous applause and standing ovations witnessed so frequently in Glennie's performances are not incidental; they are the result of a carefully curated immersive performance environment designed for multi-sensory impact: "I'm a great believer that when you attend a concert, every sense should be filled, including the eye: you hear a lot by what you see."[13] Glennie has harnessed the aural, visual and kinaesthetic appeal of

---

[13] Evelyn Glennie in Nick Kimberley (2000) Classical – Even More Bangs for your Buck in David Bedford's New Percussion Concerto, *Independent*, 3 March 2000.

The Ascendance of Solo Multi-Percussion Performance   21

multi-percussion, adopting the roles of sound sculptor, performance artist and virtuosic musician to command the attention of the audience. She has also recognized the power of being the first, both in terms of situating solo multi-percussion in new contexts and in premiering new works, a means of ensuring that her performances are enticingly unpredictable, even before a note is struck. Interest in watching Glennie perform has become intrinsically connected to the dissemination of new music, positioning multi-percussion as a living art form and shared experience of discovery for both performer and listener: "I think people should realise that it's not just new for the audience but the performers as well. I just happen to have the piece a few weeks or months before them."[14] Glennie enjoys the theatricality of the medium, aligning the role of dramatist with musicianship, virtuosity and intense immersion in each moment of performance. There is also a frisson in seeing a small female figure quietly enter the stage and then proceed to dominate an often imposing configuration of powerful instruments. For some, awareness of the fact that Glennie's listening processes are primarily tactile and vibrational is of interest (as evinced in the fact that she generally plays barefoot). Cumulatively, these sources of appeal have contributed to making Glennie the most recognizable proponent of the discipline.

Given that Glennie is often the first to perform solo multi-percussion works, she does not rely on extant recordings, videos or reflections in order to prepare (and in fact chooses not to do so even when resources are available). Score analysis, instrument selection and associated experimentation, visualization, practice and preparation of the *mise-en-scène* (lighting and costume in particular) are all part of the process. Practicalities are the first priority:

> It's really important to experiment with the setup and to come from where physically you feel comfortable, as that will impact the quality of sound. I'm not the tallest person on the planet so therefore a lot of the setups have to be suitable for my height, for the length of my arm and for the control that I want.[15]

Physical movement between instruments and setups during performance is aligned with supplementary choreography intended to unify musical ideas, intimate phrase structures and heighten a sense of anticipation. In a study of percussion practice, Schutz and Manning differentiate between two forms

---

[14] Glennie in Christopher Bowen (1998) Shock of the New, *Scotland on Sunday*, 4 October 1998, section 16.

[15] Evelyn Glennie (n.d.) *Dame Evelyn Glennie: Virtuoso Solo & Multi-Percussionist* (online). Available from: https://www.percworks.co.uk/dameevelynglennie (accessed 26 May 2022).

of performance gesture: "effective" (needed to physically produce sounds) and "ancillary" (intended as expressive movements).[16] The lack of timbral resonance for many auxiliary percussion instruments makes the use of ancillary gesture particularly important: "They can be used to accomplish *perceptually* that which is impossible *acoustically*."[17] Glennie's movements are often emphatic visual cues for the audience, but stasis is equally important. She will often remain motionless long after a note has been struck, allowing the audience to voyeuristically experience her sensations of the ongoing resonance and vibrations of the decaying sonority. The fact that Glennie is deaf means that she instinctively responds to sound through the body, which serves as a resonating chamber (what Glennie has described frequently as a "big ear"). Listening in this way means that Glennie feels sound for a longer time than it exists as an audible presence; therefore, her stillness is both theatrical effect and an indication of the fact that the music has not yet ended. A 2010 review evokes the resultant audience sensation:

> Glennie's art is both aural and highly visual. Her trigger-quick attacks with drumsticks or mallets are mirrored by her eyes, her almost choreographic arm movement and her extraordinary, incisive body language. There is nothing histrionic about her performance, nothing mechanical, just the complete immersion of a unique musical genius in what she is doing. Experiencing Glennie becomes endlessly hypnotic.[18]

Glennie is an undeniably attractive presence on stage in terms both of her gestural idiosyncrasies as a performer and her visual appeal. The potentially anachronistic juxtaposition of a petite body possessing power and control, the movement and drama of long flowing hair amplifying movements onstage, and a range of engaging facial expressions all contribute to the performance event. Whilst Glennie does not concern herself with these aesthetic elements (all of which are largely predetermined by physiology), she does give careful consideration to other visual aspects, including lighting, colour, stage design and costume. As with decisions made on physicality, costume choice begins with pragmatism. To move efficiently around the multi-percussion set-up Glennie must prioritize freedom of

[16] Michael Schutz and Fiona Manning (2012) Looking Beyond the Score: The Musical Role of Percussionists' Ancillary Gestures, *Music Theory*, 18 (1), online. Available from: http://www.mtosmt.org/issues/mto.12.18.1/mto.12.18.1.schutz_manning.php (accessed 6 November 2017).

[17] Ibid.

[18] Herman Trotter (2010) Virtuosity Reverberates in Percussive Artistry, *Buffalo News* (online), 19 April 2010. Available from: https://buffalonews.com/2010/04/19/virtuosity-reverberates-in-percussive-artistry/ (accessed 28 August 2017).

The Ascendance of Solo Multi-Percussion Performance   23

motion when choosing what to wear; secondly, she is cognizant of the fact
that costume is part of the visual language of any theatrical performance.
Despite the logic of this rationale, Glennie (as with all female performers)
has nonetheless been subjected to scrutiny in this respect, with opinions
often digressing from the central artistic objective. Performance reviews
at times are distracted by visual elements at the expense of the musical
content:

> Glennie – dressed in vivid red, her array of Chinese gongs lit in almost
> equally vivid yellow – did what seemed an excellent job.[19]

> [Glennie was] dressed as a lycra-clad alien, playing a waterphone.[20]

> In scarlet sequinned trousers and flouncy blouse, with a red spotlight
> behind her, she inhabited a little box of Chinese-opera glamour at the
> side of the stage.[21]

> Glennie was dressed in form-fitting black pants and an odd, diapha-
> nous hanging black garment. The effect was both macabre and sexy,
> suggesting something occult.[22]

The success of many Glennie album releases affirms the fact that multi-
percussion can prove captivating in the absence of spectacle, but there is no
question that this medium is most arresting as a live event. A stage devoid
of people but filled with instruments is itself a source of intrigue. The sights
and sounds of percussion are interrelated; repertoire often exploits this
premise, casting the percussionist as storyteller, character or dramatic
protagonist, a musician and actor. It is unfortunate that the male gaze
at times misunderstands the efforts of the performer to fully realize the
composer's vision onstage. Costume, lighting, instrument placement and
choreography are intrinsically connected as part of the process of musical

---

[19] Keith Potter (2003) Prom 41: Chen Yi/Evelyn Glennie, Royal Albert Hall, London/
Radio 3, *Independent*, 27 August 2003.

[20] Tom Service (2010) Taking the Knocks: The Chequered History of the Percussion
Concerto, *Guardian* (online), 1 October 2010. Available from: https://www.the-
guardian.com/music/tomserviceblog/2010/oct/01/percussion-concerto-o-duo (accessed 18 August 2017).

[21] Erica Jeal (2003) BBCSO/Tortelier: Royal Albert Hall, *Guardian* (online), 21 August
2003. Available from: https://www.theguardian.com/music/2003/aug/21/classical-
musicandopera.proms2003 (accessed 18 August 2017).

[22] P. Kennicott (2000) Percussionist Evelyn Glennie's Otherworldly Rhythms, *Washington Post* (online), 6 October 2000. Available from: https://www.washington-
post.com/archive/lifestyle/2000/10/06/percussionist-evelyn-glennies-otherworld-
ly-rhythms/e076d1e2-3227-4d02-9f0d-7353987559f4/?utm_term=.194946cd4bf5
(accessed 18 August 2017).

communication, all of which are intended to facilitate more meaningful engagement with the music: "It's a fine line, and the visual aspects can sometimes supersede the musical ones in percussion works. I mean, we all love to see beautiful clothes and exciting and exuberant performances, but in the end the music has to stand up on its own."[23]

In establishing the identity of the contemporary solo multi-percussionist, the importance of public performance has run parallel to the commissioning of new works. For Glennie, this process was initiated out of personal necessity; the Proms recital of 1989 heralded the arrival of an exciting presence in contemporary music, but also emphasized the lacuna of music available for solo percussion. As noted succinctly by one attendee: "Glennie is a phenomenal player but seems in want of good pieces to play."[24] Glennie has not pursued this mission alone; percussionists are now associated by default with commissioning and promoting new music. They take a pro-active role in directing and supporting the evolution of the discipline. At times, these works remain synonymous with the percussionist who commissions and premieres them, but in many instances the resultant repertoire is shared and disseminated.

Programming for Glennie's Proms recital exemplifies the issues faced at the early stages of her career (see Table 1). Opening with a two-minute Chopin transcription for marimba, the performance was otherwise reliant on dated tuned percussion repertoire (Paul Creston: 1940, Tanaka: 1965 and Abe: 1978). Only two works expanded beyond the familiar sonority of the marimba: an energetic two-minute snare drum solo by Paul Price and the world premiere of John McLeod's *Song of Dionysius*. Commissioned by Glennie in 1988, McLeod's multi-percussion solo presented a dynamic, theatrical and powerful statement of intent, an exciting and engaging encounter for the listener. With frequent transitions between instruments, an unsettling ambiguity in terms of tempo and metre, and two cadenzas reliant on free improvisation, *The Song of Dionysius* assertively established multi-percussion as a virtuosic discipline. If Glennie was to capture and sustain the public's attention whilst also progressing as a performer, more repertoire written specifically for multi-percussion was required; commissions were essential to achieving this objective. The priority was to eschew the limitations of tuned percussion and transcriptions in favour of a career foregrounding the diversity of the discipline. New interpretations of sound required new approaches to composition.

[23] Evelyn Glennie (2000) *Press Pack*, access kindly provided by The Evelyn Glennie Collection.

[24] David Cairns (1989) Performers Who Play with Fire, Record Choice, *The Sunday Times*, 30 July 1989.

Table 1: 1989 programme for Glennie's BBC Proms recital.

Composer	Title of work
Chopin, arr. Evelyn Glennie	*Study in C sharp minor, Op. 10, No. 4*
Toshimitsu Tanaka	*Two Movements for Marimba*
John McLeod (world premiere)	*The Song of Dionysius*
Keiko Abe	*Michi*
Paul Price	*Exhibition Snare Drum Solo No. 1*
Paul Creston	*Concertino for Marimba*

Glennie's Multi-Percussion Concerto Commissions: Overview

Since its inception in the Baroque era, the concerto has functioned as a means of exploring the unique properties of a solo instrument whilst also demonstrating the technical and interpretative acumen of the performer. In Western art music it has become the definitive means of establishing virtuoso status. For Glennie to advance her career as a solo multi-percussionist, concerto commissions were an essential means of accessing the global market and validating her place therein. High-profile collaborations with orchestras in large-scale performances, and the opportunity to work with a wide range of composers, were fundamental to consolidating her professional identity. With a virtuosic commissioner, there are few (if any) restrictions as to what the composer can ask of the soloist. This freedom is extended further in an inherently theatrical discipline where there are no limits in terms of instrumentation or extended techniques. Writing for Glennie therefore becomes both a daunting and exciting prospect, demanding that the composer negotiate a precarious balance between spectacle and musicianship. James MacMillan acknowledged this dilemma in relation to the process of writing *Veni, Veni Emmanuel* (1992), the first solo multi-percussion concerto in the history of the BBC Proms: "It worries me if it's virtuosic just for the sake of it and there's no substance to the music, but, when you get the marriage right, as it were, when the balance between virtuosity and substance is right, then it's a goal worth pursuing."[25]

Glennie's professional legacy of concerto commissions began in 1987 with John McLeod's *Percussion Concerto*, a five-movement work in which fanfares frame a dissonant and imposing soundscape. This was preceded by Kenneth Dempster's *Concerto Palindromos* (1985), commissioned by

---

[25] James MacMillan and Richard McGregor (2010) James MacMillan: A Conversation and Commentary, *The Musical Times*, 151 (1912), p. 94.

Glennie for performance as part of her undergraduate studies at the Royal Academy, in response to the fact that it did not yet allow percussionists to perform concertos. The list (which continues to expand) includes double concertos, expansive multi-percussion set-ups and compositions for single auxiliary instruments. Their average length is around twenty-five minutes, with the longest extending to approximately forty (see Appendix 1 for chronology, instrumentation and duration). In terms of the types of instruments used, there is no definitive chronological trend discernible in relation to timbre. Some composers experiment keenly with improvised and new sounds; others foreground instruments drawn from non-Western sources; several take a more practical approach by scoring for easily available standard percussion instruments. Almost half require the performer to play thirty or more sounding objects. Improvised instruments or found objects are a feature of interest to many composers, the first example being Dave C. Heath's *African Sunrise/Manhattan Rave* (1995), which requires the percussionist to select their own range of "trash" or industrial sounds. The soloist must create musical meaning on objects more readily perceived as detritus, with percussion blurring literal and metaphorical boundaries between everyday life and concert hall, noise and music, tradition and innovation. Works such as Joseph Phibbs' *Bar Veloce* (2011), where the performer explores the musical potential of items such as spirit bottles and cocktail shakers, or Clarice Assad's *Ad Infinitum* (2017), in which the soloist is invited to choose a selection of toy instruments, further extend the parameters of what can reasonably be defined as a percussion instrument. Reviews of premiere concerto performances by Glennie acknowledge unequivocally the virtuosity and charisma of the soloist; audiences enjoy the experience, but they don't always understand it. As Glennie notes in 1992: "I haven't yet received a review where they've criticized the playing. I can't believe it's because I'm so magnificent. I think it's their lack of knowledge about percussion."[26] Not all commissions reach the stage of performance, and not all performances achieve equal status as seminal events. It is not easy to write for percussion, and Glennie's decision not to premiere certain works is based on a number of compositional pitfalls:

> The main reasons [are that] there are too many mallet changes, not appropriate time to use the mallet for the particular instrument, non-cohesive with the instruments chosen, too many bits and pieces whereby colour as opposed to musical line has been the criteria. This

---

[26] Evelyn Glennie in Paul Fisher (1992) A Woman on the Move: Paul Fisher Meets Evelyn Glennie, the World's Only Full-Time Female Solo Percussionist, *Independent*, 7 August 1992.

happens less so nowadays but was a regular occurrence in the early years before composers had more access to players and instruments.[27]

Of the commissions which are premiered, critics do not tend to question Glennie's skill, but instead have at times expressed more fundamental concerns about the discipline itself. In such commentary, the diversity of multi-percussion is viewed as a negative trait, a disruption to the conventional concerto model of one voice against the forces of the symphony orchestra. Dated views of auxiliary percussion as decorative, noisy and peripheral are retained in such criticism, part of a larger argument that the diffuse nature of large configurations lacks the musical substance and clarity to persuasively control the soundscape. An indicative example is Anderson's response to the double percussion concerto *Fractured Lines* (Mark Anthony Turnage, 2000), unapologetically critical of the suitability of multi-percussion for a large-scale work: "I've yet to hear a percussion concerto that works ... The trouble is that the solo part (or parts, in this instance) in a percussion concerto can only ever be decorative."[28] Seymour's evaluation of Michael Daugherty's *Dreamachine* (2014) alludes to dissent even from within the orchestra: "Clear screens separated Glennie from the first violins but the feverish power of the ear-splitting [snare drum] beat was too much for some of the players, whose hands offered further protections for their ear-drums."[29] Glennie has continued to commission and premiere concertos, choosing to express in performance her conviction that multi-percussion is a complex and unique musical language which requires that the listener be open to new ideas and sounds: "Music isn't all about leaving the audience wanting more. It's also about making them think and giving them an experience."[30] The very fact that multi-percussion concertos are so unpredictable and difficult to categorize are part of their inherent appeal. In supporting the commissioning of new concertos, Glennie celebrates eclecticism and experimentation as attributes. To return to

---

[27]   Interview with Glennie, 14 September 2017.

[28]   Martin Anderson (2001) Royal Albert Proms (3): Selected Premieres, *Tempo*, New Series No. 215, p. 47.

[29]   Claire Seymour (2017) *Evelyn Glennie on Scintillating Form in Michael Daugherty's Percussion Concerto* (online), 18 June 2017. Available from: http://seenand-heard-international.com/2016/06/evelyn-glennie-on-scintillating-form-in-michael-daughertys-percussion-concerto/ (accessed 5 September 2017).

[30]   Evelyn Glennie in Alexander Varty (2013) Evelyn Glennie gets Unhinged with Musicophilia, *The Georgia Straight* (online), 24 September 2013. Available from: https://www.straight.com/arts/428916/evelyn-glennie-gets-unhinged-musicophilia (accessed 1st September 2017).

The Invention of New Percussion Instruments

Glennie's concerto commissions require an eclectic range of percussion instruments and repurposed sounding objects. To this already endless timbral palette, further resources are being gradually subsumed into the language of multi-percussion repertoire with the invention of new instruments. These differ from found objects in that the intention is to create sonorities that will find a more permanent place in the multi-percussionist's musical vocabulary. The effort is not one of replacement; it is an additive process intended to build on a long and culturally rich history. Though the discipline of solo multi-percussion is still relatively new, its origins are rooted in ancient traditions and musical practices; in many instances, looking back can be as inspiring as moving forwards. Drums, tuned percussion and auxiliary instruments have ancient legacies in numerous cultures and musical genres; there is an inherent universality to the medium offering multiple sources of creative inspiration for further developments. Though percussion is deemed historically important in many diverse regions of the world (including the gamelan of Indonesia, the zhonggu ensembles of China and the djembe drum circles of West Africa), its evolution in the context of Western art music presents less idealistic truths about intersections of culture and musical practice. From the tentative admission of Turkish Janissary percussion to the Classical orchestra, problematic terminology has pervaded discourse on orchestration and composition, with percussion frequently described as simplistic, primitive, exotic and even barbaric. Disparaging attitudes towards the introduction of diverse percussion instruments have oftentimes served as a metaphor for cultural imperialism; in the orchestras of the Classical and Romantic periods, the percussive other of the ensemble functioned as a musical representation of any identity which extended beyond the Eurocentric frame. In inventing new instruments and selecting timbral palettes for scoring, both percussionist and composer must be mindful of the fact that the idealistic democracy of multi-percussion – where all sounds are equal – is an ethos not always reflected in Western history; inspiration must not become appropriation.

Acceptance of extant instruments drawn from multiple cultures was the first objective, necessary before new inventions could be accommodated. The timpani, as the first and most esteemed percussion instrument of the Baroque and Classical orchestras, was emancipated as a solo instrument as early as the eighteenth century (pre-dating the invention of the tuning foot

The Ascendance of Solo Multi-Percussion Performance 29

pedal): "Georg Roth, a Nuremburg timpani virtuoso, gave a concert at the Kärntnertor Theatre in Vienna on 29 April 1798. The concert advertisement shows him performing on sixteen timpani with three sticks in each hand."[31]

Janissary instruments first featured as an entity separate to the orchestra, providing superficial militaristic sound effects which reflected the original function of bass drum, cymbals, tambourine and snare drum in Turkish marching music; the orchestral percussionist was essentially a soloist in this respect, detached and disconnected from the sonorities of tuned instruments. As new sounds and techniques for Janissary percussion were integrated into scoring, a gradual process of expansion and assimilation admitted new sounds to the palette of Western art music. The rise of auxiliary percussion was not rapid, and it was not immediately accepted; experimentation and innovation were often initially treated with disdain. When Liszt ventured to feature the triangle prominently in his first piano concerto (1849), the sobriquet "Triangle Concerto" coined by his contemporary Eduard Hanslick was intended as a derogatory descriptor. In Mahler's symphonies, similar efforts to heighten the musical value of auxiliary percussion was evident, with the cowbells of *Symphony No. 4* establishing a motif intrinsic to the journey of the work, though the instrument was played offstage. By the later stages of the Romantic era, when growing interest in expanding the orchestra's timbral palette became a more palpable aesthetic priority, a certain sense of apprehension about where such exploration would lead was at times given voice in journal articles. An 1898 opinion piece for *The Musical Times* sarcastically advised that there was now room for sirens, table legs, iron rods and steam whistles in the percussion section.[32] Such misgivings endured well into the twentieth century, with a similar 1928 article entitled "The Destinies of Music" manifesting a sense of panic in the face of change:

> This accounts for the possibility nowadays of composers who invent a method of playing the pianoforte with the elbows, or introduce new instruments into the orchestra, such as domestic utensils, electric bells, oyster shells, and whips. Before long we shall surely have choruses of dogs and frogs, pianoforte playing with footballs, and other acquirements. The musical art has offered its hand to the circus and the music-hall turn.[33]

[31] Naxos (2005) *Programme notes for Virtuoso Timpani Concertos* (online). Available from: Virtuoso Timpani Concertos NAXOS 8.557610 [RH]: Classical CD Reviews-October 2005 MusicWeb-International (accessed 13 July 2023).

[32] Additional Instruments (1898) *The Musical Times and Singing Class Circular*, 39 (662), p. 235.

[33] Leonid Sabaneev and S.W Pring (1928) The Destinies of Music, *The Musical Times*, 69 (1024), p. 505.

The emancipation of percussion began definitively with the emergence of Futurism in 1909, integrating noise and new effects to an entirely unprecedented level. The Futurists' efforts to align music with the industrialized world, in a wilful disregard for history and tradition, positioned percussion instruments as an important means of offering a more realistic, less idealized representation of society and culture. Russolo's *Art of Noises* (1913) asserted the validity of new sounds in the Western palette: "We must break out of this restricted circle of pure sounds and conquer the infinite variety of sounds."[34] Much of Russolo's vision was concerned with the creation of new instruments, most notably his own invention, the *intonarumori*. The six noise families associated with the intonarumori were to be used alongside "rumori ottenuti a percussion" (noises obtained by percussion). The Futurists freed noise in an intentionally chaotic manner; avant-garde and experimental composers subsequently harnessed its potential. In both contexts, new instruments and sounds were at the centre of innovation. In *Credo* (1937), Cage positioned percussion as a central means of eschewing the confines of tradition and convention: "Any sound is acceptable to the composer of percussion music; he explores the academically forbidden 'non-musical' field of sound insofar as is manually possible."[35] With the exponential increase in the range of timbres, objects and instruments falling under the categorization of "percussion", it is unsurprising that the percussionist became by default a curator and inventor. Cage's inventory list (started in September 1938), continued to expand in alignment with his evolution as a composer. The James Blades Collection (at the Royal Academy of Music) is an important predecessor of The Evelyn Glennie Collection, incorporating well-loved and exhaustively used percussion instruments as well as many of his own creations:

> Blades worked closely with Benjamin Britten to produce the precise sounds that were needed in many of his compositions, researching percussion instruments from many musical traditions, constructing his own instruments and experimenting with the sounds produced by unusual items. Many of these instruments form part of the Academy's museum collections.[36]

The Percussive Arts Society continues to develop the Rhythm! Discovery Center in Indianapolis, a repository of historical artefacts and instrument

---

[34] Luigi Russolo in Rose Trillo Clough (1961) *Futurism: The Story of a Modern Art Movement – A New Appraisal*. New York: Polyglot Press, p. 125.

[35] John Cage (1937) *The Future of Music: Credo* (online). Available from: https://www.liberationofsound.org/words/the-future-of-music-credo/ (accessed 21 June 2023).

[36] James Blades Collection (online). Available from: https://www.ram.ac.uk/museum/collections-index/performers (accessed 20 June 2023).

The Ascendance of Solo Multi-Percussion Performance   31

inventions currently operating as an online resource. Even the images of instruments in this virtual museum are fascinating, a reminder of the fact that percussion possesses a unique visual attraction. The Harry Partch Collection (which tends to change residency every few years between universities in the US) also reflects this appeal, preserving inventions which function both as works of visual art and innovative sources of sound. The Evelyn Glennie Collection incorporates Glennie's own museum of sounds; over 3800 instruments serve as artefacts of many decades of travel, collaboration, and invention. In cataloguing each item, archivists are researching the histories and practices associated with older sounding objects, mindful of the rich cultural palette which characterizes solo multi-percussion. The contemporary percussionist retains the legacy of the past whilst also holding the power to change and redirect the future of music-making; instruments are a key means of connecting tradition and innovation.

In the canon of Glennie's multi-percussion commissions, three inventions in particular have found an identity beyond use in a single work: the Simtak, Batonka and Aluphone. With the exception of the Simtak, which is Glennie's own design, the evolution of the Batonka and Aluphone are demonstrative of the fact that the collaborative experience of commissioning also extends to partnerships centred on creating and premiering new instruments. Composers are generally invited to Glennie's studio at an early stage in the development of a new piece, and Glennie draws their attention to interesting sounds, potential combinations and the various applications of the instruments. The fact that many multi-percussion commissions do not specify the precise configuration for the performer also means that Glennie can continue to add new instruments to existing repertoire.

The Batonka is categorized as a tuned percussion instrument. Its original prototype consisted of tuned PVC tubes struck with foam- or plastic-headed mallets. The process of creating the Batonka was initiated by Will Embliss, an inventor who specializes in unusual tuned percussion instruments. An experimental collaborative session between Embliss and Glennie resulted in the commissioning of the Batonka (see Fig. 2). Glennie selected the materials to be used for the tubes of the two-octave prototype and Embliss completed the commission.

Several years later Glennie asked for a second Batonka to be created:

> Evelyn's office contacted me asking if I could make a second instrument that could be dismantled for easier travel. So Batonka version two was designed and made. I believe that this instrument was used to compose the music for the Radio 4 music quiz *Counterpoint* with Ray Davies.[37]

---

[37] E-mail correspondence with Will Embliss (www.willembliss.co.uk), 26 April 2018.

Fig. 2: Glennie at the Batonka (October 2000). Permission kindly granted by The Evelyn Glennie Collection and Will Embliss.

The *Counterpoint* theme tune incorporated a wide range of timbres, with Batonka joined by vibraphone, marimba, wood chimes, bass drum, timbales, steel drum and exhaust pipes. The fact that Glennie was inspired to compose music centred on the unique sonority of the Batonka demonstrates the value of new timbres as an impetus for further creative evolution. Likewise, the desire to expand on the initial prototype indicates

The Ascendance of Solo Multi-Percussion Performance 33

that experimentation does not equate to passing fascinations with certain sounds, but a more enduring and conscious effort to diversify the percussion family. Stewart Wallace scored a prominent part for the Batonka in the 1996 concerto *Gorilla in a Cage*. Glennie introduced him to the instrument when he came to her home studio in the preliminary stages of composing the commission: "I chose it while visiting Evelyn at her home and rummaging through all her instruments. That was the first thing we did when we began working together."[38] The roles typically afforded to tuned and auxiliary percussion are subverted in this instance, with Batonka and chimes focused on providing resonant rhythmic motifs whilst the relative pitches of auxiliary instruments create melody lines (drawn from timbales, tom-toms, temple blocks and a range of cymbals). David Bedford was also drawn to the opportunity to compose for a new instrument, featuring the Batonka in his *Percussion Concerto* (1999). Bedford recalls the experience of visiting Glennie's studio, where the unique visual and timbral effect of the Batonka made a distinct impression: "It's a set of 24 plastic drainpipe lengths laid out as a keyboard, and covered with plastic which she bashes with what look like table tennis bats. The noise they produce reminds me of 1960s synthesisers."[39] The Batonka is the only percussive presence in the first movement of Bedford's concerto, afforded an extended cadenza allowing for full exploration of the resonance and range of the instrument.

Glennie introduces the Simtak in episode six of a series of short YouTube documentaries entitled *Playing Around the Office*. Her enthusiasm for seeking out new sounds is manifest in the video; she notes therein how she visits scrap-yards at least once a year in search of inspiration. Both the Batonka and Simtak are made from repurposed materials, which resonates with Glennie's larger mission to make musical experiences accessible to all; the prototype Simtak is simply a car muffler played with triangle beaters. Bedford's *Percussion Concerto* integrates the Simtak into a meandering second movement exploring a range of metallic timbres (including glockenspiel and cowbells). Gareth Farr's concerto commission *Hikoi* (1999), also makes use of the instrument. The title of the concerto, a Maori word meaning a communal march (often as a form of protest), is reflected in the power and energy of the scoring. *Hikoi* was premiered with the New Zealand Symphony Orchestra and subsequently featured as part of a concert for the 2000 Olympic Games Art Festival in Sydney, introducing the Simtak to a global audience. In the same year, the Simtak became the central timbral identifier of the title track for Glennie's first entirely improvised

---

[38] E-mail correspondence with Stewart Wallace, 26 April 2018.
[39] David Bedford in Kimberley (2000) Classical – Even More Bangs for your Buck.

recording, *Shadow Behind the Iron Sun* (2000). With the capacity to generate resonant power or delicate twinkling flourishes, the Simtak is a versatile auxiliary percussion instrument with a distinctive timbral identity; it can mimic the lightness of the triangle but can also achieve the sustained impact of the tam-tam at a higher registral range. The broader appeal of the Simtak is also evinced beyond the scope of Glennie's work. The Carolina Crown Drum Corps presented a programme at the 2014 Drum Corps International World Championships including a composition featuring eight Simtaks (based on Glennie's *Shadow Behind the Iron Sun*). In this display of choreography, athleticism, narrative and music, the sight of car mufflers reimagined as resounding musical instruments proved both visually and aurally powerful.

The Aluphone (see Fig. 3) has become a notable feature of Glennie's performances in recent years and has quickly been integrated into the language of contemporary solo percussion, played by many prominent soloists including Colin Currie and Martin Grubinger. A creative experiment initiated by Kai Stensgaard (marimbist and composer) and Michael Hansen (owner of an aluminium foundry), aluminium discs ordinarily used to top fence-posts were reimagined as tuned percussion resonators. Stensgaard and Hansen began collaborating with Glennie following the first unveiling of the instrument at the Percussive Arts Society International Conference

Fig. 3: The Glennie Concert Aluphone.

The Ascendance of Solo Multi-Percussion Performance   35

in 2011. By 2012, the Glennie Concert Aluphone had evolved as a direct result of their work together. This instrument extends to a length exceeding that of a five-octave marimba, an imposing and visually attractive presence in the multi-percussion set-up. It has a haunting, ethereal and beautiful sound whose vibrations tend to decay in overtones which extend beyond the strict specifications of equal temperament. Directives to potential composers provided on the Aluphone website outline its timbral range: "The sound can change a lot, depending on the types of mallets you are using. Soft mallets give you the sound of Tibetan Singing Bowls, medium hard mallets give you more of a vibraphone/bell sound and hard mallets make the Aluphone sound almost like church bells."[40] Glennie has played a significant role in popularizing the instrument. After bringing it to the attention of the creative team for the Olympic Games Opening Ceremony in London (2012), the Aluphone became the defining sonority of the closing stages of this seminal event. Mark Bowden's *Heartland* (2012), was the first Glennie commission to make use of the Aluphone in a concerto directly inspired by the Olympics Ceremony; the second section centralizes the instrument, where it is used to communicate a "long, yearning melody"[41] (see Ex. 1). This segues to an improvised cadenza which also incorporates tuned gongs, resulting in a celestial soundscape.

Glennie gave the world premiere of Anders Koppell's *Concerto for Aluphone and Orchestra* in 2014, further consolidating her relationship with the instrument in a work which foregrounds the sights and sounds of the Glennie Concert Aluphone.

Glennie continues to create new instruments, oftentimes in direct response to the stimulus of particular commissions or collaborations, but also as natural by-products of practice and improvisation. The Barimbulum (catalogued by The Evelyn Glennie Collection in 2016), presents as a rather bizarre and crudely designed entity. Inspired by experiments with the sonorities of disused materials sourced by Glennie from her brother's farm, it consists of an open-topped box with various brass rods fed horizontally through on either side. Regardless of its lack of finesse in aesthetic terms, it clearly proves fascinating to Glennie. She discusses the Barimbulum in episode 3 of *Playing Around the Office* and demonstrates its sonic properties. The sound is unquestionably strange and immersive and is later found in Glennie's 2018 score for the Royal Shakespeare Company's *Troilus and Cressida*: "The one that took me by surprise was the Barimbulum. I showed

---

[40] *Info for Composers* (online). Available from: https://aluphone.dk/info-for-composers/ (accessed 20 June 2023).

[41] Mark Bowden (2012) *Heartland: Description* (online). Available from: www.markbowden.net/music/heartland.html (accessed 3 May 2018).

Ex. 1: Aluphone solo in *Heartland Concerto* (Mark Bowden).

the Royal Shakespeare Company that instrument, and they really liked it and ended up making three for their production. One was enormous. They hung them on the walls of their set."[42] Its angular metal design and abrasive, industrial sound proved to be well suited to the landscape of war in which the play is set.

Investigating sound is integral to the practice methodology of the percussionist. Glennie's experiments with new instruments are a form of creative sustenance, adding new possibilities to extant repertoire whilst also inspiring the evolution of new music. The journey of percussion, mirrored in the narrative of Glennie's career, is a constant process of collecting. Timbres, techniques and styles belonging to its history are retained, extended with recourse to sounds and practices drawn from non-Western sources, and further enhanced with the addition of found objects and new instruments. Nothing is left behind or rejected in the evolution of the discipline. There will always be a sense of play embedded in the ethos of the solo percussionist, but likewise there is a serious intention to develop and pioneer more options for the next generation of performer. The forthcoming release of the Evelyn Glennie Hyperstellar Waterphone (an instrument with two tuned plates and sixty metal rods producing a deep registral sonority with extraordinary resonance) indicates that Glennie continues to innovate in this respect. As noted by solo percussionist Robyn Schulkowsky: "Our instrument, the percussion, is neither fully developed nor can it be perfected. We are in a permanent state of growth and fluxion. Our instrument expands with technical possibilities and human ingenuity."[43]

---

[42] Interview with Glennie, 27 June 2023.
[43] Robyn Schulkowsky (2014) Bagatelles, in Kevin Lewis and Gustavo Adler, eds. *The Modern Percussion Revolution: Journeys of the Progressive Artist*. London: Routledge, p. 219.

National Acclaim: *Veni, Veni Emmanuel* (1992)

It is impossible to describe all of Glennie's concerto commissions and premieres, but it is feasible to identify seminal works which have had a lasting impact on the evolution of the discipline and on her status as a pioneer. As the first percussion concerto in the history of the BBC Proms, James MacMillan's *Veni, Veni Emmanuel*, is important by default. However, it is more than a first; *Veni, Veni Emmanuel* has remained a consistent feature of Glennie's repertory long after its premiere. This in itself is significant, given that her programming changes so frequently to accommodate new commissions. MacMillan (1959–) is now one of Scotland's most respected composers, but at the time of the commission he was in the early stages of his career. The considerable success of *The Confession of Isobel Gowdie* at the 1990 Proms positioned him as an important presence in UK music, with his compositional style praised for its immediacy yet also demeaned for the same reason by several critics. For the first percussion concerto in the history of the Proms, accessibility of musical language was an attribute, a means of providing a sense of clarity and familiarity whilst introducing a solo medium that felt entirely new. Glennie's positive response to MacMillan's work from the beginning was unequivocal, and has not diminished over time. Speaking in 2013, Glennie notes:

> This epitomises perfection for me. If ever there has been a piece written with such emotional and physical depth, it is this one. When I gave the world premiere of *Veni, Veni Emmanuel* in 1992 I knew I was dealing with a masterpiece and I knew it was going to change the face of percussion in every way.[44]

Veni, Veni Emmanuel provides the listener with a clear programmatic construct, a conventional use of the soloist–orchestra relationship exploring the contrasts and synergy of the concerto form, and a compelling visual path as the percussionist moves with purpose between instruments (as per scored instructions); it possesses a cognitive and emotional logic that is persuasive and direct. *Veni, Veni Emmanuel* derives its primary musical motifs from the traditional plainsong of the same name and is a musical transition from the contemplative period of Advent to the redemption and hope of Easter. The percussionist is required to command an extensive range of instruments positioned in three different locations around the orchestra (stage right: auxiliary percussion, stage left: tuned percussion, tam-tams

---

[44] PRS Foundation (2013) *Guest of the Month April 2013: Dame Evelyn Glennie* (online). Available from: http://prsfoundation.com/about-us/guest-of-the-month/guests-of-the-month-2013/april-2013-dame-evelyn-glennie/ (accessed 4 May 2018).

Evelyn Glennie: Sound Creator

and gongs and rear-centre: bass tubular bells). The resultant choreography is inherently theatrical; the soloist moves back and forth between set-ups at the front before completing a processional walk upstage in the closing moments. Each multi-percussion configuration features instruments that prove both visually and aurally attractive in performance: the complexities of four-mallet marimba and vibraphone are interspersed with emphatic tam-tam strikes; the auxiliary station is so extensive that the performer is surrounded on all sides; the elevated tubular bell part demands raised arms and forceful movements. The decision to employ a multitude of percussive sonorities (thirty-eight instruments) represents a collaborative creative decision, with Glennie acknowledging that "in the early days ... I just wanted to use every instrument possible."[45] The dramatic impact of the physicality within and between percussion stations is supported with musically interesting features: rapid (often staccato) flourishes on vibraphone, challenging four-mallet writing for marimba – both beautiful and dissonant – reverberating tam-tam strikes, energetic rhythmic phrases ascending and descending through the drum station (scored for tom-toms, timbales, bass drum, bongos and congas), and flashes of sonorities drawn from a rich cultural palette (including Chinese–Javanese gongs, temple blocks and log drums) conflate as a celebration of the potentialities of the discipline. Eyes and ears are considered in the drama of the 26-minute journey.

A *fff* strike on two tam-tams opens the work. This is followed by a rapid two-mallet section for vibraphone, played with hard sticks. Intervallic gaps gradually increase in bars 8 and 9 demanding accuracy of attack from the soloist. Another loud tam-tam note resonates in bar 13 as the performer moves to the drum set-up (initially scored for tom-toms, timbales, bass drum, bongos and congas) where rapid and accented rhythms feature. Despite the aggression of these figurations, the movement between drums creates in effect an auxiliary percussion melody. Following a two-bar rest (to facilitate movement across stage), an extended tam-tam roll graduates from *p* to *fff* in bars 30–33. The use of *crescendo* rolls on a range of auxiliary instruments becomes a recurring feature (bars 168–169, timbales; bars 438–447, tam-tams; bars 453–455, tam-tams; and bars 558–564, bongos). Another transition to the Chinese–Javanese gongs, temple blocks and log drum explores a second *staccato* auxiliary percussion melody. The "heartbeat" motif is first sounded in bars 49–73 (a triplet/quaver figuration with

---

[45] Radio New Zealand Interview with Evelyn Glennie: Composer of the Week (2015), *Evelyn Glennie – Percussion Champion* (online), 19 July 2015. Available from: http://www.radionz.co.nz/concert/programmes/composeroftheweek/audio/201762818/evelyn-glennie-percussion-champion (accessed 4 May 2018).

The Ascendance of Solo Multi-Percussion Performance   39

rests creating a sense of breath between each iteration). Percussion instruments are more frequently played together in the sections which feature this idea. Cowbells and wood block are added from bar 84, further expanding the timbral palette of the soloist. From bar 142, the multi-drum motif returns, augmented this time with use of all auxiliary instruments. There is a wave-like motion to the solo line which is both musically and visually effective, functioning as a cohesive melody. At bar 220, the soloist restates the "heartbeat" melody above a relatively static orchestra. Instruments are gradually removed from the solo part until only cowbells, bongo and bass drum remain by bar 286 (in advance of the marimba entry). The tuned percussion line consists primarily of alternating rapid demisemiquaver flourishes and extended rolls. There is an uneasy balance juxtaposing tonal alignment and dissonance between soloist and orchestra, heightened by the fact that the marimba line remains *pp* for much of the section. Mark tree flourishes enter intermittently during this more reflective middle passage, anticipating the bell sonorities to follow in the later stages of the work. Vibraphone enters at bar 469 in a section marked "brutal", emphatically transitioning back to the energetic and aggressive mood of the concerto opening. The section from bar 565 sees the soloist playing a huge range of instruments – wood blocks, temple blocks, cowbells, cymbals (used for the first time), bongos, congas, tom-toms, timbales, snare drum, and bass drum – exploiting aggressive septuplet, sextuplet and triplet figurations. The soloist is exposed, supported only by sustained chords and occasional outbursts from timpani. From bar 581 the percussionist is required to sustain a *ffff* dynamic on simultaneously struck cowbells, bongos and bass drum for ten bars – a restatement of the "heartbeat" motif.

The potent final tableau is the defining moment of the concerto, situating the soloist centre-stage (in both literal and musical terms). Following the auxiliary percussion cadenza, all orchestral members put down their instruments (in itself an arresting gesture) and begin to play handheld bells. As this meditative and haunting soundscape emerges, the soloist moves slowly upstage, where the tubular bells stand alone. Directed to improvise on the six notes of the plainchant (a presence throughout the concerto), the percussionist must transform the contemplative delicacy of the orchestra into a triumphant and jubilant ending. It is in this deceptively simple moment where the skills of the performer are most important. The finale must echo the spiritual ethos of the concerto, giving life to the symbolic association between bells and religious ceremony; the percussionist needs to demonstrate the beauty of the instrument even whilst playing loudly and rapidly; clarity of gesture is essential as a means of marking the end of the work for the audience. Glennie's rehearsal scores tend not to be filled with annotations, but there are several markings added to the final pages of *Veni, Veni Emmanuel* providing evidence of decisions made in both private practice and ensemble rehearsals. Stored in The Evelyn Glennie Collection (when not in use), the blue front cover of the original score is battered, with sections of binding missing; within, page edges are frayed and torn. Despite the physical decline of the manuscript, this first response to the concerto remains for Glennie the most authentic. On the final page, annotations include practical considerations, with dynamic markings circled, significant beats highlighted (in pink), reminders inserted for forthcoming instrument entries, and bar lines extended using a black marker. A scrawled note in pen (clearly written whilst the score was positioned on the music stand) notes that the "back bench start bells first"; Glennie uses this cue to begin her transition to the tubular bells. Elsewhere, interpretative responses to the music are added. In bar 581, Glennie writes "final heartbeats EMPHATIC" (referencing the rhythmic motif which appears throughout the concerto), followed in bar 594 with a reminder to "keep intensity".

When the tubular bells enter in bar 602, Glennie conflates practical and personal directives: "Bells must come out over other bells in orch. Come from within." On the final pause, Glennie leaves two options available: "Bells in orch. and solo can be cut off or let ring." In the premiere, Glennie let the bells ring long after the final note is struck, holding the audience in a suspended state of heightened attention. The ecstatic audience reaction on 10 August 1992 – requiring both Glennie and MacMillan to return to the stage three times – was a clear indication of Glennie's success in realizing the composer's musical vision, whilst also an important validation of multi-percussion as a viable concerto medium. As Glennie attests: "It was the piece that firmly established the notion of solo percussion in people's minds."[46]

The legacy of *Veni, Veni Emmanuel* is extensive, performed hundreds of times by Glennie with orchestras around the world (see Fig. 4), and associated with her name as much as that of its composer (though UK percussionist Colin Currie has since performed and recorded the concerto). Perhaps most importantly for the promotion of the discipline, the work has enjoyed an appeal which extends beyond the boundaries of percussion, featuring on the AQA A-Level Music Syllabus since 2016 alongside compositions by Olivier Messiaen, Dmitri Shostakovich and Steve Reich. *Veni, Veni Emmanuel* is the product of a constructive and engaged collaboration between composer and performer, an important and recurring feature of Glennie's most popular works.

[46] PRS Foundation (2013) *Guest of the Month April 2013: Dame Evelyn Glennie.*

Fig. 4: Glennie rehearsing *Veni, Veni Emmanuel* in Beijing (1997) using instruments from her own collection.

The International Stage: *UFO* (1999)

Veni, Veni Emmanuel was a decisive moment when multi-percussion became part of the British cultural consciousness; subsequent commissions with international orchestras and high-profile composers extended its reach further, whilst also positioning Glennie as a global commodity. Even with the visual intrigue of the soloist moving between set-ups and the drama of the finale, MacMillan's work is relatively understated; display and physicality are by-products of the musical directives; scored instructions to the soloist are unambiguous and pragmatic. Other commissions celebrate the potential of multi-percussion as performance art to a much greater degree, integrating choreography, costume and acting roles. American composer Michael Daugherty poses one such challenge with *UFO*, a multi-percussion concerto in five movements which casts the soloist as an alien entity. The 1999 premiere in Washington, DC (as part of the National Symphony Orchestra's Percussion Festival) introduced a striking and eccentric iteration of the concerto genre, with soloist functioning as both virtuoso and actress. Daugherty did not deviate from his personal style or aesthetic as a composer in this respect; a six-time Grammy winner, many of his works are concerned with the visual elements of performance, and with programmatic narratives derived from American popular culture. *UFO* is one such homage to America's abiding fascination with aliens, spaceships and other dimensions. As is often the case with the commissioning process, Glennie worked extensively with Daugherty in developing and preparing the work, particularly in relation to the timbral palette. The resultant score lists over forty percussion instruments, to be augmented further with "trash" and "alien" sonorities (see Table 2).

Whilst Daugherty's writing in the three scored movements is meticulous, focused primarily on virtuosic xylophone and vibraphone passages in "Unidentified" and "Flying", it is in the moments of free improvisation where the work of the percussionist is most intense. In this space, the soloist explores sound, gesture and synergies between performer and instrument in real time; the discoveries of the alien are represented in the experiments of the percussionist. There is a magnetism in the way that auxiliary percussion can captivate the listener when it is used in this way. Without the instinct to listen for a returning melody or tonal motif, time is somehow suspended; in the blank canvas of the first and fourth movements, the remit of the soloist is to harness this power. Virtuosity in this respect feels very different to that of other instrumental disciplines, wherein the audience can be equally enthralled by both extraordinarily complex tuned percussion writing and apparently simple timbral effects:

> I think the thing with percussion, because it's so visual, we can be tripped up with the word "virtuosity", so we can see something that's absolutely unbelievable visually and think it's very good. I think virtuosity for me is when an individual is able to portray an emotional journey, an emotional story. That doesn't mean that everybody has to like that journey, but just simply that there is a real, genuine sense of structure there, of a real story, a real command of what you're doing.[47]

For "Travelling Music", Daugherty's instructions to the performer are broad, concerned largely with atmospheric effect: "Soloist enters from rear of performance space and slowly moves towards Percussion station III. Movements should be mysterious and unpredictable. Improvise *ad lib.* on a waterphone or other hand-held "alien" sounding percussion instrument."[48] The difference between success and failure in this improvisation is based on intentionality; if the performer believes in the story they are projecting, the listener is better able to acquiesce to the experience. Glennie's annotations

---

[47] Interview with Glennie, 3 May 2019.
[48] Michael Daugherty (1999) *UFO* (score). London: Boosey and Hawkes, p. 1.

The Ascendance of Solo Multi-Percussion Performance   43

Table 2: Structure and instrumentation, *UFO* (Michael Daugherty).

Movement	Solo Instrumentation
I: *"Travelling Music"* (improvised)	Waterphone, mechanical siren, additional handheld percussion
II: *"Unidentified"*	Xylophone and a range of metallic sonorities including ice cymbal, earth plate and Chinese gong
III: *"Flying"*	Vibraphone, cymbals, mark tree
IV: *"???"* (improvised)	Non-pitched "alien" instruments
V: *"Objects"*	Five tom-toms, eight octobans, bongos, kick drum, cymbals, temple blocks, cowbells, mechanical siren, waterphone, range of metal objects (chosen by performer)

are simple, comprising several dynamic markings, a cue to watch the conductor at bar 17 and a pair of glasses to denote the *ff* dynamic in bar 22. In the top right corner of the score is the most important note: "Have a good display of effects/experimental touch and sheer virtuosity, musicality and emotion. <u>Be</u> from outer space."

For the fourth movement, creative control is once more left entirely in the hands of the performer (supported only by contrabassoon playing angular melodic motifs, trills and repeated notes with frequent pauses). Only two cursory directions are provided in Daugherty's score: to improvise on "various non-pitched 'ALIEN' percussion instruments", and later to "move slowly, mysteriously, and dramatically to Percussion station IV".[49] Glennie's instrumentation list for the premiere (dated 15 January 1999) required eighty objects, with scope to add more under the headings of "selection of miscellaneous scaffolding if possible" and "other strange instruments"; reference is also made to lighting (shadows and colour spots).

UFO is a work written with live performance (and Glennie) in mind. A video released by The Evelyn Glennie Collection (performing with the Kent County Youth Orchestra in 2000) offers a useful means of engaging with the concerto in this context.[50] For this performance, the first improvisation was compelling and appropriately bizarre. Chanting through a headset microphone whilst bowing a waterphone and moving purposefully through the auditorium, Glennie emerged from the darkness dressed

---

[49]   Ibid., p. 127.

[50]   Evelyn Glennie (2012) *Evelyn Glennie performs UFO by Michael Daugherty with the Kent County Youth Orch – 09/2000* (video online). Available from: https://www.youtube.com/watch?v=GyRlozJxDio (accessed 1 June 2022).

in a silver trouser suit (subsequently featured as the cover image for the 2001 Klavier recording). On reaching the stage, her foot kneads an air-filled rubber glove as she moves a metal spring in arcs around the body, creating a tangible sense of expectation. With every movement, the anticipation of sound possesses an energy as resonant as the subsequent musical outcome. The string section emerges in parallel with a *crescendo* on mechanical siren; as this fades, Glennie moves towards the central multi-percussion set-up. Metallic and brittle sonorities dominate the second movement (cymbals, xylophone, metal sheets, cowbells and temple blocks); the third ("Flying") continues to feature metal instruments, but these now evoke an ethereal and celestial atmosphere (with wind chime flourishes, cymbal rolls and vibraphone). Later in this movement, the soloist bows the edges of the vibraphone (a technique used in many percussion scores), wherein theatricality supersedes musical complexity. Glennie bows both front and rear, moving the sound through the body (of both performer and instrument) with slow determination. As with the experimental opening, the bowed notes are not difficult to execute, but this means that the soloist must capture the imagination of the audience in different ways. Virtuosity here is in the ability to hold the attention of the listener without recourse to complicated technical display.

In the fourth movement, "???", Glennie investigates sound, gesture and resonance. At the front of the stage, various objects (including cimbalom, handheld rattles and instruments manipulated using the feet) become sources of alien exploration. Glennie clearly enjoys the instability and fluidity of the moment, alternately standing and crouching as the improvisation progresses. Following the final movement (which features a compelling auxiliary percussion melody on tom-toms and octobans), Glennie returns to the mechanical siren at the front of the stage, once more experimenting with the collection of instruments on the floor.

Daugherty's score requires the soloist to embrace multiple creative identities as improviser, actress, musician and sound creator; all of these descriptors are relevant to Glennie's performance style. The work is a concerto, but it is also a living film score, wherein the percussionist is the protagonist; Daugherty's approach foregrounds the visual, tactile and aural power of the discipline. *UFO* has become linked directly to Glennie's interpretation, both in the context of live performance and recording. Released initially as an arrangement for soloist and wind band (2001) and subsequently with its original orchestration (2002), reviews were mixed (as was the case with appraisals of live performances). In many instances, the popularity and accessibility of the work was once more categorized as problematic, as was the emphasis on free improvisation in a genre which for centuries curtailed

The Ascendance of Solo Multi-Percussion Performance   45

the creative autonomy of the performer; critical response might best be summarized as confused. Nevertheless, subsequent composers remain drawn to the conceptual framework of Daugherty's concerto, positioning Glennie as protagonist in a range of dramatic contexts (several of which will feature in later chapters). In many ways, *UFO* is the first of many acts of creative rebellion wherein otherness is celebrated and diversity of response embraced:

> I can't really please everyone; it's not really possible to do that. You can try, but ... I used to try very hard to please people and I got myself in hot water, really. It didn't quite work because it meant that sometimes I wasn't receiving musical satisfaction ... It takes a lot of experience and a lot of experimentation.[51]

Glennie's Solo Multi-Percussion Commissions: Overview

The concerto is an established musical form in the context of Western art music; the introduction of an alternative solo voice represented progress for percussion, but not a shocking departure from convention in broader terms. Solo works for multi-percussion instead posited a new genre that was an unprecedented and essentially unregulated experimental medium. Early repertoire for solo percussion initiated interest in diverse instrumental configurations, extended techniques and new methods of scoring, with attempts to exploit the potential of the discipline most often resulting in expansive set-ups, extreme contrasts and virtuosic tasks. This legacy was continued in many of Glennie's early solo commissions. Subsequent investigations of sound have evolved to incorporate intimate explorations of auxiliary instruments; with the acceptance of solo percussion, less has become more. There is room for both; in the context of Western art music history, solo multi-percussion remains in its tumultuous and unpredictable infancy.

Glennie's solo commissions are reflective of a desire to embrace this state of flux, and also offer important insights into her personal interests as a performer. Whilst concerto commissions are generally undertaken with the support and collaboration of a particular orchestra or event, solo works are more often conceived with less defined objectives. As such, the chronology of these commissions trace Glennie's evolution as sound creator, metamorphosing from virtuosic flamboyance towards more focused

---

[51] Evelyn Glennie in Bruce Duffie (1994) *Percussionist Evelyn Glennie: A Conversation with Bruce Duffie* (online). Available from: http://www.bruceduffie.com/glennie. html (accessed 19 December 2016).

studies of timbre and extended improvisation (though this timeline is not strictly linear).

Solo commissions completed prior to 2006 tend to be scored for a large number of percussion instruments (see Appendix 2), part of a shared discovery of the sounds and sights of the medium for composer, performer and audience as the discipline evolved. Virtuosic percussionist and academic Steven Schick (whose career timeline is contemporary to Glennie's) summarizes this initial impetus to intrigue and entertain: "It used to be that you had to convince people it was worth listening to. I mean this in a general way, but you did this in a sort of vaudevillian approach: 'Look what that crazy guy can do', and that was at least one step closer to something interesting."[52] Early commissions were also key to defining the Glennie brand, an important musical form of self-promotion and publicity. Diversity and novelty of repertoire were required in order to fulfil this remit. Several composers responded by positioning Glennie at the drum kit to explore her proficiencies as a cross-over artist; *Drum Dances* (John Psathas, 1993) and *Reaching Out* (David Horne, 1996) are two such examples, where the techniques of art music merged with patterns drawn from jazz and rock repertoire. The sight of Glennie in command of an instrumental configuration most often associated with male performers was itself potent. Many enjoyed the theatricality of conjuring musical life from unlikely objects (as in Django Bates' *My Dream Kitchen*, 1996 or Heath's *Darkness to Light*, 1997). Works such as Robert Carl's *Written on Wood* (2000) or Steve Heitzig's *Free!* (2000) filled the stage with over forty instruments, choosing to foreground the timbral diversity and visual intrigue of the medium.

When the number of instruments is reduced, the range of techniques and communicative strategies must be expanded; in many ways, later works amplify the inherent vulnerability of solo performance. Replacing dramatic spectacle with more conceptual studies of sound is entirely more difficult than it may first appear. The soloist must hold the attention of the listener only with hi-hat for Julia Wolfe's *Iron Maiden* (2011), and crash cymbal for Allan Bell's *Littoral Liminal* (2017), the latter based on a direct instruction from Glennie:

> I wrote to her and asked what she would be interested in and she replied with the explicit challenge: one cymbal with no stick changes. She stated that she wanted a piece that was not just an exercise in

---

[52] Steven Schick in Will Romano (2014) Steven Schick: Interview, *Modern Drummer Magazine* (online), May 2014. Available from: https://www.moderndrummer.com/article/may-2014-steven-schick/ (accessed 30 May 2018).

stick/mallet exchange, but rather one that was a genuine exploration of the sound of the instrument.[53]

Joan Tower's 2016 commission *Small* was a playfully literal diminution of the multi-percussion set-up, with the soloist performing on a range of miniature instruments. There is a sense of growing confidence in the recent repertoire emerging for solo percussion, with composers now stimulated by the challenges of writing for individual instruments and scoring timbral nuance with clarity. Diversification and evolution do not always demand that more be added. At its most elemental, percussion is colour, rhythm and timbre; sometimes this is enough. It is difficult to choose case studies from Glennie's solo commissions, since each is unique. For the purposes of this chapter, two examples are chosen as a means of illustrating some of the ways in which composers have interpreted the identity of the solo multi-percussionist. Others will be referenced where relevant in subsequent chapters.

Creative Autonomy: *Darkness to Light* (1997)

The first solo commission to attract the attention of British audiences, *The Song of Dionysius* (McLeod, 1988) initiated an abiding interest in writing for percussion within a programmatic framework:

> *The Song of Dionysius* is a shorter piece based on the story of the Greek Dionysius the Elder, who was so suspicious about what people might be saying about him that he built a subterranean cave in the form of a human ear, with the acoustic designed so that he could clearly hear what was being said by the prisoners he kept in the chamber above the cave.[54]

A striking and impressive feature of her 1989 Proms recital, the world premiere of McLeod's fifteen-minute composition also exemplified the early priority of establishing Glennie's credibility as a virtuosic performer. Beginning and ending at the piano, Glennie was otherwise positioned in a cave of instruments, surrounded by marimba, gong, stones, claves, cowbells, temple blocks, tom-toms, suspended cymbal and wind chimes. Tuned and auxiliary percussion function largely as distinct entities (creating in effect two resonating chambers), allowing the soloist to demonstrate proficiencies in both facets of the discipline. *The Song of Dionysius* remained a key feature of Glennie's recital programming for almost a decade, performed

---

[53] E-mail correspondence with Allan Gordon Bell, 25 May 2018.
[54] Glennie (1990) *Good Vibrations*, p. 3.

148 times between 1989 and 1998, and included in her second solo album *Light in Darkness* (1991: RCA Victor Red Seal). In Glennie's words, she "played it to death until more repertoire was written".[55] McLeod offered an accessible and engaging work, but his scoring did not yet fuse tuned and auxiliary sonorities into a unified musical language.

Subsequent solo commissions moved towards a more holistic sound-scape and a keener blurring of the boundaries between tuned and untuned, instruments and found objects, sound and music, art and popular music, composer and performer. Whilst the title of Heath's *Darkness to Light* establishes a defined programmatic dichotomy, in musical terms the work is an exploration of synergies between potentially disparate elements. Heath's effort to connect art music to other genres closely associated with percussion (most notably jazz and rock references) is perhaps the most significant manifestation of this impetus, felt keenly in passages scored for drum kit. Whilst the kit is, by default, a multi-percussion set-up, it is a discipline with its own cultural and social history. It also requires a specific set of skills; the use of all four limbs to create layers of sound deviates from the standard positioning of the solo multi-percussionist (who most often stands to perform). As another means of exploring Glennie's range as a performer, the drum kit is a useful addition (already employed in earlier solo works by Psathas and Horne); its inter-genre implications are even more important, resonating with her efforts to elude classification and to expand the remit of solo multi-percussion performance. In *Darkness to Light*, passages are scored for waterphone, drum kit, mark tree and vibraphone; the performer is otherwise free to create their own configuration. As Glennie notes: "In this piece I use a lot of toys ranging from autoharps, battery-operated spinning tops, fire extinguishers and thunder sheets to cracked marimba bars clunked together and little squeaky toys and whirlies, as well as voice effects."[56]

Space for free improvisation in all three sections further heightens the degree of performer-determination: the darkness of the opening (dominated by the abrasive metallic resonance of the waterphone), the metamorphozing middle passage (featuring drum kit) and resolution into the light (heard most definitively in the vibraphone line with pitches indicated but rhythms undetermined). Glennie's annotations for the first percussion entry offer

---

[55] Evelyn Glennie in Kenny Smith (2018) Dame Evelyn Glennie Shares Her Early Years, *Scottish Field*, 5 October 2018 (online). Available from: https://www.scottishfield.co.uk/culture/music/dame-evelyn-glennie-shares-her-early-years/ (accessed 13 June 2022).

[56] Evelyn Glennie in Lynne Walker (2001) Hit Me With Your Rhythm Schtick, *Independent*, 10 March 2001.

The Ascendance of Solo Multi-Percussion Performance   49

an evocative sense of the dark atmosphere which she seeks to create; notes such as "use other weird instruments", "lots of space" "bring audience in" and "lonely and weird" are highly subjective prompts. These also indicate that improvisations genuinely evolve in the moment of live performance. Glennie's cues do not dictate musical content, but rather define the mood that she wants for the section. Heath offers a similarly open-ended series of directives, requesting certain timbral effects in the first twenty-six bars and a number of specific rhythmic entries, but otherwise providing a blank canvas for the performer. The most engaging feature of the work (certainly in its early performances) was the sight and sound of Glennie as kit player, a symbol of the status of percussion as a discipline which traces multiple histories, styles and legacies. By default, this positioned Glennie as a performer with interests extending beyond the parameters of art music.

The drum kit (heralded by snare drum in bar 27) dominates the central section with an insistent jazz–rock fusion in dialogue with syncopated piano chords. A ten-second improvisation between the two performers in bars 45–46 segues to a powerful piano ostinato with an insistent and arresting rhythmic outline. Much of the solo part is notated as a series of wavy lines in this middle section, wherein the relationship between piano and drum kit evolves during the live event. There is a powerful sense of escape, freedom and connection which is both musically and programmatically transformative in this brief but significant section; transecting genres becomes a metaphor for the transition from darkness to light. Five breaks (spaces for the kit player to improvise) are indicated on the score, the last of which extends over forty bars (with Glennie's annotations including prompts such as "wilder and wilder" and "heaps of cymbal crashes"). The sense of light in the finale is beautifully rendered with mark tree entries leading into an ethereal vibraphone melody in its highest register supported by sustained piano chords. Flourishing arpeggiated figures are then shared between the performers in a delicate interplay.

Over the course of eleven minutes the listener witnesses three distinct worlds, but each overlaps and intersects. *Darkness to Light* was one of a limited number of scored compositions included in the three-night series *Evelyn Glennie's Hitlist* (2001), concerts focused primarily on collaborative improvisations with a range of guest performers. The *Hitlist* was a statement of creative intent which prioritized the live performance event: "It's important to realise that these concerts are not for critics ... They are simply a celebration and the audience is almost eavesdropping on this informal music-making."[57] *Darkness to Light* reflects this ethos in microcosm, pre-

---

[57]   Ibid.

50 *Evelyn Glennie: Sound Creator*

senting a nuanced balance between Glennie as virtuosic solo multi-percussionist and the more exploratory identity of sound creator. There is a defined structure in *Darkness to Light* which scaffolds the improvisations, but the performer is essentially asked to paint with sound in each of the three sections. The soloist guides the musical journey, and the composer trusts them to do so.

Interdisciplinarity: *Sounds of Science* (2014–2016)

Almost twenty years later, programme music was still a central feature of commissions, and continued to offer a means of extending the role of the multi-percussionist into a wider range of cultural and social contexts. Maintaining her vision of percussionist as storyteller, Glennie has not stayed in the concert hall or within the parameters of art music; her commissions have likewise evolved into works intended to reach untapped demographics and new listeners. *Sounds of Science* (2016) was an interdisciplinary commission with this ambition in mind, a collaboration envisioned as a multi-faceted creative experience in both artistic and pedagogical terms. The programmatic construct in this instance is factual, following the chronology of human innovation. In *Sounds of Science*, the audience was provided with a pre-show narration and visual timeline of scientific discovery (by historian Christopher Lloyd), a live solo multi-percussion performance (by Glennie), and a recorded audio accompaniment featuring both orchestral and ambient sounds (by composer and jazz pianist Jill Jarman).

World history author Christopher Lloyd initiated the project in 2014 as a result of an informal encounter with Glennie (from whom he purchased a marimba for his daughter). Lloyd is best known for his visual timelines of scientific discovery and historical events for the *What On Earth?* wallbook series. Jarman is an established composer and academic whose output demonstrates an ongoing interest in the confluence of science and sound as evinced in earlier works including *Soundwaves of Light* (2006), based on the light frequencies of the stars, *H2O* (2010), which is inspired by a water molecule's behaviour in different states, and *Resonance* (2015), a composition for cello based on the science of cymatics. Both individually and in collaborative sessions, the first stage of evolution centred on the selection of sounds suited to each of Lloyd's ninety-two events, all of which needed to be accommodated in an audience-friendly duration of twenty minutes. *Sounds of Science* is scored as a single movement, structured in chronological accordance with the visual timeline. The stage for the premiere (Edinburgh International Science Festival, 30 March 2016) was filled with various instruments and objects; some were immediately recognizable (snare drum, tambourine, bass drum and Aluphone), whilst the function of others remained unclear until they were used (see Fig. 5).

The audience could follow Lloyd's illustrations (included in the programme) or watch and listen to Glennie's performance onstage in order to discern each event; the intention was that they use a combination of

Fig. 5: Instrument configuration for *Sounds of Science* world premiere.

both sight and sound to progress through the timeline. A number of seminal events were easily and directly translated by percussive sounds: two stones struck together for "Hammering of Tools"; a hollow metal cylinder and glockenspiel stick denoting "Blacksmiths"; a long guiro played with thimbles creating the rhythmic pattern of "Indian Spinning Wheels". Found objects featured throughout, creating both visually and aurally appealing sources of interest: a plastic bag was crushed forcefully between the hands for "Making Controlled Fire"; a two-litre bottle of water both gesturally and sonically portrayed "Sailing Boats"; for "Abacus", this invention was repurposed as a percussion shaker. Sounds drawn from scientific innovation became musical instruments: a bottle of pills was the instrument for "Penicillin", wallpaper for "Chinese Paper-Making" and the opening of a can for "Carbonated Drinks". The recorded soundscape also balanced the literal and atmospheric. Direct translations included rushing water for "Archimedes Pump", a ticking clock for "Pendulum" and an explosion for "First Nuclear Bomb". Elsewhere, creating the ambience of events was instead the focus: the opening "Big Bang" was represented by *glissando* strings descending to a dark *tremolo*; "Wheels" was realized in a rippling orchestral figuration; a brass motif heralded the invention of "UK Wind Turbines". Gesture is integral to the soloist's role as narrator; beginning in a kneeling position downstage left, Glennie moved from one installation to the next. Some movements were timed to coincide with recorded sounds (as for "Flushing Toilet"), whilst others employed techniques to physically and aurally denote "Scything" (sweeping sticks methodically along a length of wood) and "QWERTY keyboard" (where a typewriter represented both the innovation and the instrument).

As seen in earlier commissions (including *UFO* and Vincent Ho's 2011 concerto *The Shaman*), Glennie is interested in integrating vocal effects into the solo percussionist's role. This is a recurrent feature in *Sounds of Science*, heard both in the recorded accompaniment (for "*Greek Philosophy*") and in the live performance (answering a ringing telephone, a haunting melody for "House of Wisdom", a loudspeaker instruction for the "London Underground" and elements recited from the "Periodic Table"). Though the intention is that the performance feels instinctive and improvisatory, much of the solo part is meticulously scored (extending even to pitches for the voice in "House of Wisdom", seen in Ex. 2 and rhythmic patterns for spoken sections). The practicalities of combining gestures, transitions and sticking in alignment with the recorded track present considerable logistical challenges. Though this represents the primary difficulty of the work, Jarman also scored moments where technical agility was also required, particularly

Ex. 2: Scoring for voice in *Sounds of Science* (Jill Jarman).

in the closing section which features increasingly frenetic rhythmic figurations around timbales, tom-toms and bass drum.

Entries are cued in several ways based on practicality, with reference to bar numbers, events in the backing track and titles from Lloyd's timeline. There are several short moments for improvisation, with the longest at bars 553–571, where thunder sheet and bass drum recreate "Earth Tremor" and "The Mallard" (a steam locomotive).

Glennie added relatively few annotations to her score, circling tempo directives, exaggerating bar lines with thick black marker and adding larger bar numbers/counts for *tacet* sections. However, as the piano begins in bar 512 for "Motion Pictures" (Lloyd's description) or "Silent Movies" (the term employed in Jarman's score), Glennie inserted several notes: "calm down and enjoy" and later "(oooh!)" for the left-hand figuration in bar 518 (see Ex. 3). At this stage, much of the timeline is completed.

Speaking of the premiere, Jarman reflected the positive energy radiating from the live performance experience:

> I became an audience member for a while, stepping back, watching the audience of all ages following the program's timeline. There were young people swaying in their seats to the clockwork section, making gestures for the fireworks. There was rapt attention from the "adults", a palpable excitement, and overall a sense of the shared discovery as the concert unfolded.[58]

For Glennie, the resounding impact of the commission was in the opportunity to introduce percussion to an entirely new audience and into disciplines wherein music is not always viewed as significant. The Institution of

---

[58] Jill Jarman (2016) *Sounds of Science: Telling Our Story Through Music* (online), 23 June 2016. Available from: https://www.evelyn.co.uk/sounds-science-telling-story-music/ (accessed 12 May 2018).

Ex. 3: Percussionist as pianist in *Sounds of Science* (Jill Jarman).

Mechanical Engineers described the work as "a musical masterpiece",[59] and Glennie's guest appearance on an episode of the *Love and Science* podcast (a detailed and somewhat obsessive series exploring contemporary directions in scientific research), was further testament to the fact that *Sounds of Science* resonated within this community.[60] As is the case with a number of commissioned composers (including Heath, Daugherty and Ho), Glennie's work with Jarman has since extended to other projects, including *Echoes from the Birdcage* (2017), *Beat of Hope* (2020) and *Across the Divide* (2022).

Combining collective energies to experiment and expand the repertoire for solo multi-percussion is a fundamental feature of Glennie's creative evolution. She is a solo performer, but music is an ecosystem which requires collaboration in order to succeed.

---

[59] *Sounds of Science Translates the Story of Engineering into a Musical Masterpiece* (online). Available from: http://www.imeche.org/news/news-article/the-sounds-of-science-translates-the-story-of-engineering-into-a-musical-masterpiece (accessed 18 May 2018).

[60] Andrew Glester (2017) *Love and Science: LISA's Gravitational Waves, Dame Evelyn Glennie and Hannah Peel* (podcast), 26 June 2017. Available from: https://loveandscience.podbean.com/e/lisas-gravitational-waves-dame-evelyn-glennie-and-hannah-peel/ (accessed 20 May 2018).

The Emancipation of Auxiliary Percussion: *Fifty for Fifty* (2015) and *Playing Around the Office* (2016–2019)

The expansive instrumentation for soloist in *Sounds of Science* reflects a statement made earlier in the chapter, noting that evolutions in Glennie's style and performance practice are not strictly linear. Though recent movements towards improvisation and timbral exploration have often meant a smaller arsenal for the performer, there is still room for large set-ups (as in *Sounds of Science*) which continue to celebrate the diversity of percussion. This final section does, however, look at small-scale works for minimal resources which also initiate a greater degree of independence from scored repertoire. From imposing virtuosic commissions to the emancipation of individual auxiliary instruments, there is room for all in the identity of the contemporary solo percussionist. Following the necessity of attention-seeking drama in the early promotion of solo multi-percussion, Glennie can now enjoy the freedom of returning to the fundamentals of the discipline (as both commissioner and improviser); resultant works and performances are focused on the nuances of sound creation. By reducing the performer's arsenal to a single object, spectacle and showmanship defer to sound and sensation; timbre assumes precedence over all other musical elements. Solo commissions such as Wolfe's *Iron Maiden* (2011) for hi-hat and Bell's *Littoral/Liminal* (2017) for one crash cymbal are indicative examples, but the *Fifty for Fifty* project (2015) is the most ambitious. As a means of celebrating Glennie's fiftieth birthday, fifty composers were asked to write fifty bars of music for a solo instrument, each instructed to choose between one tuned and one untuned option. To date, forty of these works have been added to Glennie's list of commissions, twenty-three of which are scored for auxiliary percussion. Whilst framed as a birthday gift, it was Glennie's intention that these works should appeal to other solo percussionists; obtaining a single instrument is much more feasible than sourcing the wide variety often required for multi-percussion pieces, and the short duration of each allows for their inclusion in recital programmes:

> I really wanted something that was long-lasting and that was more legacy built. So I basically thought, well, you know, commissioning has been such an important part of my growth as a musician, but also the growth of percussion, and I just thought, well wouldn't it be interesting if we approached fifty composers to write fifty bars of music.[61]

---

[61] Radio New Zealand Interview with Evelyn Glennie: Composer of the Week (2015), *Evelyn Glennie – Percussion Champion*.

56   *Evelyn Glennie: Sound Creator*

Though many commissions become synonymous with Glennie (based on her role in their premieres, recording legacy and in terms of the rights of exclusivity retained in several instances), the *Fifty for Fifty* works were intended to be shared with immediate effect. Eight have already been published; of these, five are scored for auxiliary percussion instruments. *Whisper* (by English composer, violist and pianist Sally Beamish) is written for three suspended cymbals; *Fifty Fifty: Leth-Chaud – Rima Tekau* (by Gareth Farr, a New Zealand composer, percussionist and drag artist) is for bongos; Matthew Hindson (academic and composer) reflects his instrument selection in the title, *The Accelerating Hi-Hat*; Áskell Másson's contribution (from one percussionist to another) is scored for four mallets (on any surface); *Colours of Naobo* (by the Chinese–American composer and violinist Chen Yi) explores a pair of Chinese cymbals. Glennie's directives on instrument choice required composers to become sound creators. As Farr attests: "What it makes you do as a composer is really think about all the different sounds you can get out of that one instrument."[62] Másson's *Fo(u)r Mallets* removed instruments from the work entirely. He chose instead to write for four different beaters (arranged from softest to hardest left to right), which can be played on any surface. This is a composition which can therefore be executed with the simplest of tools.

Glennie has recorded a number of the *Fifty for Fifty* commissions for her YouTube channel; each performance is preceded by a spoken introduction offering insights into the experience of preparing and executing the work. *Fo(u)r Mallets* is performed on a plastic timpani cover using marimba mallets; a post-instrumental work, this is a captivating homage to the technical skills of the contemporary percussionist and also an ode to the most consistent feature of their art – the stick. The composer asks the performer to begin with mallets raised; Glennie interprets this in a reverential manner, looking at each in turn and building a powerful sense of expectation. The silence itself assumes a musical identity, where the anticipation of sound is potent. Scored meticulously, the subsequent conflation of *accelerando* passages, polyrhythms, dynamic contrasts and drum rudiments (primarily the flam and drag) creates a sense of melody even in the absence of any defined instrumental sonority.

Whisper achieves a similar objective, in this instance creating a musical dialogue between three suspended cymbals. Glennie uses the word "respect" in the introductions to *Whisper* and *Fo(u)r Mallets*, a term applied to the relationship between performer and instrument, but also as an advisory to the listener. These works are short, but they invite concentrated listening,

---

[62] Ibid.

wherein they become meditations on sound. In *Whisper*, the section where Glennie bows the cymbals whilst using her other hand to feel the vibrations emanating from the centre of the instrument, evokes this sense of absolute concentration (see Ex. 4).

Each one of the short works celebrates percussion from the particular aesthetic perspective of the composer. Ho's *Sandman's Castle* (for tam-tam), retains the intention of being an accessible work, but nonetheless reflects awareness of Glennie's interest in experimentation and his own fascination with exploring timbre. As a result, there are no time signatures indicated and few bar lines, but directives on parts of the instrument to be used, dynamics and techniques are extensive. Glennie's performance notes list ten different striking implements as possible options (including chop sticks, prongs and a chicken foot). David Lang's *touch not the cat* is similarly adventurous, written for spoken word, tambourine and a number of specific gestures. In this instance, there is no score; an instructional paragraph and the text of the poem are instead provided.

From the listener's perspective, many of the *Fifty for Fifty* works could be mistaken for short improvisations, despite the fact that almost all are scored using the conventional five-line staff (albeit with numerous additional directives and symbols pertaining to sticks, placement, effects and gestures). There remains an enigmatic quality to works of this nature; they feel organic and spontaneous, even when notation is specific. The second reason for assuming that the works are improvised is more pragmatic:

Ex. 4: Opening of *Whisper*, using a range of effects on cymbals (Sally Beamish).

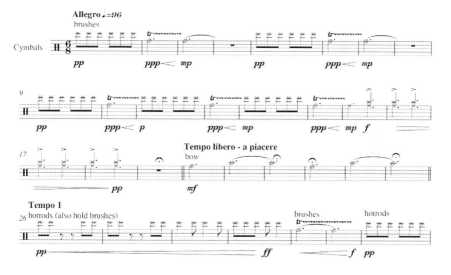

58   *Evelyn Glennie: Sound Creator*

many listeners do not know how timbral studies are notated. Glennie notes that this uncertainty extends beyond the *Fifty for Fifty* series:

> So many people, even after playing a concerto or something, will come up and say 'Was that music notated?' or you know, did I make it up? You would never say that to a violinist or a pianist after they've played a concerto ... I think it's this sort of feeling where they may not necessarily know how multi-percussion is notated, whereas they do know with piano or any other pitched instrument.[63]

For Glennie, an interest in improvisation co-exists with a passion for commissioning, resulting in a performance language that is both defined and exploratory. Therefore, it is not necessarily a problem when the listener does not discern the difference, as long as the work proves engaging and immersive.

The *Playing Around the Office* YouTube series (initiated in 2016) removes this ambiguity entirely, replacing notated repertoire with free improvisation in playful sonic explorations. They retain a connection to the *Fifty for Fifty* works in their brevity and attention to the sonorities of a single percussion instrument. All are auxiliary percussion, with the exception of the timpani (part 5), though the melodic range of this instrument is not the focus (see Table 3).

Conflating pedagogy and performance, *Playing Around the Office* offers vignettes of Glennie as sound creator, informal and accessible glimpses into what this identity means. Glennie is clearly still inspired by her work and continues to find new ways to explore sound: "like a lot of percussion, you just have to let the imagination go" (part 2); "it's really again up to the imagination to just try and be curious to what might happen" (part 4); "the instruments speak themselves and go on their own journey" (part 5). The timbral effects generated by various sticks and techniques are paired with responses to the inaudible sensations of resonance (also integral to Glennie's concert performances). In part 4, after playing the tam-tam with several implements, Glennie stands motionless in front of the instrument, allowing the vibrations to make a physical, embodied connection; a longer episode on the gong drum (part 15) also demonstrates the balance between hearing and feeling sound. At first glance, *Playing Around the Office* departs considerably from Glennie's primary professional identity as virtuosic soloist, but the essence of the multi-percussionist remains the same in both instances. *Playing Around the Office* is a distillation of the foundations of percussion practice, centred on the endless creative possibilities of striking,

---

[63]   Interview with Glennie, 3 May 2019.

The Ascendance of Solo Multi-Percussion Performance 59

Table 3: Instrumentation for YouTube series *Playing Around the Office*.

Part	Instrument
1	Cajons
2	Waterphones
3	Barimbulum
4	Tam-Tam
5	Timpani (with objects placed on skin)
6	Simtak
7	Exhaust Pipes
8	Thunder Sheet
9	Marimbula
10	Lambeg
11	Liam's Pipes
12	Wood Blocks
13	Spring Drums
14	Log Drums
15	Gong Drum
16	Metal Drums

shaking or scraping an object to produce sound. As the examples in this chapter demonstrate, the art of solo multi-percussion accommodates multiple modes of musical expression, including free improvisation, structured freedom and notated repertoire.

Concluding Thoughts

By the beginning of the twenty-first century, multi-percussion had an ever-increasing range of available solo repertoire and was firmly established in terms of pedagogical and performance practice. As audiences grew accustomed to the sounds and sights of solo multi-percussion set-ups, and students worldwide studied the discipline, innovation and progress manifested in often unexpected ways. Whilst concert and recital performances have remained a significant part of Glennie's touring commitments, commissions for solo multi-percussion represent one part of a much larger vision. Emerging with increasing frequency from 2012 onwards are inter-genre and interdisciplinary collaborations, new creative paths which further expand the remit of Glennie as sound creator. Glennie's interest in commissioning works for smaller instrumental forces, partnered with solo and ensemble improvisation, consolidates the importance of the live performance experience. Active listening, engaging with the properties of sound, and reinvigorating a sense of curiosity about the potential of relatively simple instruments, are the larger objectives.

It is possible to trace an evolution whereby virtuosic performances facilitated the commissioning of new works, which subsequently expanded into a search for new contexts and settings for multi-percussion. Concertos and recitals firstly positioned the discipline centre-stage; from this foundation, Glennie has looked beyond the concert hall and into the larger cultural sphere.

2

"I just basically followed my own instincts."

Diversification, Improvisation and Collaboration

An entrepreneurial spirit has directed Glennie's career in relation both to the art of sound creation and the demands of the contemporary music industry. As such, Glennie's professional portfolio encompasses multiple identities: she is a performer, commissioner, composer, improviser, collaborator, instrument inventor, motivational speaker, teacher, jewellery designer, and philanthropist. Each new pursuit involves both risk and opportunity.

In terms of music specifically, Glennie has eschewed the relative safety of a career in one milieu, choosing to evolve from the domain of art music into popular idioms, jazz, inter-cultural collaborations, electronic dance music and interdisciplinary performance. Though the genres and disciplines are diverse, and the role of improvisation changes dependent upon context, collaboration is the unifying element. No musician operates in isolation; Glennie's profession as a solo multi-percussionist has always been collaborative, even in the context of art music, where the virtuosic performer is often physically and hierarchically distinguished from their peers. Networking and interaction are essential to any performer's professional development: liaising with composers for commissions and working with conductors and orchestras for concerto premieres are just two obvious examples of how soloists collaborate and interact with other musicians in art music. However, the parameters of control exerted on commissions and concerto performances incorporate scores, rehearsals and concert dates, meaning that little is unforeseen or spontaneous; Glennie's later collaborative projects seek greater freedom in this respect.

In a book titled *Greatness*, D.K. Simonton hypothesizes that artists take around ten years to develop their mature, idiosyncratic style.[1] If this timeline is applied to Glennie's professional development, dating from her definitive emergence into the public consciousness with the Proms recital of 1989, the period from 1999 onwards indicates a consistent move towards group improvisation and shared creativity. Glennie's first album release subsequent to Simonton's proposed stage of artistic maturation is the collaborative improvised album *Shadow Behind the Iron Sun* (2000), made in conjunction with producer Michael Brauer, and musicians Philip Smith and David Motion.

Glennie's work in recent years encompasses a diverse range of projects centred on creative experimentation, many of which rely upon the synergies of collaboration. Though the Romantic trope of the isolated genius lingers in the literal and metaphorical distinction between a virtuosic soloist and their peers, more recent discourse on the hive mind, swarm intelligence, and group flow more accurately reflects the inherently shared nature of creative endeavour. One of the primary benefits of collaboration is the interactive confluence of practices, experiences and interests wherein art emerges from the convergence of several sources, allowing cross-fertilization between musical and artistic genres to render terms such as "art music" or "jazz" less restrictive (or necessary). The most important is the opportunity for a shared learning experience:

> I think that the majority of the collaborations have been rewarding and I think that when you are collaborating it is important to realize that even if something doesn't work in the way that you felt it might do, you've lost nothing; you've learned something about that collaboration ... You always have that step where you just sort of see if the chemistry is right and if something can grow there and then you build on that chemistry. And then you commit to the collaboration.[2]

A democratic and egalitarian process of music-making, an analogy can be drawn between Glennie's collaborative creativity and her analogous work as an advocate and philanthropist. This is noted succinctly in Sawyer's observation that "musical collaboration can help us to understand all collaboration".[3] This chapter will offer insights into the rich creative artefacts which have emerged as a result of Glennie's experimentation, which serve to situate the art of multi-percussion in new contexts.

[1]   D.K. Simonton (1994) *Greatness.* New York: Guilford Press, pp. 68–69.
[2]   Interview with Glennie, 3 May 2019.
[3]   R. Keith Sawyer (2006) Group Creativity: Musical Performance and Collaboration, *Psychology of Music*, 34, p. 164.

Improvisation, Art Music and Percussion

From its emergence in art music, works for solo percussion involved a heightened degree of performer-determination: there are numerous versions of instruments and sounding objects; decisions made regarding configurations and physical gestures are highly subjective; timbral scoring directives can be ambiguous; composers often include passages for improvisation in notated works. Whilst all percussionists play with sound as part of the fluid nature of the discipline, the ability to improvise is a skill that must be practised and developed over time. It is incorrect to assume that all are improvisers by default, a notion which undermines the complexities involved, and returns to dated perceptions of percussion instruments as noise makers and objects to be struck with wild abandon (and limited musical intent).

Glennie notes that the concerto cadenza, in which composers so often offer guidance to soloists in other disciplines, tends to be an entirely blank canvas for percussionists. Though this of course reflects Glennie's own performance style and interests in the case of commissioned repertoire, it does raise some interesting questions as to why composers so readily place the onus of creation on the soloist in this milieu. For other instruments, the cadenza is most often framed and anticipated with clarity, so that the audience clearly understands the delineation between the score and the performer's interpretation. There is an expectation that the percussion soloist does not need such scaffolding to present the drama of their art; the ramifications of this in terms of improvisation is that it is presumed to be a less significant and specific skill, an instinct as opposed to an art form: "Somehow for percussionists, composers feel 'Oh well, they improvise all the time'. A lot of times after I've played a concerto, sometimes audience members may say, 'So, was that piece written down or did you just make it up?'"[4]

To devalue the complexities of improvisation as something which the performer "makes up" is problematic, as is the inference that percussionists do not read notated repertoire in the same manner as their peers. For any instrumental discipline, the identity of improviser is to be claimed, studied and practised as a unique mode of expression which definitively positions the performer at the centre of the musical experience, a much more complicated proposition than simply filling time with sound. When executed proficiently, improvisation is a profound means of forging a direct connection between performer and listener wherein spontaneous freedom

---

[4] LMEA Music (2021) *Healing Power of Music, An Interview with Dame Evelyn Glennie* (video online). Available from: https://www.youtube.com/watch?v=RRFYmn-RNNn8&t=1553s (ccessed 8 February 2023).

co-exists with the accumulation of all prior learning skills. It is emotional and intellectual, known and discovered, conscious and sub-conscious, a living archive of retained memories. It is communal and personal, simple and intricate, familiar and unknown. Improvisation is poetry and practicality, art and life; anyone can improvise badly, but it requires much effort to do it well.

Whilst now a presence in multiple genres and interdisciplinary environments, Glennie began her career as a virtuosic percussionist working in the context of art music, wherein the role and status of improvisation has been particularly unstable. In the seventeenth century, extemporization, ornamentation and embellishment were standard aspects of Baroque performance practice. The score provided the performer with the impetus to imbue music with their own interpretative acumen. But as printed music developed as an increasingly lucrative industry, composers began to exercise greater control over the musical product; ornamentation became more prescriptive and less improvisational. The Classical era continued to explore improvisation as a manifestation of the skills of the virtuoso primarily by means of the concerto cadenza, defining the parameters where freedom was permitted, whilst the burgeoning generation of amateur musicians grew increasingly cautious of advancing beyond the guidance of the score. Manderson eloquently describes the hierarchy at this point in Western art music history:

> We think of classical music as the very opposite of improvisation, as the creature of a calculated perfectionism of creation and reproduction. The composition is carefully set down and deviation is not permitted. The performer is enlisted as the servant dedicated to reviving as faithfully as possible this precise and immobile object.[5]

Manderson's description of the performer as "servant" marks an important paradigm shift. The musician was no longer a co-creator; they were now subservient to the directives of the composer. The growing search for perfection in the musical product made improvisation increasingly problematic, and when the composer assumed status as genius in the Romantic era, attitudes towards its value diminished considerably. With the ascendance of the score as the central artefact and representation of the musical work, even the most distinguished performers were relegated to serving as the conduit through which the composer's vision is conveyed. Despite the popularity of virtuosic performance in the Romantic era, critical

---

[5] Desmond Manderson (2010) Fission and Fusion: From Improvisation to Formalism in Law and Music, *Critical Studies in Improvisation,* 6 (1), p. 1.

attitudes towards the notion of the performer appropriating the musical work to display their own skills resulted in a gradual decline in respect for improvisation.

In the opening decades of the twentieth century, abstract expressionism in the visual arts and existentialist writing in literature invited spontaneity and immediacy in cultural creativity. However, the impulsive energy which emerged so forcefully in the experimental aesthetics of the literary and visual arts did not arrive so readily for the discipline of music. Even the most rebellious composers of the twentieth century did not fully abandon the security of a semblance of musical structure. Rather than freely admitting improvisation to performance, experimental music opted not to explode the system, but rather to expand it. Growing interest in noise and non-traditional instruments, and a move away from standard nomenclature, extended the scope for controlled degrees of freedom. Quite understandably, there was unwillingness amongst even the most progressive composers to fully relinquish creative control; to do so would render them irrelevant.

Given that percussion was peripheral in art music until the twentieth century, its history is not necessarily imbued with the conventions of other solo instrumental disciplines. However, all musicians working in art music are faced to some extent with the burden of the canon, positioned for several centuries in direct opposition to the notion of performer autonomy. Glennie is not the first percussionist to transect the boundaries between notated repertoire and improvisation, but this transition is not intrinsic to the discipline. Whilst the contemporary solo percussionist is certainly invited to explore improvisation, they are not compelled to do so (beyond the liberties of the concerto cadenza). Performers choose this path, much in the same way as many opt to specialize in a particular genre or on an individual instrument. For this reason, it is relevant to consider some predecessors whose efforts anticipated Glennie's own.

From the 1920s, the xylophonist George Hamilton Green integrated the practice of extemporizing melodies into performances and pedagogical publications. Though not the first xylophone virtuoso in history (Michael Joseph Gusikov and Charles De Try had already demonstrated the capacity of the instrument for nineteenth-century European audiences), Green emerged when the new sounds of ragtime combined with the increasing popularity of recorded music to reach a much larger demographic. For this reason, his name remains synonymous with the instrument. Along with over one hundred recordings, Green's interest in improvisation is reflected in sections of *George Hamilton Green's New Instruction Course for Xylophone* (first published in 1924), and in *George Hamilton Green's New Series of Individual Instruction Courses for Xylophone and Marimba: Modern Improvising and Application of Ideas to Melody* (first published in 1936). Green determined that improvisation was a natural extension of the development of technical acuity; scales and arpeggios were learned with the specific intention of utilizing these skills for improvising effectively. Due largely to a revival of his works pioneered by Bob Becker (founding member of the venerable Nexus Percussion Ensemble), percussion students continue to engage with Green's repertoire and pedagogical materials. In 1976, Nexus prepared a programme consisting entirely of ragtime pieces which led to an album released the same year, entitled *Nexus Ragtime Concert*; this was followed by the 1989 album *Nexus Plays the Novelty Music of George Hamilton Green*. Though his career began with transcriptions of art music repertoire, Green's legacy belongs primarily to the lineage of popular culture (including jazz, bebop and swing) in which improvisational ability is acknowledged and respected as a distinct and particular attribute. To some extent, this positions him as a marginal predecessor of the improvising percussionist in the context of art music, a discipline with precedents much less willing to accommodate the inevitable imperfections of the process.

One might argue that the Nexus Percussion Ensemble also function as tangential predecessors to Glennie, given the fact that collective creativity differs from the experience of solo improvisation. However, the Nexus Ensemble has always included virtuosic performers recognized in their own right as pioneers of the discipline (as soloists, orchestral players, teachers and academics); they remain an integral part of the timeline of contemporary percussion. In the inaugural two-hour Nexus concert (22 May 1971), Bob Becker, Bill Cahn, Russell Hartenberger and Garry Kvistad presented an entirely improvised programme, positioning spontaneous creativity at the centre of their philosophical and aesthetic identity.

Over time, Nexus have commissioned challenging new music for percussion ensemble, paralleling Glennie's interest in developing the canon. Though scored works have become increasingly important, improvisation retains its status as a defining feature of their evolution. There are three primary reasons for this: the influence and inspiration of non-Western practices, an interest in collecting and developing new percussion instruments, and a desire to celebrate the unique nature of the performance event in the fullest possible sense. A fourth, less tangible, rationale might also be added – the intention to surprise and engage the listener using sound in new ways. Though it might seem redundant to state that musicians embrace improvisation as an opportunity to play more, this is particularly important for percussionists more typically employed by orchestras (as is the case for most Nexus members over the years).

With the enduring predominance of works from the Classical and Romantic period, orchestral percussionists still perform perfunctory roles in the orchestra. Improvisation is a means of being present in every moment of performance, of making use of instrument collections, and of retaining a sense of engagement that is sometimes difficult to find when faced with hundreds of *tacet* bars. Hartenberger (founding member of Nexus and orchestral percussionist with ensembles including the Oklahoma City Symphony and Toronto Symphony) recalls "wanting to play more – not just counting rests and playing little fragments of interesting phrases, and not wanting to be tone colour but to be an essential ingredient in the music."[6] For Nexus, improvisation was a means of rebelling against the strictures of the canon; for Glennie, there was a similar impetus to elude the confines of genre. Performing without a score emancipates both the sounds of percussion and the identity of the percussionist from convention. This is key to the Nexus ethos. As stated by Robin Engelman: "I feel that sound, the essence of music, is too often subjugated. Relationships between players and their instruments, audiences and music, are undermined by excessive intellectualism or incompetence."[7]

Engelman's reference to the "essence" of music is reflected in Abe's practice, another significant predecessor who has fully integrated improvisation into her professional identity as an art music virtuoso. Abe's biographer Rebecca Kite describes improvisation as a means of "turning toward her essential self"[8] A direct influence on Glennie at the early stages of her musical development, Abe's work as both composer and performer affords freedom to develop intuitive connections between instrument, musician and listener in the moment of performance. Glennie was unquestionably affected by Abe's perspective: "One of the differences between Japanese and Western performers is the attitude to playing music. Japanese musicians don't regard performing as in any way a job or task that has to be got through; it is more a state of being, a total involvement, almost a religion."[9]

Abe's *Michi* (1978) for solo marimba has retained a place in Glennie's programming since she first performed it in 1986. The title, meaning "the path" or "the way", is reflected in the freedom to improvise at both the beginning and end of the work. In doing so, the performer creates their own journey through the performance. Improvisation offers space to breathe, firstly to anticipate and subsequently to reflect, on the considerable technical

---

[6] Russell Hartenberger in Rick Mattingly (1996) Nexus, *Percussive Notes*, August 1996, p. 16.

[7] Ibid.

[8] Kite (2007) *Keiko Abe*, p. 76.

[9] Glennie (1990) *Good Vibrations*, p. 137

demands of the central section of the work. In *Michi*, performance becomes a balance between time which is controlled and time which is suspended; virtuosity is realized both in the execution of the score directives and in the ability to submit to the present. For Abe, it is essential to her evolution and practice as a performer: "I had to find a way to ensure 100% concentration during performances, and to achieve a creative space in my playing that transcends mere technique. I did not achieve that goal until I began to improvise, both alone and in ensemble."[10]

Again, Abe's path differs from Glennie's (as with Green and Nexus); focusing on one tuned instrument demands different skills to those required for the multi-percussionist. What is common to all predecessors is the impetus or compulsion to improvise for self-fulfilment, creative autonomy and connection. For improvisation to reach the audience in a meaningful way, the performer surrenders to the fluidity of the moment; they become both vulnerable and powerful. Though all percussionists play with sound, it is the willingness to make this private experience public, to follow their own *michi*, which denotes seminal figures in this respect.

Glennie and Improvisation: Overview

From the very beginning, Glennie has lived performance as a subjective and responsive process. In interviews discussing her musical development, Glennie frequently recounts her early experiences with peripatetic tutor Ron Forbes, which began with explorations of the snare drum (without sticks), feeling resonance through walls, instruments and the body. There is an improvisatory quality to her performance style even when interpreting scored repertoire, a sense of connecting with sound that supersedes technical accuracy or skill. She is an instinctive performer, for whom the live experience must feel different and new each time:

> Every time you're with a snare drum or a wood block or whatever, you want to think, well that's the first time you're experiencing it. You want to feel as though there's yet another layer to explore, another way to strike it or another tool to use to strike it, or another angle for it to be positioned or whatever. That's really important.[11]

---

[10] Keiko Abe in Lauren Vogel Weiss (1993) *PAS Hall of Fame: Keiko Abe* (online). Available from: https://www.pas.org/about/hall-of-fame/keiko-abe#:~:text=The%20first%20woman%20ever%20inducted%20into%20the%20PAS,with%20the%20confident%20way%20she%20approaches%20the%20marimba (accessed 13 June 2017).

[11] Interview with Glennie, 3 May 2019.

Increasing experimentation in collaborative projects, solo performances and recording outputs in recent decades indicates that improvisation resonates in a particularly profound manner with Glennie's maturation as a performer. Whilst Glennie views this as a natural and organic progression, issues have arisen in commentary on her work in this domain, many of which pertain to dated perceptions of virtuosity in art music. Does improvisation represent an act of creative insurgence? Is it an effort to transcend musical boundaries? Can a virtuosic performer associated with art music make such a transition? In many ways, Glennie sees improvisation as a question stated in musical form, asking the audience to engage and participate actively in the experience. Glennie's work in this domain is an articulation of the importance of listening, the centrality of the performative act, and the inherently social nature of music-making: "By seeing myself more as a sound creator rather than a percussionist, all the walls come tumbling down as it opens up other avenues of music."[12]

Glennie's discography indicates an interest in improvisation from the beginning of her career as a recording artist. Works by Abe (with improvisations on marimba) feature in two early releases: *Rhythm Song* (1990) and *Wind in the Bamboo Grove* (1995). In 1995, a cross-over collaboration with Björk relied on improvisation to create two tracks, "My Spine", included on Björk's 1996 release *Telegram*, and "Oxygen", on Glennie's compilation album *Evelyn Glennie: Her Greatest Hits* (1998). "Oxygen" is a haunting dialogue between voice and a chorale-like marimba accompaniment; "My Spine" features a relentless ostinato on bells and various metal resonators. Speaking of the project, Glennie notes: "Everything we did we recorded; this piece, with all the pops, rattles and other unrefined noises, shows that this was a totally spontaneous effort ... This is how I like to make music."[13] Björk recounts the experience of collaborating with Glennie in similar terms: "I just went to her house and we ate a lot of biscuits and drank a lot of tea and she took out exhaust pipes and made up that song ["My Spine"] and recorded it in ten minutes."[14] Glennie's work with Björk alludes to the value of improvisation as a means of connecting musical genres, expanding the potentialities of multi-percussion beyond the confines of the concert hall. It also anticipates a growing interest in collaborative projects which develop in alignment with increasingly experimental live and recorded performances.

[12] Evelyn Glennie in Kenny Smith (2018) Dame Evelyn Glennie Shares her Early Years.
[13] Evelyn Glennie (2002) *Oxygen* (online). Available from: http://www.bjork.fr/Evelyn-Glennie,2716 (accessed 28 November 2018).
[14] Björk (1996) *Björk on the Aftershock of Hate Mail and Love Affairs* (online). Available from: http://www.bjork.fr/Blah-Blah-Blah-1996 (accessed 28 November 2018).

A number of very brief improvisations (referred to as "Sorbets") are included on Glennie's solo album *Drumming* (1996), offering fleeting expositions of auxiliary instruments (such as Simtak, wood block, hi-hat, llama hooves and Chinese cymbals). These improvisations retain some sense of the instinctive and responsive energy of live performance, so often compromised when works are recorded. The most important rationale for improvising in Glennie's view is the opportunity to share the process of music-making with the listener in a particularly profound communal journey of discovery. Though improvisation feels to some like a significant change in Glennie's career direction (emerging definitively from 2000), exploration of sound has always been intrinsic to her performance practice; it is the transition from (relatively) private to emphatically public which marks a new stage in her evolution.

Statement of Intent: *Shadow Behind the Iron Sun* (2000)

When one examines the early part of Glennie's discography it is clear that her professional identity was focused primarily on commercially viable projects with wide general appeal. The release of her *Greatest Hits* in 1997 attests to this, indicating her popularity as a virtuosic art music performer and exemplifying the frenetic pace of Glennie's emergence into the public domain. In many ways, the "Sorbets" (six of which are also included on her *Greatest Hits*) serve as a tentative prelude to the arrival of *Shadow Behind the Iron Sun* (2000), a provocative artistic statement marking a seminal moment in Glennie's evolution as sound creator. At the height of her performing career, with a rapidly increasing number of commissioned works to premiere, this entirely improvised album was an assertive declaration of diversification. From this point onwards, experimental collaborative projects have allowed Glennie to record and perform in contexts which extend far beyond the parameters of art music. She has not rejected her status as a virtuosic art music performer and commissioner; she has extended it: "What type of recording is it? Is it a pop recording? Is it classical? Is it new age? Is it contemporary? I mean, what is it? I haven't a clue. It's just one of those things that people accept it as it is, and there won't be another one like it, and that's the beauty of it."[15]

Shadow Behind the Iron Sun served several important functions for Glennie; it allowed her to avoid categorization in any one musical genre;

---

[15] Evelyn Glennie (2012) *Evelyn Glennie Documentary on the Making of the Album "Shadow Behind the Iron Sun"* (video online). Available from: https://www.youtube.com/watch?v=xGuUX1NEock (accessed 16 February 2023).

it afforded the freedom to make use of her burgeoning instrument collection; it further diversified the voice of multi-percussion in the context of contemporary music. Whilst she is ambiguous about whether this was a determined effort to rebel, there is the sense that her success as a virtuosic art music performer was becoming increasingly restrictive, a situation that she wanted to avoid:

> By this time, I had been collecting instruments for a while; the collection was growing. I was finding things that I wasn't using necessarily on the concert platform, but yet they were still really interesting objects that created interesting sounds and I wanted an outlet to use these kinds of things. I felt that I really didn't want to be hemmed in as a particular kind of musician … It was just something that felt right to do. I just felt this need to get what was inside of me out, not really knowing what was inside of me, but just knowing that there was this kind of creative streak that wanted to just have complete and utter freedom, not to be hinged to a notated score, and literally see what happens.[16]

Shadow Behind the Iron Sun, though marketed as a solo album, was collaborative in nature. The sonorities of multi-percussion dominate, but producer Michael Brauer (an established presence in commercial popular music) played a significant role in realizing Glennie's creative vision in the studio. It took time to persuade the production company BMG that the idea could work, even with a prominent performer and successful producer in place: "BMG was very sceptical. They just couldn't get the concept, and I couldn't find a way to make the idea more clear whereby the remit was to go into the studio with a barrage of instruments and spend two days improvising … The outcome of it was something that no one could really imagine."[17] Ultimately, Glennie's proven success as a recording artist, and her power as a cultural commodity at this time, meant that BMG acquiesced. The resultant *Shadow Behind the Iron Sun* was entirely different from Glennie's earlier releases. The instrumentation focuses on metallic sounds (capable of evoking both light and darkness) including Simtak, suspended rows of cymbals, earth plates (small textured metal sheets) and wind chimes; tempering these sonorities are a range of drums (including bass drum and congas), used most often to develop ostinato figurations. Titles such as "Icefall" and "Crossing the Bridge" suggest visual imagery for the listener, but are reflective of the results of improvisation rather than the impetus which inspired them. The collaborative interaction between Glennie and

---

[16] Interview with Glennie, 10 March 2023.
[17] Ibid.

Brauer is echoed in an immersive blurring of acoustically generated sounds and post-production effects. From the beginning of the process, Glennie stipulated that every moment of the experience should be captured as a recording; this included ambient sounds, movements through the space, and discussions between producer and performer. For three days (with two more for post-production), Glennie was fully immersed in the process of improvising.

Brauer condensed Glennie's work into tracks with an average duration of three minutes (the only exception being the expansive "Land of Vendon"), aural vignettes presented in an accessible and direct manner. "Battle Cry" is particularly compelling in its immediacy, opening with solo wood block and seguing into an intense jungle beat with various vocalisations and sound effects (including piano and guitar motifs). Subsequent album pressings included a bonus mix of "Battle Cry", a more heavily produced interpretation which transforms the improvisation into a dance track. It is ingratiating to the ear (particularly in the remixed version), given the clarity of structure (insistent ostinati), fixed time signature (4/4) and consistency of instrumentation. Glennie's vocal effects are also refined to become coherent and melodic. As with several of the shorter tracks, "Battle Cry" serves as an engaging connective between art music, popular music and free improvisation; it does not present considerable challenges for the listener. Conversely, "Land of Vendon" is perhaps more interesting because it demands more active engagement. Extending to almost thirty minutes, it comes closer to capturing the essence of the creative process, allowing ideas to evolve and emerge at a slower rate of change. Stasis, silence, noise, and unfolding dialogues between performer and instrument intersect with moments of intensely energetic repetition. It is atmospheric, strange, unpredictable, and at times discomfiting, an articulation of the wonderful eccentricities of multi-percussion. In this track, Glennie explores the diversity of sonorities in a multi-percussion set-up featuring drum kit, found objects and over forty other instruments. "Land of Vendon" exemplifies one of the most discernible differences between the specificity of scored repertoire and the freedom of improvisation: the liminal space between anticipation and sound assumes a heightened level of significance even in the absence of gesture. In extended improvisations, the performer plays both with music and with time itself. Though improvisation should not be linked directly to Glennie's processes as a deaf performer, it does offer her the scope to feel every vibration emanating from the instrument. Listening through the body means that the music is felt for longer than it exists as an auditory presence. Improvisation provides the opportunity for this embodied response to become part of the musical event. In "Land of Vendon" the spaces in between are intrinsic parts of the experience (for both performer and listener).

In a documentary on the making of *Shadow Behind the Iron Sun*, Glennie is clear on the importance of creative autonomy in her professional identity: "There are no categories to what I do."[18] To some extent, this assertion has become a manifesto, extending from Glennie's identity as performer into her role as business and brand. In correspondence prior to the album release, Glennie was clear in her conviction that *Shadow Behind the Iron Sun* must be marketed differently: "This CD should be in the Classical Department and Pop ... Under no circumstances should it appear in the Classical section only."[19]

Whilst the album is, by definition, a fixed creative artefact (a distilled iteration of improvisation), live performances are the ultimate statement of intent. Following the release of *Shadow Behind the Iron Sun* in March 2000, Glennie began to integrate improvisation into her touring schedule, initially on a small scale, framed by multitudinous concerto premieres, recitals and public appearances. A multimedia event simply titled *Shadow Improvisation* (Queen Elizabeth Hall, London, 23 July 2000) marked the beginning of this expansion, a determined effort to broaden Glennie's portfolio. In email correspondence ahead of this show, she states: "I feel a need to get away from the predictable form of presentation and when I am booked to do something; there must be an element of surprise there."[20] This first solo improvisation did not prove entirely successful:

> To be perfectly honest, it was a complete disaster. Having done the *Shadow Behind the Iron Sun* CD where the studio was filled with instruments, I thought I could do the same on a concert platform. And so basically I had absolutely everything I could find (including half of a Mini car filled with instruments). The stage looked incredible. However, I think that was the biggest mistake I made and it definitely made me realize that less is more. So I had no concept of time (that is, duration); I had completely misjudged structure; I had completely misjudged that there was an audience there and what felt or appeared interesting to me onstage was not the case with the audience. Everything was sort of self-indulged I would say.[21]

---

[18] Evelyn Glennie (2012) *Evelyn Glennie Documentary on the Making of the Album "Shadow Behind the Iron Sun"*.

[19] E-mail dated 25 February 1999, kindly provided by The Evelyn Glennie Collection.

[20] E-mail dated 20 March 2000, kindly provided by The Evelyn Glennie Collection.

[21] Interview with Glennie, 10 March 2023.

Glennie's honest appraisal of this experience is testament to the fact that improvisation is an art which requires practice; it is not only in the first concert where the performer must acknowledge the process as one of trial and error. Subsequent collaborative events lingering on the *Shadow* theme continued in 2001–2006; undeterred, Glennie channelled the learning experience of the initial show to evolve as a performer: "It was probably one of the most successful learning curves of my life, and so for that I'm grateful. It really did help me spring forward with improvised concerts thereafter. They became, and are, my favourite form of playing I would say."[22] At the TROMP Percussion Festival (Eindhoven, 2006) Glennie collaborated with Fred Frith and Trilok Gurtu in an improvised performance for her peers, again referencing the lasting impact of *Shadow Behind the Iron Sun*. A six-minute compilation of the TROMP performance is captured on YouTube, offering some sense of the compelling visual elements of free improvisation, and of Glennie's increasing command of this musical language.[23]

Collaborative improvisation which extended beyond the foundations of *Shadow Behind the Iron Sun* also became part of Glennie's recital programming, beginning soon after the album release. In March 2001, Glennie presented a series of three performances in the Wigmore Hall, London, uniting with a number of instrumentalists including Hakan Hardenberger (trumpet), Christian Lindberg (trombone), Oren Marshall (tuba), Emmanuel Ax (piano) and Margaret Leng Tan (toy piano). Removing the programmatic impetus of *Shadow*, the improvisations in these concerts confounded several critics: "There's a lot of good music around now involving percussion (Glennie should know – she commissioned much of it) but by being so staunchly eclectic, and relying on the goodwill of her audience, she risks losing her powers of discrimination."[24]

In many ways, critique has served as motivation for Glennie; the enduring perception of notated works as superior, questions as to the suitability of "informal" music-making in the concert hall and narrow perceptions of the skills which constitute virtuosity are ideologies to be challenged. The metaphorical journey from the shadows of uncertainty and ambiguity to creative emancipation, stated symbolically in this album, remains part of

---

[22] Ibid.

[23] Evelyn Glennie (2011) *Evelyn Glennie Shadow Behind the Iron Sun Show with Fred Frith & Trilok Gurtu Eindhoven 2006* (video online). Available from: https://www.youtube.com/watch?v=RviHoQQ2SNs (accessed 18 February 2023).

[24] Evelyn Glennie review (2001) *Guardian* (online), 15 March 2001. Available from: https://www.theguardian.com/culture/2001/mar/15/artsfeatures4 (accessed 18 February 2023).

Glennie's impetus to improvise: "There is also a shadow that occurs before an improvised performance. It can drape like a cloak of anxiousness and concern about what will happen if I cannot think of something to play. As soon as the performance begins it evaporates and the creativity and music takes over."[25] *Shadow Behind the Iron Sun* initiated a consistent and definitive move towards experimental ensemble collaborations, resulting in numerous creative artefacts which celebrate multi-percussion and sound creation in unanticipated ways. For Glennie, improvisation is a musical metaphor for a career which revels in experimentation, innovation and diversification.

The Cinematic Experience: *Touch the Sound* (2004)

In a cavernous abandoned industrial space, two people meet and become acquainted through the language of music. A film crew documents every moment of the experience as it unfolds. This determinedly experimental concept serves as a synopsis of *Touch the Sound* (2004), an atmospheric documentary which focuses on capturing the essence of experimentation and musicianship. The sugar factory in which the improvisations take place becomes both an instrument and a resonating chamber for the sounds of percussion, voice and guitar. Glennie is partnered with Fred Frith, a British musician and composer whose ethos is well suited to the unusual remit of the documentary: "I embrace the idea of the 'work' as an unfinished and constantly mutating entity. Collaboration, improvisation, sculpting sound in the studio, and treating composition as an open-ended process remain central to how I make music."[26] Improvisations between Glennie and Frith are positioned as moments of calm and focus, interspersed with interviews and insights into the otherwise hectic pace of life as a touring musician. There is a meditative quality to Thomas Riedelsheimer's directorial style, juxtaposing Glennie's work beyond the walls of the disused factory with the escapism of collaborative improvisation. Glennie and Frith use instruments, voice and the intrinsic musicality of the industrial space, collated by Riedelsheimer into a visually and sonically stimulating journey which positions improvisation less as a conscious change of stylistic direction for Glennie and more an artistic compulsion, a manifestation of her desire to interact with the experience of making music on the deepest possible level.

[25] Evelyn Glennie (2012) *Shadow Behind the Iron Sounds* (online blog), 18 April 2012. Available from: https://www.evelyn.co.uk/shadow-behind-the-iron-sounds/ (accessed 5 November 2021).

[26] Fred Frith (n.d.) *About Fred* (online). Available from: http://www.fredfrith.com/ueber-mich/ (accessed 13 July 2023).

76   *Evelyn Glennie: Sound Creator*

Touch the Sound is significant, since it documents many of Glennie's views on the freedom of improvisation whilst also definitively addressing her specialized processes of listening through the body. Glennie talks openly about how she experiences music, but Riedelsheimer frames the discussion carefully to position Glennie as expert listener and not deaf musician:

> Normally this is a big issue in her life, and she's not very much pleased to lay too much stress on it, and it's always this, 'Well, that's the deaf musician. How can that be so?' so that's the first issue ... So my idea was always not to start with that and not make it the main issue of the film. I think you go through the film for half an hour or something like that, twenty minutes, and then you learn about her deafness and it doesn't play that big role in the rest of the film.[27]

Interactions between Frith and Glennie exemplify the ways in which all listening is multi-sensory; through eye contact, body language and instruments, sound is received and understood. There is no difference between Frith and Glennie in this context; deafness is irrelevant to the experience. The resonance felt through the body as Glennie listens is realized acoustically in the soundscape of the documentary, which creates textures and layers of ambient sonorities throughout. The only moment of silence is deliberately incongruous, positioned at a pivotal moment following an awkward question posed during a telephone interview: "How can a profoundly deaf person become a musician?"[28] There is a voyeuristic pleasure in watching Glennie experience the vibrations emanating from the gong in the opening moments, or immersed in a snare drum solo imbued with the surrounding energy of Grand Central Station. In scenes featuring Frith and Glennie, they interact with a playful sense of enthusiasm, seeking to draw sounds from every part of the space. Beginning with a joint improvisation on a flight case and Frith's body, they make music even before the audio equipment has been set up; a clear feeling of joy and energy emanates from both. As Frith notes:

> Artists are people who are in touch with the energy they had when they were children; it's never left them. And so that sense of seeing something or hearing something for the first time and being excited by it, I think, you know, you should try to hang onto that.[29]

---

[27]   Michele Norris and Melissa Block (2005) *NPR: All Things Considered: Thomas Riedelsheimer Discusses Stretching the Senses in 'Touch the Sound'* (online), 30 September 2005. Available from: https://www.npr.org/2005/09/30/4931402/stretching-the-senses-in-touch-the-sound (accessed 1 September 2019).

[28]   Riedelsheimer (2004) *Touch the Sound* (DVD).

[29]   Frith, ibid.

The longest improvisation, with a duration of around four minutes, positions Glennie and Frith seated side by side. Incense burns as the two converse through sound. Extended techniques on guitar are answered by Glennie using a range of sticks on gamelan gongs. There is a sense of independence and yet a synergy between instruments. The moments that feel connected (to both instrument and partner) are extended; elsewhere, intermittent strikes and experimental sounds resonate and fade as new ideas emerge. It is an atmospheric and invitingly strange scene, making the experience of improvisation an almost intimate journey.

Whilst these collaborative moments are a recurring feature of *Touch the Sound*, the documentary is primarily a study of Glennie's life and work; the music created between Frith and Glennie is tantalisingly brief. A soundtrack of the film (also released in 2004) features the ambient sonorities captured by Riedelsheimer and includes solo performances by Glennie, but only six tracks (of twenty-three) centre on the shared improvisations. In 2007, an album titled *The Sugar Factory* focuses specifically on the music created by Frith and Glennie during filming, with six evocative tracks offering a more holistic iteration of the three-day improvisation.

Whilst album releases like *Shadow Behind the Iron Sun* and *The Sugar Factory* broaden the genre categories in which Glennie can be marketed, it remains in the elusive and transitory domain of live performance where improvisation is most important. In the liner notes for *The Sugar Factory*, Frith acknowledges the importance of developing and nurturing collaborative synergies in this context: "Evelyn and I have performed together several times since these recordings were made. A language is developing between us, and every concert brings new discoveries."[30] This chemistry was potently expressed at the Moers Jazz Festival in 2013 (posted in its entirety on YouTube).[31] It is a study in sound and interaction, but also an unfolding which demands patience on the part of the listener. Here, improvisation is not curtailed by time or shaped by a particular narrative frame. The Moers performance develops excruciatingly slowly at the beginning, but the persevering listener is rewarded when the musical dialogue intensifies (around six minutes into the concert as Glennie begins to play the vibraphone). Long before ASMR (autonomous sensory meridian response) was connected to subtle, repetitive and amplified sonorities, this improvisation has the same impact, creating an intensely enjoyable

---

[30] Fred Frith (2007) Liner notes, *The Sugar Factory* (CD) New York: Tzadik.
[31] Evelyn Glennie (2013) *Evelyn Glennie at Moers Jazz Festival, Germany – May 2013* (video online). Available from: https://www.youtube.com/watch?v=JkPXuPwaUCM (accessed 22 February 2023).

sense of connection between listener and performer, even a decade after the live event; in these moments, we are part of an intimate, exploratory and entirely honest musical encounter. The flow state of the musicians is transferred without filter to the listener. Improvisation becomes virtuosity on the performer's terms, an instinctive, responsive, patient forum. In the concert hall, Glennie is extraordinarily powerful, goal-oriented and dominant; in improvisation, another side of her performance style is allowed to flourish. There is no question that these concerts embrace the vulnerability of the performer, inviting all participants to submit to the process of connecting with sound in real time. As is always the case, Glennie is not leaving one identity behind in moving towards collaborative improvisation; she is extending her remit: "I would like to think moving forward that, you know, that balance between improvisation and playing a notated piece of music will always remain in my journey as a musician because I feel one needs the other in a way."[32]

Improvisation as Interdisciplinary Art: The Animotion Project (2012)

Without a defined instrument or standardized professional remit, solo multi-percussion is a practice and ethos which positions the performer as sound sculptor and performance artist. These roles remain consistent regardless of whether the percussionist reads from a score or creates music in the moment of performance. The diverse skill set of the contemporary percussionist, and the open-ended nature of the discipline, means that this art form is positioned well to find a place beyond the confines of the concert hall. If sound is everywhere, so too is the percussionist. Percussion readily intersects with other disciplines and modes of creative expression, and Glennie is keen to explore the ways in which it can become a part of contemporary culture at large. The search for new environments in which percussive timbres can resonate (in both literal and metaphorical terms) is fundamental to Glennie's activism as an advocate for the potentialities of sound creation, an extension of her efforts to remove ideological divides between musical genres and modes of performance. From 2012 onwards, Glennie's career reflects increased diversification; collaborations with visual artists, dance ensembles and theatrical productions are particularly resonant features. In each instance, the inherently multi-sensory nature of solo percussion is heightened. Glennie assumes various roles in these projects as both performer, improviser and composer; in all instances she remains a sound creator.

[32] Interview with Glennie, 10 March 2023.

The Animotion project aligned Glennie's work with Russian painter Maria Rud and projection artist Ross Ashton, connecting sound and vision in the context of environmental theatre. A term first used in the 1960s and associated primarily with the philosophies and installations of Richard Schechner, environmental theatre was concerned with resituating performance events in new contexts. The main aim was to reinvigorate the reciprocal relationship between performer and spectator by removing any sense of division or hierarchy, a theatrical medium which celebrated the intersections between art and life. Environmental theatre can happen anywhere; it escapes the conventions of stage design and framing so that the gaze of the spectator is not regulated or controlled. The audience can choose what to engage with and determine their own level of participation. Given the convention of the concert hall platform in art music, which establishes both a physical and hierarchical distance between performer and music, there is a parallel interest in removing such boundaries in this context.

In the Animotion project, Rud's spontaneous paintings (in direct response to musical stimulus) were superimposed onto building fronts or large interior spaces. Improvisation was applied in several aspects of the performance event; it was part of the performative language of both musician and artist. The theatrical space was likewise fluid and responsive; fixed architecture became living scenography, wherein the site of performance was itself a transitory entity. Environmental theatre, rejecting physical or psychological barriers between performer and audience, is a collaboration which extends to include all present. In the outdoor Animotion performances, artists and musicians were arranged to form a promenade stage, allowing freedom of movement between these living installations; it was intended to be immersive and determinedly open-ended. Indoor venues, whilst providing seating, also invited the audience to move and explore the space as the creations evolved. Rud's painting style is direct and dynamic, employing bold colours and frequently referencing elements drawn from her Russian heritage (in terms of iconography and symbolism). The instinctive nature of her approach echoes Glennie's processes as an improvising performer:

> [Rud's] paintings are not the product of the intellect, but visceral expressions of images received "fully formed" in her mind. Despite the obvious technical excellence, there is a simplicity that can be understood without explanation. Each and every painting can be read and interpreted by anyone on a purely emotional level.[33]

---

[33] *Maria Rud biography* (online). Available from: https://www.mariarudart.com/about (ccessed 1 March 2023).

Just as musical improvisation allows creativity to exist as a unique, singular and transitory experience, Animotion embraced the same concept in visual terms. Rud's paintings evolved to construct complete tableaux which were then almost immediately transformed or erased. Following a number of experimental performances by Rud (initiated in 2010), her collaboration with Glennie (joined by cellist Phillip Sheppard and vocal ensemble Canty) in October 2012 presented the first high-profile Animotion event. The Grand Gallery of the National Museum of Scotland (a long, resonant atrium painted white) became the living canvas on which Rud's response to music was projected in real time; images were created, amended and erased as the performance developed. Programming for Animotion accommodated scored repertoire and improvisation on a wide range of percussion instruments (often including collaborations with other performers). In all instances the emphasis was on an instinctive dialogue between musician(s) and artist. Designed as a determinedly multi-sensory and immersive event, Glennie's quotation for the media release defines the rationale of the collaboration. Again, an interest in challenging and diversifying her remit as a performer was the central objective:

> The Animotion project is very exciting and pushes the boundaries of all participants, including myself. Our aim is to bring art and music together in an extremely new and unique way, almost theatrical, in that the players are all artists of notoriety in their own right, the auditorium teeming with art works and eclectic musical instruments. To premiere this new work ... will be a thrilling experience for us and, we trust, for the audience.[34]

A new interpretation of programmatic music, in this project the trope was reversed: the visual narrative did not inspire the composition, but instead the imagery was created in response to the music. For the first Glennie and Rud Animotion event, improvisation featured in Glennie's solo performance of *Michi* on marimba and between Glennie and Sheppard (cello). Tuned instruments (marimba and vibraphone) were juxtaposed with toys, thunder sheets, wine glasses and a halo drum (also known as an American hand pan). The performance at the National Museum of Scotland opened with a vivacious two-mallet transcription of Vivaldi's *Concerto in C major* (arranged by Glennie for vibraphone), mirrored in Rud's energetic movements and bold colour palette.

---

[34] Evelyn Glennie (2012) *Animotion: Evelyn Glennie and Maria Rud at the National Museum of Scotland* (media release), 11 October 2012. Kindly provided by The Evelyn Glennie Collection.

Másson's *Prim* for solo snare drum (1984), previously performed by Glennie in Grand Central Station for *Touch the Sound*, offered a distinct contrast to Vivaldi. At times, the sonority of the snare drum threatened to overwhelm the echoing space, but in the later stages of the work Glennie's movements and dynamics became delicate and elegant. A short but theatrical work, *Prim* is fully notated, but it incorporates a range of timbral effects which are both visually and aurally potent (including rim shots, rubbing of skin and striking on various parts of the head). Rud used paintbrushes and the fingertips to mirror the intensity and shape of Glennie's sticking, a dance between artist and musician resulting in various projected images. A proud cockerel in yellows and reds represented the powerful opening of the solo; as the music acquiesced to a more contemplative mood, Rud's movements were smaller, with paint being removed rather than added. A new image emerged in the later stages, with warriors preparing for battle (a reference to the military origins of the instrument), tempered by a deep blue sky painted using the hand.

The halo featured in the final work *Orologeria Aureola* (composed by Sheppard and Glennie) for halo and tape (marimba), punctuated by intermittent cello entries. An upturned metal bowl with various indentations creating a range of pitches, the halo is played with the hands (and fingertips); this compact interpretation of the steel drum was invented in 2007 (by the American company Pantheon Steel). The result of improvisations and discussions between Glennie and Sheppard, *Orologeria Aureola* is a beautiful and intense composition, driven by repetitive rhythmic patterns and a melody which emerges intermittently in the upper register of the halo. In response, Rud firstly created a tableau of four soldiers in dark silhouette, with swords held high; red filled the light box as the image transitioned several more times, mirroring the sense of motion in the soundscape. Just as Glennie played the halo with the hands, Rud painted using the palm and fingertips.

In 2013, St. Giles Cathedral in Edinburgh was reimagined as a multi-media installation. Glennie's multi-percussion improvisation with Heath (playing a range of flutes) became a lone warrior riding his horse through the night, metamorphosing to a stark profile of the soldier with head bowed in contemplation. As the intensity of the improvisation developed, yellow and orange bursts of colour were added with similar vigour by Rud, enveloping and enlivening the image. A review of the event attempted to capture the sensations generated as the collaboration evolved:

> Musical ideas flashed like quicksilver between them in this highly charged, virtuosic performance. It veered from Glennie's rock star turn on the drum kit to a mesmeric, almost shamanistic passage, as

Heath's growling bass flute buffeted the eerie sighing from a whirly tube [boomwhacker] twirled by Glennie above her head. This was mirrored in elegant sabre-waving figures that emerged from Rud's constantly evolving paintings.[35]

Durham Cathedral was repurposed as a site of performance art in April 2014, and included improvisation on a number of auxiliary percussion instruments. At the Edinburgh Fringe Festival (14–29 August 2015), Glennie aligned scored repertoire with explorations on waterphone, wood, Aluphone and Barimbulum. Each night of the residency offered attendees new musical and visual experiences (see Fig. 6).

Glennie notes that programming for the Fringe residency, performed during the summer, facilitated a more patient and relaxed interaction between artist and audience than was possible at colder sites such as Aberdeen, where attendees were less willing to move around: "People could literally come right up, so you could be more small with your sounds, and more intimate. You could play off the audience a bit more, so there was room to do things where you were just literally sitting on the ground."[36] Tenney's *Having Never written a Note for Percussion* (a 1971 composition for any instrument but most often performed on tam-tam or gong as in this instance) featured several times in the summer performances. Tenney's conceptual work, centred on exploring gradations of tone, essentially blurs the boundaries between scoring and free improvisation. Originally written for percussionist John Bergamo (to whom it was sent on a postcard), the directive to the performer is to move from *pppp* to *ffff* and back by means of a sustained roll.

In Animotion, improvisation not only provided scope for Glennie to move between musical genres (or to elude them entirely); it was also part of the performance language of the painter, the movements and decisions made by the audience, and the changing nature of the theatrical space. The collaboration became a collective form of synaesthesia, wherein the soundscapes of multi-percussion were communicated as colours, shapes and images. Instead of boundaries, there were multiple continuums – between scored repertoire and improvisation, painting and music, participant and spectator, art and life. Glennie has always considered the visual narrative (gesture, costume, positioning, lighting and use of space) to be intrinsic to the performance experience; Animotion was an amplified iteration of

---

[35] Susan Nickalls (2013) The Animotion Show, St Giles' Cathedral Edinburgh – Review, *Financial Times* (online), 19 December 2013. Available from: https://www.ft.com/content/d987e920-6806-11e3-8ada-00144feabdc0 (accessed 5 November 2021).

[36] Interview with Glennie, 27 June 2023.

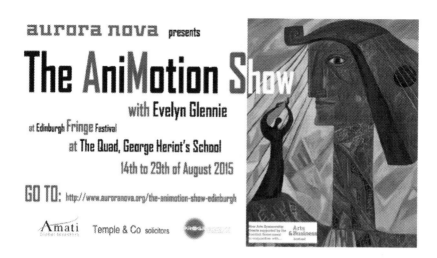

Fig. 6: Poster for Animotion residency at Edinburgh Fringe Festival.

this. It was a living film, a concert, an exhibition, a masterclass and a work of theatre. The role of improvisation in this project (both through music and painting) exemplifies its significance as a means of making art which is entirely present, reflective of the time in which it is created with unabridged clarity. The performer must fully submit to the sensations and emotions of the moment, trusting that ideas will evolve: "Improvisation can be liberating and exciting but it can also be frightening at the same time because I am never sure where the inspiration is directly coming from."[37]

Music and Movement: Multi-Percussion and Dance

Percussion instruments first ascertained some degree of emancipation in Western art music as colouristic sound effects for staged productions, most notably in opera and ballet. Jean-Baptiste Lully's tragic opera *Thésée* (1685) introduced the timpani to the orchestra, whilst the late eighteenth century opera scores of Christoph Willibald Gluck, including *La Cadi Dupe* (1761), *Echo and Narcissus* (1779) and *Iphigenie en Tauride* (1779) added bass drum, cymbals, tambourine and triangle. Richard Wagner made the glockenspiel part of the orchestra in all four operas of *Der Ring des Nibelungen*, premiered in 1876. The origins of orchestral percussion are therefore directly

---

[37] Glennie (2012) *Shadow Behind the Iron Sounds*.

connected to dramatic works; their history began in a theatrical setting. In ballet, percussion was valuable both for its timbral diversity and its capacity to efficiently articulate rhythmic patterns and pulse (essential means of aligning sound and movement). Stravinsky's early ballets are dominated by percussion, most notably in *The Rite of Spring* (1913), where auxiliary instruments captured the primal and elemental narrative through relentless ostinati and powerful dynamic aggression. The resultant timpani part presented an exposed and challenging role; percussionist Charles L. White, in an article on the work, humorously recalls anecdotes of timpanists who quit their jobs upon seeing the score, of performers suffering heart attacks, and of orchestra members being fired for inadequate execution.[38]

Rhythmic precision is at the heart of both multi-percussion performance and the physical body in dance; there are natural synergies between the two. They are both languages of gesture in which the body is the communicative medium. Glennie's performance style, as evinced in her work with Rud, can be understood as a form of choreography, wherein movements and connections with the instruments are embodied, physical gestures; in Animotion these were reciprocated in the painting style of her collaborator. Aligning the physicality of multi-percussion with dance ensembles is another organic expansion of the theatrical and visual elements already intrinsic to the discipline. 2012 – a year which also included performing at the Olympic Games Opening Ceremony in London, Animotion, the Joshua Light Show, three album launches and international dates with ensembles including the Pittsburg Symphony Orchestra, Manitoba Chamber Orchestra and Nuremberg Symphony Orchestra – offers a seminal example. In the case of *Fusional Fragments*, percussion was no longer the offstage soundscape for a dramatic work; it became part of the dance. Whilst improvisation was featured in the live event, the performance was the culmination of extensive advance planning (to facilitate set design, lighting, choreography and narrative). There were logistical and pragmatic considerations which co-existed with creative decision-making, particularly important when disciplines converge.

Fusional Fragments, composed and premiered in 2012, aligned Glennie with the Marc Brew Company, formed in 2008. Combining contemporary dance with elements drawn from a range of genres, the company seeks to create "a series of physical conversations, encounters and interventions that reflect what it is to be human."[39] Brew is a dancer, choreographer, pro-

---

[38]   Charles L. White (1971) The Rite Timpani Player, *Percussionist*, 8 (4), p. 131.

[39]   *Marc Brew* (online). Available from: https://www.disabilityartsinternational.org/artists/profiles/marc-brew/ (accessed 5 March 2023).

ducer and director whose works interrogate attitudes to the physical body, seeking to make the discipline of dance an inclusive and socially engaged mode of artistic communication.

Brew's vision for *Fusional Fragments*, realized by Glennie (as soloist and co-composer), composer Phillip Sheppard, light designer Andy Hamer, and five dancers, was autobiographical, exploring his processes and experiences as a disabled performer and choreographer. In much the same way as Glennie views deafness as one of many diverse aspects of her personal identity, Brew has adopted a similar approach to his wheelchair use (the consequence of injuries sustained in a car crash at the age of twenty): "One of the things that appealed to me about working with her was that she had made a very successful career for herself, one not based at all around her disability but rather her musical talent. That's always been my aim as well."[40] The work emanated from the words "dislocated, broken, shattered", themes sent initially to Glennie as impetus to begin improvising and selecting sounds.

The Evelyn Glennie Collection retains all paperwork and administration associated with each of Glennie's collaborations. The extensive correspondence related to *Fusional Fragments* (first initiated as a concept early in 2011) offers insights into the process, including discussions on instrumentation, stage design, use of space, narrative arc and atmosphere. Sheppard and Glennie frequently reference visual elements (including dancers, positioning of instruments, gesture and lighting) in planning musical decisions. The resultant score presented ten scenes, and the instrumentation balanced visual intrigue with the practicalities of the percussionist moving around the stage. Marimba and snare drum were juxtaposed with spinning tops, waterphone, kalimba, music boxes, halo drum and wood blocks. Auxiliary percussion dominated, focused on instruments with limited resonance, sonorities which emphasize attack rather than decay; driving rhythms were juxtaposed with static moments wherein silence became part of the musical narrative.

Though Glennie remained onstage throughout, she was not always central to the movements of the ensemble. Balancing theatricality with the ability to perform effectively was key. Though the work represents a fusion of disciplines, Glennie was keen to ensure that her role as multi-percussionist did not defer to that of dancer or dramatist. In determining the extent to which she would feature onstage, Glennie was clear about this priority:

---

[40] Marc Brew in Nick Duerden (2012) How We Met: Marc Brew and Dame Evelyn Glennie, *Independent* (online), 22 August 2012. Available from: https://www.independent.co.uk/news/people/profiles/how-we-met-marc-brew-dame-evelyn-glennie-8073470.html (accessed 10 November 2021).

I am happy to be as open minded as possible. My only thought at this point is that some of the instruments will be on stands such as the snare drum, cymbals and a few other bits and pieces. Therefore, they will have to be in place and remain there. Also, as I shall have several "sound effect"-type instruments … then we must think how to practically pick them up and put them down in close proximity. They need to be played in a manner that makes them speak so a part of me will have to be practical and realistic as to what is actually possible.[41]

Scene 1 began with Glennie (on a tenor drum) in close proximity to a solo dancer enclosed in a metaphorical box representing isolation and distance from society; through music and lights, the space was gradually opened and the dancer moved towards the centre of the stage. In the second scene, Glennie was positioned upstage; for this section, the naturally emphatic movements required to play a range of handheld instruments (including waterphone and hand chimes) provided a natural choreography as the ensemble moved through a series of ballet poses. A subsequent duet between two male dancers placed Glennie at the centre of the frame, playing a number of music boxes and spinning tops. For scene 5, Glennie used a head mic to create ethereal vocal sounds as she moved downstage, once more part of a physical duet with the opening soloist. In scene 6, Glennie was in a fixed position, playing the halo drum (amplified by a condenser mic underneath) as a duet was performed between the male and female protagonists. The sonorities of the halo drum continued into scene 8, where Glennie was once more visually integrated into the scene as the central axis between a trio and duet performed concurrently. In scene 9, Glennie moved diagonally downstage, crossing paths with the female lead; lights surrounded both performers. She was then positioned at a multi-percussion station at the front of the stage. The work ended as it began, with the male protagonist returning to his safe space as Glennie observed and responded through a plaintive improvisation (all performed over pre-recorded audio accompaniment). A black-out closed the performance.

Whilst much of the experimentation in this project functioned as a precursor to composition, four scenes accommodated improvisation. The support of a backing track ensured that tempo and duration were consistent in each performance (to facilitate the choreography). In scene 4, Glennie improvised on snare drum, accompanying an energetic and jagged confrontation between two of the male dancers. In scene 7, the toy piano played a series of descending flourishes to support the interactions of three dancers.

---

[41] Email correspondence between Evelyn Glennie and The Marc Brew Company (2012), kindly provided by The Evelyn Glennie Collection.

For the penultimate scene, after traversing the stage diagonally, Glennie performed at a multi-percussion station on piccolo snare drum (with snares off to create a leaden timbre), cymbals and wood blocks. In scene 10 Glennie continued to improvise at this set-up, creating an atmosphere of reflective sadness as the protagonist returned to the perceived safety of their closed world. Improvisation in *Fusional Fragments* is structured in terms of duration, but its central intention is to respond to the atmosphere and journey of the characters at pivotal moments in the narrative. It is unlikely that the audience would have been aware of the delineations between scored repertoire and free improvisation in this instance, but it was of great relevance to the performers who created a unique synergy in these interactions.

Fusional Fragments premiered as part of the first Unlimited Festival (designed to celebrate diversity in relation to disabled identity as part of the 2012 Olympiad). It was both an interdisciplinary art work and a determined statement on inclusion and the disabled experience. There was no divide between able-bodied and disabled, hearing and deaf, classical ballet and contemporary, dancer and percussionist; as with all successful collaborations, it celebrated creativity converging from a range of sources. The work clearly demonstrates Glennie's efforts to sustain and diversify the remit of the contemporary performer, but it also alludes to the next stages in creative collaboration: addressing issues of social justice and legacies of exclusion.

Long-Term Alliance: Glennie and Trio HLK (2017–present)

Whilst *Shadow Behind the Iron Sun* and *The Sugar Factory* fall under multitudinous genre categorizations (marketed variously as popular, avant-garde, experimental and classical), and the convergence of art and dance in Animotion and *Fusional Fragments* brought multi-percussion into interdisciplinary contexts, Glennie's alliance with Trio HLK at first glance represents further diversification into contemporary jazz. Trio HLK (Rich Harrold on piano, Ant Law on guitar and Richard Kass on drums and percussion) are often described in the media as a jazz group, but in fact prefer not to define their sound or musical style in such specific terms, echoing Glennie's own wilful eclecticism. In a documentary on her work with the trio, Glennie states: "The music is difficult to categorize, and why should we categorize it?"[42] Harrold is both pianist and composer for the group, and his remit is determinedly diverse:

---

[42] Trio HLK (2019) *Trio HLK and Evelyn Glennie* (video online). Available from: https://www.youtube.com/watch?v=wTeb6OtsLQ4 (accessed 10 July 2019).

People are always going to try and categorize things. I think it's a shame actually. I mean I understand it because we improvise with a lot of that jazz vocab, and the instrumentation represents a jazz trio to some extent, and it's amplified music instead of proper chamber music, and the album recording is like a studio album instead of that kind of live sound you get with a classical recording. So there are a lot of things that make it sound like that, but when you strip away that surface for me it's coming from a different place actually. It's coming from twentieth-century classical music really. That's how I write it.[43]

Trio HLK are interested in experimenting with classic jazz standards but complement this by integrating numerous influences drawn from Indian music, art music, rock and avant-garde. As is the case with many of Glennie's commissions, the trio often combine scored repertoire and improvisation in performance. Formed in 2015, Trio HLK first approached Glennie and alto saxophonist Steve Lehman to contribute to their debut album *Standard Time* (released 11 May 2018). A challenge deviating from the determined freedoms of *Touch the Sound*, improvisation in this context was structured (in terms of harmonic outline and duration), framed by complex and precise notation. For the album, Glennie performed (and improvised) only on tuned instruments (vibraphone and marimba), differing from her usual multi-percussion identity: "I have always felt comfortable improvising sonically and rhythmically but melodically less so because I have had less need to do that throughout my career."[44]

In the final mix, Glennie featured on three tracks ("Extra Sensory Perception Part I", "Extra Sensory Perception Part II", and "The Jig"). Harrold composed "Extra Sensory Perception" in 2013, realized on the album as "Extra Sensory Perception Part II". The score was inspired by "E.S.P.", written by saxophonist Wayne Shorter and first interpreted by the Miles Davis Quintet. "Extra Sensory Perception Part I" emerged during the process of recording in Glennie's Cambridgeshire studio, with improvisation seguing to the development of a scored arrangement (see Ex. 5).

The track opens with a piano and vibraphone duet, focused on a repeated C around which the four-minute work evolves. Increasingly complex ascending figurations on both instruments become frantically loud and dissonant, before dissolving into a bell-like final section. The track is

---

[43] Interview with Richard Harrold, 23 March 2023.

[44] Evelyn Glennie (2018) Music Interview: Dame Evelyn Glennie, *The Yorkshire Post* (online), 2 November 2018. Available from: https://www.yorkshirepost.co.uk/arts-and-culture/music-interview-dame-evelyn-glennie-i-knew-i-would-be-out-my-comfort-zone-thats-always-good-thing-any-musician-experience-230770 (accessed 23 February 2023).

Ex. 5: Opening of *"Extra Sensory Perception Part I"* (Richard Harrold/Trio HLK).

atmospheric, harmonically complex and timbrally beautiful. Though the vibraphone is a sonority readily associated with jazz performance (pioneered by virtuosic musicians including Red Norvo, Lionel Hampton and Milt Jackson), the piece does not connote any specific idiom. This reflects the larger post-genre mood of the album, with critics applying expansive descriptive parameters including dubstep, techno, prog-rock, punk, Latin, Cuban and jazz in their interpretations.

The album track "Extra Sensory Perception Part II" remains largely respectful of the specifics of Harrold's original score, with an open repeat for solos at bar 30. Glennie plays marimba in the first improvisation on the album, moving from intermittent, sharp, accented attacks within a limited range to more expansive use of the instrument's registral and dynamic extremes. Hi-hat cymbals and snare drum (played with brushes) are gradually added by Kass, followed by a series of intermittent piano chords scored in Harrold's draft to denote the ending of each improvisation. Electric guitar then assumes the lead role, and all instruments gradually enter before the music returns to the directives of the score from bar 35 (at 4'23"). Whilst this track is intense yet beautiful, the final album track "The Jig" (also featuring Glennie) is a driving exploration of polyrhythms and changing time signatures punctuated by an aggressive *tutti* motif. Harrold's inspiration in this instance was derived tangentially from J.S Bach's *Cello Suite No. 1*. Glennie's marimba part is exacting and precise at the opening (see Ex. 6); as with "Extra Sensory Perception Part II" there is space for a relatively short improvisation following the first collective statement of the theme. In Glennie's score, annotations emphasize the rigour and concentration required in both the studio and subsequent live performances. Cues, bar numbers and repetitions are denoted in thick black marker to ensure accuracy; these notes also indicate decisions made as a group in rehearsals. Bars 149–152 are each repeated once; bar 153 thrice; bar 154 four times; the final bar 155 is sounded five times for an abrupt *tutti* ending.

Initially conceived as a one-off encounter, Glennie's time with Trio HLK in the recording studio became a more enduring collaboration. Commencing with the album launch tour (which included Glennie in half of the twenty-four performances), this relationship has continued to evolve. Performances on this first tour adhered largely to the order and content of the album, but Glennie's remit was extended with multi-percussion and drum kit added to several more numbers in the set. Harrold acknowledges that Glennie has become an integral part of their artistic development: "The live shows have massively changed from the recordings. There's so much extra stuff she's bringing to it, every rehearsal she'll come in with something else, it's incredibly creative and collaborative. Even at the gigs, she's constantly throwing new things out there."[45]

Dates with Trio HLK were among the first casualties of the COVID-19 lockdown, but Glennie rescheduled these appearances, continuing to perform with the group throughout 2022–23; it is clear that the synergies between what is often referred to by the band as Trio HLKG continue to provide creative sustenance for all involved (see Fig. 7).

Glennie's instrumentation list for a performance in the Stoller Hall, Manchester on 1 December 2022 demonstrates the fact that the identity of tuned percussionist (as in *Standard Time*) has definitively metamorphosed in to that of multi-percussionist. From her own collection, Glennie integrated a wide range of timbres, creating a sense of fluidity and freedom even as the set-list and musical forms remained fixed. The sounds of *Standard*

---

[45] Richard Harrold in Chris Broom (2018) Dame Evelyn Glennie Teams Up With Jazz Group Trio HLK at Petworth Festival, *The News*, Portsmouth (online), 26 July 2018. Available from: https://www.portsmouth.co.uk/whats-on/gigs-and-music/dame-evelyn-glennie-teams-up-with-jazz-group-trio-hlk-at-petworth-festival-1-8580199 (accessed 3 March 2019).

Ex. 6: Opening marimba line for *"The Jig"* (Richard Harrold/Trio HLK).

Time were augmented with a varying range of additional percussion instruments including Japanese cup bells, halo drum and waterphone. There is a particular energy generated between improvising musicians who have time to interact and evolve as an ensemble, allowing new ideas to emerge

Fig. 7: Trio HLK(G).

organically from the confluence of several sources. As Trio HLK develop new repertoire for their next album, Glennie is once more an integral part of the process; multi-percussion, improvisation and live performance have inspired new creative directions. As Harrold notes: "She just basically started bringing instruments and throwing them in [on tour]. So we just wanted to capture some of that as well, because it's such an amazing aspect of the live stuff."[46] Glennie's work with Trio HLK is another challenge to the conventional remit of the virtuosic art-music performer. Moving beyond

[46] Interview with Richard Harrold, 23 March 2023.

a single genre descriptor and exploring the creative synergies of collaboration advance both the art of multi-percussion and its potential target demographic. It is a risk, but also an important opportunity to evolve and diversify further:

> I do always want to be in a position where I feel uncomfortable now and again – where I feel as though I'm pushing my boundaries as well in how I might be dealing with something, with a particular skill, or an aspect of playing. That's really important. So I think it's that kind of combination of familiarity and absolutely "I haven't a clue what's going to happen here", and that's really important I think for any musician.[47]

Electro-Acoustic Experimentation: Roly Porter (2019)

While Glennie's long-term collaborations continue (with ensembles such as Trio HLK and O/Modernt and also with composers including Jarman), there remains interest in exploring the immediacy of short-term improvisation projects. Meeting in the studio (or on the stage) and becoming acquainted through the language of music is a powerful communicative forum. Glennie's work with Roly Porter (*ODB 17: Evelyn Glennie Roly Porter One Day Band*, recorded in 2018 and released on 1 March 2019) is a pertinent example, wherein the musical language of two diverse artists converged. Their collaboration was part of a broader concept, entitled One Day Band, initiated by London-based label Trestle Records in 2014. The primary aim of this series is to unite artists from diverse backgrounds "to facilitate an environment for musicians to meet and collaborate on an improvised endeavour."[48] These one-day projects have culminated in an archive of improvised works; each results in an album reflecting the studio experience of meeting and interacting through music. Electronics are the most prominent instrumental and production medium in the collaborations, followed closely by the relatively consistent presence of drums and percussion, an indication of the importance of both in the context of contemporary music. Most favour larger ensembles, with Glennie and Porter one of only three duets to date. In a summary of each session provided by Trestle Records, reference is frequently made to the many multi-instrumentalists involved in the projects, and numerous artists are described as producing works which span the musical spectrum; both Porter and Glennie reflect this eclecticism.

---

[47] Interview with Glennie, 3 May 2019.
[48] *One Day Band* (2019), online. Available from: http://www.trestlerec.com/one-daybands.html (accessed 28 March 2019).

Roly Porter is an artist associated primarily with electronic dance music (EDM) and electro-acoustic composition. His career began as one half of Vex'd, a duo formed in the mid-2000s, whose style is most often described as industrial dubstep. The group released two albums, *Degenerate* (2005) and *Cloud Seed* (2010). Dubstep is rooted in rhythmically intense structures, where melody is secondary to the elemental and driving force of insistent rhythmic patterns. Low registers and a general atmosphere of menace are also ideas readily associated with the genre. In his solo projects after 2008, Porter has gravitated towards a freer and more improvisatory approach to composing and producing music, moving away from the often formulaic structures associated with dubstep and electronic dance music. Despite the fact that they come from seemingly distant musical worlds, Glennie and Porter share several aesthetic and artistic beliefs: neither has remained tied to any one musical genre; their disciplines are directly connected to the emancipation of noise in the twentieth century (solo percussion and electronic music-making); they are both sound sculptors. As a solo composer–producer, Porter has rejected the drum machines and synthesizers associated with EDM in favour of working with sounds that he designs, realized in acoustic terms with Glennie's invention of new instruments. The collaboration celebrated both the contrasts and similarities of two musical worlds. Glennie notes: "I think from my perspective I was quite intrigued by the prospect of coming together with Roly, and I just love the idea that you can take an object and it can be manipulated and have its own life again. There's just layer upon layer upon layer of creativity."[49]

Combining live performance with electronic and ambient sounds is not new to Glennie (nor to contemporary music in a wide range of genres). Performance with tape, as in *Orologeria Aureola* (Glennie and Philip Sheppard, 2011) or the orchestral and *musique concrète* recorded accompaniment for *Sounds of Science* (Jarman, 2015), are just two examples of her prior experience of connecting acoustic and electronic sound worlds. Electro-acoustic music is a fusion of the skills of the live performer and those of the sound producer, a means of further expanding and investigating the timbral qualities of various percussion instruments; improvisation functions as process, compositional methodology and creative artefact in this environment. Glennie used instruments from her own collection in the recording, opting for timpani (with smaller objects placed on the heads), waterphone, music box, Tibetan singing bowl and kalimba. The most discernible and

---

[49] Trestle Records (2019) *ODB 17 – Evelyn Glennie/Roly Porter Interview* (video online). Available from: https://www.youtube.com/watch?v=KblVihczuQg (accessed 28 February 2019).

Diversification, Improvisation and Collaboration   95

consistent percussive timbre is the waterphone, featured in parts 1 and 4 (the final track) of the album. This instrument (featured on the front cover) is often part of Glennie's multi-percussion performances (selected both by commissioned composers and by Glennie for improvised experiments with sound), and features on part 2 of *Playing Around the Office*. The waterphone, invented in the 1960s by Richard Waters, is inspired by the sounds of the Tibetan water drum and the African thumb piano. It has an impressive dynamic and timbral range, producing sound by means of plucking, striking or bowing bronze rods of various sizes which extend from the central stainless steel bowl, which is usually filled with water. It can be held close to the body or at arm's length, each position generating differing levels of resonance and decay; vibrations emanating from the instrument are felt either through the mid-section of the body or along the length of the arm. This establishes a powerful physical connection between performer and object. As Glennie notes: "It almost feels as if the instrument is a living thing, always communicating in ways that are ethereal and wonderful."[50] The Tibetan singing bowl is a hollow open-topped instrument played by passing a soft wooden beater along the upper rim. Associated with ancient healing and meditation rituals, the instrument emits a warm, soft and consistent metallic timbre, providing an effective contrast to the expansive resonance of the waterphone. The kalimba, a compact African thumb piano, is an even more subtle instrument, beautiful in its simplicity; often held in both hands, it is played with the fingertips. Small metal rods of varying sizes produce a range of pitches with an ethereal tone. The sounds of the kalimba mirror those of the music boxes also used in the recording, creating very soft melodic fragments which extend beyond the specificities of equal temperament to haunting effect.

Capturing the essence of percussion in any recording is a demanding task; this is one of the main reasons why Glennie did not opt to transfer her touring schedule to an online medium (as many artists did) when COVID-19 changed the nature of live performance: "It has been frustrating being asked to present certain performances digitally 'at home' whereby the quality is under par in every way."[51] Whilst Glennie's live performance was the most obvious output of the collaboration, its success was equally dependent upon Porter's work in recording and producing the tracks. The waterphone exemplifies the challenge: the performer moves the instrument

---

[50]   Evelyn Glennie (n.d.) *Waterphone* (online). Originally available from https://waterphone.com (accessed 1 April 2019). At the time of publication, this website is in the process of being updated.

[51]   Interview with Glennie, 12 October 2020.

in various directions towards and away from the body; they use different mallets and sticks to create sound; each metal rod vibrates at a particular frequency, generating multitudinous overtones; the dynamic range is expansive; the degree of reverberation changes according to the size of the recording space and the temperature in the studio. These issues are magnified further when multiple instruments are employed (as is the case with One Day Band). Given that Glennie experiences the sounds in the moment of live performance but does not have the option of listening (in full) to the results thereafter, there is a heightened degree of trust involved in recording collaborations. Porter was keenly aware of his dual role in the studio, and created four tracks which honour the fidelity of the original sound whilst extending the connections between acoustic and electronic timbres (feeding the recordings through amps and using various pedal effects). In this way, Porter retained the multi-sensory and organic energy of the live event, and explored alternative modes of responding to it, functioning as producer, composer and improviser.

The first three tracks begin with focus on the acoustic properties of a single percussion instrument; part 1 features waterphone; part 2 opens with kalimba and part 3 highlights the warm resonance of the Tibetan singing bowl. As each evolves, layers of increasingly distorted sounds rapidly blur the boundaries between live and processed timbres. All four parts end with an elongated period of silence, another means of evoking the live experience, wherein Glennie uses gesture and anticipation in the process of improvising. Porter's own interpretation of the final album reflects his awareness of Glennie's embodied engagement: "I think it extends our listening skills and it makes us really almost become the sound."[52]

Part 1 opens with delicate metallic strikes, difficult to hear at first. Gradually the texture becomes denser, with layering of drones and sustained pitches. This is a relatively static work, evoking a haunting atmosphere and sense of expectation. The manipulation of pitches as the track progresses veers between evocation of birdsong and the sound of a distant scream. The first discernible drum pattern is heard at 2'31". By 2'54" the listener is fully immersed in an alien atmosphere; any concept of the difference between acoustic and electronic sound is almost impossible. Percussive sounds are transformed into timbres reminiscent of wind or stringed instruments. The sonic landscape gradually unfolds and can be likened to the impact of film scoring, creating a sense of heightened awareness, expectation and trepidation. The tension subsides from 4'45" as the sounds subside to silence.

---

[52] Trestle Records (2019) *ODB 17 – Evelyn Glennie/Roly Porter Interview.*

Part 2 begins with the sounds of the kalimba, emerging with an intermittent three-note pattern which grows into a melodic improvisation. Porter allows the natural acoustics of the instrument to remain relatively unaltered. Consonant sustained notes emerge in the background from 2'16" and the Tibetan singing bowl is heard clearly from 2'52". Metallic taps enter in the later stages of the track, but the dynamic level remains soft. A sense of emptiness is made tangible through the sound of white noise in the final eight seconds.

Part 3 opens with the sonority of the Tibetan singing bowl, but layers of increasingly distorted sounds rapidly blur the boundaries between live and processed timbres. An auxiliary percussion rhythm pattern emerges from 1'54". From 3'20" metallic scrapes contribute to a growing feeling of uneasiness; again the sense of an alien landscape is viscerally created. The work reaches a textural and dynamic climax by 4'20" and then there is a return to the relative calm of the opening. There is no sound for the final fourteen seconds.

Part 4 represents the culmination of the collaboration, drawing together the various sonorities and effects used throughout the album. This final track is the longest (6'46") and focuses on the juxtaposition of stasis and frenetic attack. The presence of bells is clear from 32" after an almost inaudible opening, and the evocation of a distant wind is heard in the background. Cymbal rolls emerge from 1'29", and contribute to an increasingly dense texture, layering a range of percussive and electronically processed sounds. Abrasive feedback features from 4'16" and a *crescendo* climaxes around 5'. By 6'19" the static sense of emptiness returns; ten seconds of silence complete the journey. This work once again demonstrates that collaborative projects are a vital means of forging new creative paths, that improvisation is a process and art form which transcends and eludes genre specification and instrumentation, and that fusion and hybridity in music are the essence of contemporary sound. Solo percussion functions herein as both an acoustic and electronic medium. The abrasive yet ethereal sonority of the waterphone already inherently resembles electronically generated timbres; this collaboration advances that idea one step further.

Glennie is familiar with the demands of recording percussion in the studio environment, a necessary means of promoting and disseminating the commissions that have become synonymous with her professional identity. In these instances, the emphasis is on precision in terms of fidelity both to the score and to the sonorities of the instruments featured, though Glennie notes that the time, financial support and attention given to recordings is no longer guaranteed:

Well, you know, the whole recording scenario has really changed since I made some of the early recordings whereby we might have performed the piece in concert a few times and then we would have actual recording sessions. So those sessions might have still happened in a concert hall or sometimes in a studio, but basically the sessions were dedicated recording sessions. Now, you know, we very rarely have that. It puts an awful lot of strain I think on everybody to be honest, because everything's recorded.[53]

Bringing improvisation into the studio offers much greater scope for creative investigation and frees Glennie from the search for perfection in the studio; it is framed and understood as an intentionally fluid experiment, a joint adventure for both performer and producer. Glennie has channelled her interest in improvisation into composing for various media projects, finding ways to introduce multi-percussion to the larger cultural consciousness. With creative control in this context, recording becomes a process which can be executed on her own terms. The theme music for *Trial and Retribution*, a UK crime drama spanning twelve seasons (1997–2009), is an early example which emphasized the unique sonority of the waterphone to chilling effect; Glennie's score was nominated for a BAFTA Award in 1998 (for Best Original Television Music). Various film soundtracks connect music and vision in powerful ways, all dependent for success upon constructive collaboration between performers and producers – examples include *The Trench* (1999), *A Dangerous Journey* (2012), *Finding Altamira* with Mark Knopfler (2016), *Sounds of Metal* (2020) and *The Marvels* with Laura Karpman (2023). Glennie continues a long-term collaboration with Audio Network, a music library company providing excerpts for the film, television and advertising industry. To date, 1317 Glennie tracks (all with numerous additional mixes) are available for purchase.[54] Harnessing the energy of improvisation in particular (as opposed to ensuring that score directives translate to the listener) allows the creative unfolding of ideas to be crystallized, wherein Glennie's performances can continue to evolve through further experimentation in production.

As an entrepreneur, Glennie is aware of the fact that consumers now access music primarily through digital media; there exist opportunities to connect with new audiences in this way. In the later stages of the COVID-19 lockdown, Glennie experimented with technology, briefly using the hashtag #foleyartist in November–December 2020 to promote three short

---

[53]   Interview with Glennie, 10 March 2023.

[54]   See   https://www.audionetwork.com/track/searchkeyword?keyword=evelyn%20 glennie&sort=52 (accessed 27 February 2023).

videos exploring ambient sounds (*Christmas Food!*, *Christmas Cocktails* and *Sleigh Ride*). Evocative vignettes, Glennie used percussion instruments to provide sound effects for boiling food, champagne bubbles, a horse-driven sleigh and church bells, temporarily assuming the identity of foley artist. In 2022, this interest in the nuances of percussive sounds, and the intersections between live music and production, evolved into a collaboration with Spitfire Audio. The Resonate sound library provides a collection of miniature improvisations for use by sound producers and composers. Glennie's experiments in these instances extend the quality and range of percussive sounds which will subsequently be heard in the cultural zeitgeist. Focusing primarily on effects using a range of sticks, mallets, bows and the body, the sounds of the water tank, thunder sheet, timpani and barrel (with various objects added to their surfaces) were recorded using underwater microphones, contact microphones and boundary microphones. The user can explore these acoustic sonorities further using signal paths and after-effects. From Glennie's improvisations, worlds of sound emerge, described admiringly in one review as "a new virtual instrument".[55]

Concluding Thoughts

As noted at the beginning of this chapter, improvisation eludes definition. It serves numerous functions and assumes significance at various stages of the creative process. Improvisation can be part of a personal and private process of discovery, or a social and collaborative experience; it can inspire a composed work or represent the final creative artefact; it may manifest expertise in a specific discipline or represent the convergence of multiple spheres. In alignment with her evolution as an improvising performer, Glennie continues to commission and premiere scored works, balancing the identity of virtuosic solo multi-percussionist with that of sound creator (though the two intersect in many instances). It is wrong to assume that freedom from composer directives makes the latter path easier; the art of improvisation demands commitment, effort and dedication. The musician is entirely liable for the success or failure of the musical experience; Glennie's transition into this domain has earned recognition because she has taken this responsibility seriously. Glennie is honest about the fact that it has been a challenging metamorphosis, but a creative risk

---

[55] William Stokes (2022) *Spitfire Audio teams up with legendary percussionist Dame Evelyn Glennie to create Resonate* (online), 9 June 2022. Available from: https://musictech.com/uncategorised/spitfire-audio-percussionist-evelyn-glennie-resonate/ (accessed 1 March 2023).

which presents new rewards. She has actively sought eclecticism, creating a unique path wherein art music co-exists with post-genre experimentation, solo performances are juxtaposed with collaborative creativity, the identity of percussionist is both virtuosic and elemental, and music is understood as a connective between disciplines. In many ways, improvisation has been the most important means by which Glennie has sustained and diversified the profession of solo multi-percussionist. It has also provided the context for a more enduring performance career, allowing her to offset the inevitable long-term challenges faced in any physically demanding profession. In response to the question as to whether Glennie will make music forever, her response reflects the role that collaborative experimentation will play in her future:

> Well, it obviously can't be forever, but I think the music will still be there. I think the playing will eventually just ease off; I think, physically, that will naturally happen in its own way. Even certain pieces now, you know, I'm just sort of shelving. I feel I've had my time with that piece thank you very much. And I quite like that, because you're aware that this is a natural transition. I wouldn't want to be in a position whereby it's just suddenly cut off; I think that it would just be a winding down or an emphasis going in another direction. And possibly the collaborations are a case in point.[56]

It is clear that Glennie contextualizes collaborative improvisation as part of a "natural transition", though it is certainly not the direction that virtuosic art musicians have tended to pursue. At the same time, there is no question that the eclectic and diversifying potential of improvised projects has provided a means of engaging with new challenges and opportunities. Glennie's work in this domain is innovative, exciting and unpredictable, regardless of how it may connect to more pragmatic considerations; it mirrors precisely her desire to continue to experiment and evolve. Glennie investigates, curates and explores sound, all of which is facilitated in the freedom of improvisatory and experimental collaborations. New music is a means of challenging stereotypes and ideologies pertaining to its own history but possesses the power to extend beyond these parameters; Glennie recognizes and harnesses this potential. Embracing more fully the social nature of music-making ensures that solo multi-percussion continues to evolve as both an independent entity and an intrinsic feature of contemporary culture; it remains a part of the discussion. Collaboration and improvisation are additive processes, articulating and modelling the multi-faceted nature of what it means to be a percussionist and sound creator.

---

[56] Interview with Glennie, 3 May 2019.

3

"I'm simply a person who wants to encourage females to do whatever they want to do."

The Issue of Gender

I don't think I'm a feminist as such, no. I think I'm simply a person who wants to encourage females to do whatever they want to do, you know, I really do. But I feel that ultimately everyone has to try their best, it's as simple as that.[1]

In many ways it is unsurprising that Glennie would be reluctant to assume the title of "feminist". Her work as a percussionist and sound creator is centred on a wilful effort to elude standardization or classification, a remit which also extends to personal identity. Whilst cognizant of her status as a role model, Glennie's mission to teach the world to listen is multi-faceted; it cannot and should not be restricted by genre or discipline, gender or disability.

As the most successful full-time solo multi-percussionist in history (male or female), discourse on gender is arguably less resonant in this respect: Glennie is the first to achieve this level of renown and therefore does not have imposing patriarchal histories to address. The relatively recent emergence of the discipline also suggests that there are fewer cultural legacies to revoke.

But the reality is that women in music (particularly in roles of prominence) are still dealing with the implications of centuries of oppression derived from the legacy of the Western art canon; casual sexism (regardless of whether it is addressed or ignored) remains problematic in performance

---

[1] Interview with Glennie, 3 May 2019.

critique; gendered stereotypes relating to certain musical genres and instruments linger (not least in relation to drums and percussion); female leaders and entrepreneurs continue to be under-represented. Whilst Glennie has opted not to view gender as an issue of relevance to her career development, she is unquestionably an important female role model. She is a pioneer and innovator, the first to sustain a solo career in an instrumental milieu traditionally associated with masculinity, and a public presence subjected to reception and critique from the perspective of the male gaze.

This chapter will appraise Glennie's status in advancing opportunities for women in music. Whilst secondary to her larger contribution to the evolution of contemporary performance, there is value in acknowledging and discussing the fact that the pioneer of solo percussion, the figurehead of the discipline, and an innovator without precedent in the context of Western art music, is female. Discourse will intersect both musical and extra-musical examples of empowerment.

Situating Glennie in the Landscape of Contemporary Feminism

For many centuries in Western culture, the view of women as subservient to men was rooted in the concept of Cartesian mind–body dualism, subsequently applied in broader and much more simplified terms to define men as representative of mind and culture, and women of body and nature. The notion of woman as detached from culture proved particularly problematic in allowing access to creativity and artistic innovation. All subsequent forms of discrimination have descended largely from this othering of the female. The first wave of feminism (at the turn of the twentieth century) strove to articulate the commonalities between men and women in order to achieve gender parity in relation to education, politics and social status. The second wave (in the 1960s) was unafraid to celebrate difference, adopting a more polarizing agenda seeking female empowerment; the sense of a collective mission was resonant in this wave wherein the progress of the movement mattered more than the agenda or interests of the individual. Many of the negative connotations associated with feminism are derived from misconceptions about the intentions of the second wave, in particular the trope of the angry woman.

Born in 1965, Glennie is chronologically positioned as a child of the second wave, but her adulthood and professional career are associated with the third wave of the 1990s, a period characterized by a more personalized and subjective approach to feminist identity. The intersectionality of gender with a myriad of social, political and cultural imperatives allowed for much more complex and diverse interpretations of feminism. For many women, a third-wave identity meant that it was sufficient to live by the values of gender equality without needing to publically claim them. As ethnomusicologist Ellen Koskoff summarizes: "We came to understand that although one need not always consciously assert an identity position, one always spoke and acted from one."[2] Whilst this understated and personal iteration of empowerment represented one facet of the third wave, public and political expressions of feminist activism were also by-products of intersectionality and diversification. The Riot Grrrl manifesto of 1991 (a year in which Glennie released two solo albums, *Dancin'* and *Light in Darkness,* and was featured on the seminal BBC series *This is Your Life*) reminded the public that issues with gender continued to limit opportunities for women in culture and society: "We are angry at a society that tells us Girl=Dumb, Girl=Bad, Girl=Weak."[3] For some, the third wave of feminism continues, providing a sufficiently flexible ethos to admit multiple representations of female identity in society and culture. Yet for others, the rise of the #metoo movement, strating in 2006, heralds a fourth wave of activism, invested in confronting casual sexism and cyber-misogyny in contemporary discourse.

Glennie has opted not to position herself anywhere on the ever-evolving feminist spectrum; comfortable with uncertainty, her career identity (in all respects) is constructed on eclecticism, metamorphosis and creative risk-taking. She is a role model who happens to be female in much the same way that she is a musician who happens to be deaf; for Glennie, there is no symbiotic connection between these aspects of self and her success in the domain of music. Yet to others, her resonance in both these respects is as powerful as her musical contributions.

Percussion as a Male or Masculine Entity

Feminist musicology (an academic iteration of activism) arrived later in the timeline of gender studies than for many other disciplines, emerging forcefully in the 1990s with Susan McClary's *Feminine Endings* (1991) and Marcia Citron's *Gender and the Musical Canon* (1993). This delay was due to a number of reasons, both aesthetic and practical. The primary rationale for excluding music from any debate on gender was the culturally conditioned assumption that it was an art form which transcended societal or personal issues; positivist musicology in particular viewed the content of

---

[2]   Ellen Koskoff (2014) *A Feminist Ethnomusicology: Writings on Music and Gender.* Urbana: University of Illinois Press, p. 62.

[3]   *Riot Grrrl Manifesto* (1991), online. Available from: https://www.historyisaweapon. com/defcon1/riotgrrrlmanifesto.html (accessed 20 May 2019).

the musical score to be the central focus of academic inquiry. Combined with this perspective, the patriarchal structure of the Western art canon made this domain potentially impenetrable for feminist criticism. Both McClary and Citron were intent on exploding the gendered myths of Western art music. The rationale for examining art music through a feminist lens was immediately justifiable; women have been largely absented from the canon. Early feminist musicology was particularly invested in reclaiming and resituating women in the history of the art: "Prior to 1970 very little was known – or, at least, remembered – about women in music history. Women had vanished; virtually no traces remained on concert programs, on library shelves, or in the textbooks that musicians (more than practitioners in most other fields) absorb as gospel."[4]

Views on public performance as a male profession and the perpetuation of gender stereotypes for certain instruments (of most relevance to Glennie's work) were also subjected to closer scrutiny. Feminist musicology recognized and challenged the fact that normative cultural behaviours are learned; understanding of male and female gender roles is based upon the examples set by peers and predecessors. The danger of cultural conditioning is that the situation is often not borne of conscious aggression or oppression, but through a subconscious response to the gendered structuring of society. As stated in Doubleday's study of the intersections between instrumental performance and gender: "To possess or play a musical instrument is to wield power."[5]

If instruments are inherently possessed of power, there is little question that multi-percussion can articulate this in a particularly assertive manner, given that the size, volume and ancestries of many percussion instruments strengthens their association with dominance and control. The assumption that drums and percussion are inherently masculine, and thus the province of male performers, is a key example of the ways in which certain behaviours have been subsumed into the Western consciousness over the course of several hundred years. The fact that the origins of orchestral percussion can be traced directly to the battlefield (with the Baroque timpani followed thereafter by military and Janissary percussion), established a particular relationship between drums and masculinity. However, this connection does not accurately reflect the role played by female drummers in earlier civilizations. As noted by Angela Smith:

---

[4] Susan McClary (1993) Reshaping a Discipline: Musicology and Feminism in the 1990s, *Feminist Studies*, 19 (2), p. 399.

[5] Veronica Doubleday (2008) Sounds of Power: An Overview of Musical Instruments and Gender, *Ethnomusicology Forum*, 17 (1), p. 3.

Archaeological findings and ancient illustrations from Egypt and Mesopotamia provide indisputable evidence that women have been drumming for thousands of years. In numerous cultures – African, South American, and North American Indian, for example – the drum was considered a feminine object, and the beat of a drum for many cultures was representative of the heartbeat of mother earth.[6]

Eurocentric perceptions of drummers as male are refuted in numerous cultures, including Middle Eastern practices wherein the frame drum has been connected with women since the third millennium BCE.[7] Chronologically closer to the timeline of Western art music, evidence of women playing an active part in music-making activities during the medieval era has been compiled by academics (citing the word *timpestere*, meaning "female drummer").[8] A seventeenth-century ballad titled *The Famous Woman Drummer* infers their presence into the Baroque period.[9] Yet when the foundations of orchestral percussion were established, the association between these instruments of power and their military origins meant that drums no longer "belonged" to female performers.

In the Classical and Romantic eras, professional solo performance – on any instrument – also became a male preserve; aside from preoccupations with the potential interruption of femininity (and the associated connotations of the gentle and passive female), women were not viewed as sufficiently assertive to perform as soloists. Though musicianship was a desirable attribute for educated women, any instrument that was loud, physically imposing or a threat to appreciation of the female form was deemed inappropriate, as was performance beyond the private sphere. Such views persisted into the twentieth century, as expressed in *Etude* in 1952: "Instruments requiring physical force are a dubious choice, partly because women lack strength for them, partly because the spectacle of a girl engaging in such physical exertions is not attractive."[10]

If the central intention of female music performance is to celebrate and highlight traditionally feminine attributes, as established in the Romantic period, drumming and multi-percussion threaten this on almost every

---

[6] Angela Smith (2014) *Women Drummers: A History from Rock and Jazz to Blues and Country*. Lanham: Rowman and Littlefield, p. 1.

[7] Veronica Doubleday (1999) The Frame Drum in the Middle East: Women, Musical Instruments and Power, *Ethnomusicology*, 43 (1), p. 105.

[8] Edith Borroff (1975) Women Composers: Reminiscence and History, *College Music Symposium*, 15, p. 26.

[9] Christopher Marsh (2011) "The Pride of Noise": Drums and Their Repercussions in Early Modern England, *Early Music*, 39 (2), p. 210.

[10] Raymond Paige (1952) Why Not Women in Orchestras?, *Etude*, 70, p. 302.

level. The sheer size of many percussion instruments and set-ups entirely distort or disguise the performer; solo percussion demands control, precision, assertive gestures, physical prowess, power, volume and intellectual acumen. All of these features challenge widely held views on a woman's place in music-making. As such, the glass ceiling imposed by Romantic conventions is entirely shattered. Solo percussion also rejects older dichotomies which still endure, upsetting the hierarchy of mind as superior to body, since the performer (regardless of gender) feels, thinks and experiences sound through the physical self in performance. Any enduring apprehensions regarding women and power (in terms of public performance and instrumental medium) or professional aptitude based on gender, is refuted entirely in Glennie's success as a female solo multi-percussionist. As women continue to assert their presence as composers and conductors in the twenty-first century, the discipline of performance offers an equally potent arena to demonstrate progress – particularly in relation to the patriarchal legacy of art music. Solo multi-percussion has the capacity to transcend any number of dichotomies; in relation to gender, boundaries are blurred in terms of male and female, masculine and feminine, mind and body, culture and nature, power and submission. Without needing to say a word, a powerful statement can be made through the language of music.

Sexism in Classical Music

Put in concise terms by author and journalist Inge Kloepfer as recently as 2018, with respect to art music, "men are still the geniuses, women still the muses."[11] Even though female composers, conductors and performers are increasingly visible figures in contemporary music, there is no question that they are often subject to different modes of scrutiny than their male peers. A search for the term "musician" in the Everyday Sexism Project (launched in 2012) indicates that sexism, gender stereotypes and explicit misogyny continue to create obstacles for women in all sectors of the music industry.[12] Examples of casual sexism pervade many aspects of social and cultural commentary, and art music is no exception. A light-hearted overview of the worst album covers ever (conducted by Classic FM) offers

[11] Inge Kloepfer (2018) So Sexistisch ist die Klassik, *Frankfurter Allgemeine Zeitung*, 13 June 2018. Translated from German by Elizabeth Osman and cited in Liane Curtis (2018) *A View From Germany: Classical Music is So Sexist* (online). Available from: https://wophil.org/a-view-from-germany-classical-music-is-so-sexist/?doing_wp_cron=1561375680.6319100856781005859375 (accessed 24 June 2019).

[12] *The Everyday Sexism Project* (2012), online. Available from: https://everydaysexism.com/?s=music (accessed 8 March 2023).

The Issue of Gender   107

several examples of the ways in which women have been objectified for the purposes of marketing.[13] These visual representations of gender roles in art music are indicative of a history in which dichotomies have been institutionalized to an almost obsessive degree; articulating difference and identifying otherness is a recurrent trope in Western art music.

Boundaries between male and female professional identities and instrumental disciplines extend even into the fabric of composition itself, with gendered terms used in relation to cadence, tonality, melody and musical form. These dated cultural legacies have lingered, with casual sexism in reception and critique of Glennie tending to follow one of three central (and historically familiar) narratives: the subjugation of the female figure under the male gaze, incredulity at the ability of a "feminine" woman to demonstrate typically masculine attributes, and the propagation of negative female stereotypes linked to suppressed anger and hysteria. Though Glennie states that she has not experienced any gender discrimination during her career, an early recollection suggests that it had the potential to become an issue in relation to marketing and image:

> Honestly, the only thing I can really remember is when I was asked to wear certain types of clothing for a photo shoot for my first solo CD, you know, and it wasn't particularly a type of clothing that I felt comfortable wearing, and I think it was just so important to be completely straight and upfront.[14]

Since opting to employ her own administrative staff in 1989 (a decision not well received by her agents and management team at the time), Glennie has assumed control of her own correspondence, branding and identity. From the earliest stages, Glennie has carefully curated her public image, yet follows the reflection above with the acknowledgement that she felt it necessary (in the early days) to rationalize and justify her reasons for asserting such views: "I could use the instruments as an excuse because if you wear certain things as you're sitting at a drum kit or timpani or something it's just completely and utterly absurd and impractical."[15] As business woman and brand, Glennie has exercised creative control over marketing decisions. Early album covers demonstrate that she favoured representations which align contemplation and assertiveness; the body and face (when featured)

---

[13] *These Terrible Album Covers Will Make you Laugh and Then Violently Cringe* (online). Available from: https://www.classicfm.com/discover-music/latest/worst-classical-album-covers-ever/derek-bell-plays-with-himself/ (accessed 16 July 2019). Album covers 8, 22 and 23 are particularly relevant.

[14] Interview with Glennie, 3 May 2019.

[15] Ibid.

were part of tableaux designed to celebrate the equally compelling beauty of multi-percussion. Her first two solo albums (*Rhythm Song* released in 1990 and *Light in Darkness*, 1991) are indicative of this juxtaposition (see Fig. 8).

It is important to note that both early albums favoured tuned percussion repertoire, a medium already connected to prominent female performers (such as Vida Chenoweth, Abe and Linda Maxey). Glennie's transition to more experimental works exploring a wider range of percussive sonorities in subsequent album releases presented a more empowered female identity, supported by increasingly eclectic imagery. *Drumming* (1996) is indicative of this metamorphosis, with Glennie emerging from behind an enormous anvil (in stark black and grey lighting). In some sense, Glennie becomes the instrument in this image; the focus is on the body as a source

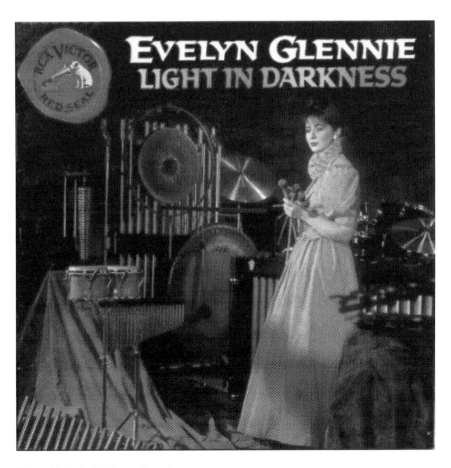

Fig. 8: *Light in Darkness* (1991).

of strength and creativity, rather than an object to be admired. The visuals mirror the album content, with experimental soundscapes encompassing a broad range of auxiliary instruments, and tuned percussion now a much less obvious presence.

Whilst Glennie has controlled and directed promotional materials, she is not in a position to evade critical commentary on live performances, a context in which the male gaze has often focused on physical attributes and allure rather than more relevant observations on the music. Though representative only of subjective and determinedly opinionated responses, the recurrence of reviews distracted by Glennie's visual appeal are nonetheless problematic. A 1992 newspaper article made little effort to disguise implicitly sexual commentary: "As ever, the dazzle factor is high; Miss Glennie has, by any definition, the most remarkable wrist action in the business. As a virtuoso, she is unparalleled, though I am always most taken with the way she has of shaping a soft, curvaceous phrase."[16] In 1997, a journalist noted how she "sashays disruptively through the strings waving gourds in the air".[17] Ten years later, reception of Glennie (even from female reviewers) retained an overtly sexist tone: "It's hard to know how seriously it is meant: the sight of Glennie hitching up her dress and striding round to thwack the bass drum suggested it might be about nothing more than a poetic domestic row."[18] Glennie's performance style has also been framed in terms of gender, with references made to rage and hysteria. The inference that energy and power are demonstrative of emotional instability rather than interpretative accuracy reflects writer and social commentator Roxanne Gay's observation that "all feminists are angry instead of, say, passionate".[19]

Obviously, hyperbole and an interest in salacious detail are key selling features of print media, and so dismissing these subjective irrelevancies would seem to be the most logical path. However, Glennie has always been a public commodity; her professional identity is inextricably connected to responses from beyond the musical establishment. The fact that her divorce in 2003 was seized upon by the UK tabloids is both a statement on her popularity and a damning indictment of invasive commentary on the lives of high-profile women. With a career spanning over five decades, Glennie has transitioned through various stages of womanhood in public. In a parallel

[16] Michael Tumelty (1992) Dazzle Factor. Evelyn Glennie, RSAMD, Glasgow, *The Herald*, 18 November 1992.

[17] Tim Ashley (1997) Arts Review Classical: NSO Washington, Royal Festival Hall, London, *Guardian*, 20 October 1997.

[18] Erica Jeal (2007) Prom 63: BBCSO/Belohlavek, Royal Albert Hall, London, *Guardian*, review section, 3 September 2007.

[19] Roxane Gay (2014), *Bad Feminist*, New York: Harper Collins, p. 305.

narrative associated almost exclusively with prominent women, for many years Glennie was questioned on the subject of children (a clear indication of the fact that the dualist association between woman and nature was retained). Though this is irrelevant to her professional identity, Glennie has always addressed the issue with honesty. Success has demanded compromise, and Glennie is candid about the fact that her chosen career has required sacrifices:

> I mean, I don't have children for example, and I think that my journey might have been quite different if I had children … I think that in general the relationships over the years have been challenging because of the time I'm away and that's a pity, but so that's the choice that you make.[20]

It is not difficult to understand why Glennie has distanced herself from discourse on gender until recently; her silence has been a form of patience, allowing musical achievements to supersede fascinations with the concept of a deaf female virtuosic percussionist. It is instead through the language of performance that Glennie's statements on a woman's role are articulated with the greatest potency.

Music as Metaphor:
From *My Dream Kitchen* to Glennie's Kitchen Sink

In 1966, historian Barbara Welter defined the nineteenth-century virtues of women in what she described as the "cult" of womanhood: piety, purity, submissiveness and domesticity.[21] The final virtue connected not only to culturally acceptable behaviour but also to the position of the female in society; if a woman's place was in the home then she would not be present in public life or represented in cultural production on any significant scale. First-wave feminists endeavoured to escape these confines; pioneers such as Mary Wollstonecraft and Frances Wright, who sought roles of responsibility beyond the home, were consequently condemned as "only semi-women, mental hermaphrodites".[22] Even in the twenty-first century, misogynistic commentary often returns to the image of the maternal home-maker. When sports presenter Lynsey Hipgrave was critical of a controversial penalty by Lionel Messi in 2016, she was subjected to considerable online misogynistic abuse simply for fulfilling her professional role. Comments

[20] Interview with Glennie, 3 May 2019.
[21] Barbara Welter (1966) The Cult of True Womanhood: 1820–1860, *American Quarterly*, 18 (2), part 1, p. 152.
[22] Ibid.

Fig. 9: Glennie in rehearsals for *My Dream Kitchen*.

such as "somewhere there's a kitchen and it's missing something" indicate that stereotypes regarding the gendered division of labour between work and home life persist.[23]

To some extent, any Glennie performance is a case study in female empowerment and leadership, particularly in the context of works which require extensive instrumentation and virtuosic display. Many of the case studies in this chapter can certainly be understood through a feminist lens, but they are equally important as musical works whose value extends beyond one particular reading. Of greatest interest in considering Glennie as a role model in this respect are performances which simultaneously address extra-musical narratives, challenging or reframing societal ideologies. *My Dream Kitchen* (a solo commission composed by Django Bates in 1996) positioned Glennie in a custom-made set-up of kitchen utensils and instruments, replacing the stereotype of an acquiescent and passive homemaker with a female percussion soloist who is an assertive force of energy and power. The private domestic sphere was reimagined, functioning both as a novel interpretation of percussion practice and a form of cultural commentary, achieved on conceptual, visual and musical levels (see Fig. 9).

[23] Twitter comment cited in Kate Whiston (2016) *A Woman's Place is in the Kitchen: Changing Culinary Culture* (online), 7 March 2016. Available from: https://blog.geographydirections.com/2016/03/07/a-womans-place-is-in-the-kitchen-changing-culinary-culture/ (accessed 21 July 2019).

Django Bates is a composer and multi-instrumentalist whose works are often infused with a playful sense of humour reflecting influences drawn from multiple genres. Glennie provided few specifications for the commission, asking only for a work that could be personal to her. The interactivity of the commissioning process resulted in a satirical interpretation of Glennie's skills as a cook: "Normally I hate cooking so this is all about my fury in the kitchen."[24] In addition to functioning as an ironic homage to Glennie's culinary apathy, the work also played on the assumption that percussion is little more than striking random objects (referred to in early orchestration manuals as the "kitchen" of the orchestra). *My Dream Kitchen* was a central feature of Glennie's first solo tour (1996), a series of eleven concerts performed throughout the UK. In the stage plan for the tour, *Ev's Cafe* is prominently positioned at the front of the stage. One of two works highlighted in the *Evelyn Glennie Newsletter* which preceded the tour, there is no question that *My Dream Kitchen* was particularly well suited to the earlier stages of Glennie's career, when the drive to make solo percussion a visible and viable performance medium was of keenest value; a balance of skill and playfulness are attributes of value to a young and ambitious performer. It represents the essence of Glennie's style in many ways: an experimental work, a mode of theatre, an invitation for the audience to connect with percussion on multiple sensory levels, and an opportunity to present new music. The one extant version of the score (in handwritten form) is retained by The Evelyn Glennie Collection; Glennie remains the only performer of *My Dream Kitchen* to date and has since retired the work. Speaking in 2009, she notes:

> I can't play it anymore. I had to build a prop cafe to hang the various utensils, pots and pans. The prop got so flimsy after playing it for a while on tour and it became dangerous. During the piece I had to bake a cake and put a candle on it at the finale. The fire regulations in some halls meant that it required special permission. It was a lot of fun but I finally had to leave it behind.[25]

My Dream Kitchen was conceived as an expansive multi-percussion soundscape, with unconventional objects viewed definitively as musical instruments. Details on pitch variations for saucepans and palette knives, and specifications on the contents of various objects ("a few coins in your

---

[24] Joanna Pitman (1996) Banging About in the Kitchen: Profile, Evelyn Glennie, *The Times*, 4 May 1996.

[25] Evelyn Glennie in James Ellis (2009) Evelyh [*sic*] Glennie, *Metro* (online), 27 October 2009. Available from: https://metro.co.uk/2009/10/27/evelyh-glennie-241150/ (accessed 1 August 2019).

pocket" and "egg box with one egg inside it") were part of an extensive instrumentation list which aligns marimba, glockenspiel and cymbal with various kitchen utensils. The inclusion of extras such as the Delia Smith cookbook (an icon of feminine domesticity), costume directives (apron and hat) and decorative features (basket of artificial fruit, candle and kitchen roll) infer the work's function as a satirical installation of performance art and visual spectacle in addition to a musical event. These details indicate the humorous undertone of the composition, as do the brief programme notes provided by Bates for Glennie, which include the opinion that "on the whole musicians do not make good cooks".

The score combined standard notation with narrated performance directives; the multi-percussion opening on saucepans and roasting tin (a recurring motif: see Ex. 7) is followed by a section where the soloist is instructed to "slice an apple (nice chopping sounds). Drop it into cake. Throw core into pedal bin."

Bates achieves an effective balance between showmanship and musicality; the multi-percussion saucepan motif is immediately followed by a four-mallet jazz-inspired marimba interlude which also recurs as a unifying device (see Ex. 8).

The performer then takes the time to crack an egg, bin the shell and "twang" the palette knife overhead, getting gradually quieter until it is allowed to vibrate to silence. This *diminuendo* could be entirely unconvincing if not executed with resolve. It is intended to be hypnotic, heightening audience anticipation; the power here lies in reverence for the moment – an honouring of the journey from sound to silence. Not all percussionists want to embrace such eccentricities. It is perfectly plausible to doubt the virtuosic acumen required to crack an egg or grate a carrot. Based on Glennie's annotations she revels in such theatrical interludes. On page 2 of the score, Glennie adds the note "silence important!", a statement on her

Ex. 7: *My Dream Kitchen* saucepan motif (Django Bates).

Ex. 8: *My Dream Kitchen* marimba melody (Django Bates).

perceived role as a conduit between music and gesture in the kitchen environment. A later annotation simply stating "normal!" is equally indicative of Glennie's awareness of her dual role as actress and musician.

Before the recipe is complete, there are further comedic and musical elements to implement in the score. The carrot is grated to the accompaniment of a repeated pattern on pedal bin and a cheese grater repurposed as a guiro (section F). A *pp* interlude on marimba segues to five bars of the original melody extended with rising figurations, *glissandi* and a *crescendo*. Section H combines the timbre of dried beans with the sonority of the glockenspiel. More rapid alternations between auxiliary percussion rhythms and marimba entries follow as the work moves towards its climax. The performer then pauses momentarily to roll an egg box flat (with eggs inside) and add a watch to the mixture. For the next frenetic iteration of the opening saucepan statement (making use of disjointed combinations of quintuplets, triplets and accented quavers) Glennie's annotations intimate an energetic interpretation of the *forte* dynamics and accents whilst fully embracing the comic value of the moment, with "yeah!" and "wipe brow" pencilled in. After the expenditure of such energy, section N opens quietly with the grinding of coins using a mortar and pestle; the vibrating palette knife returns, now layered with a passage for two plates and bowls.

The performance direction for these bars is "naïve". When the coins have been added to the cake mixture, four timers are set; their ticking serves as a metronome for the reprised saucepan theme. The relative stability and familiarity of the rhythmic ideas herein, combined with a sustained 6/4 time signature, suggest that the kitchen is under control. Section P disturbs the sense of balance and order with the instruction to tip a pile of bun trays onto the floor. When the performer has placed the mixture in the oven, they are instructed to put the recipe book into the bin. *My Dream Kitchen* closes with a cake miraculously appearing from the ingredients box; the performer leaves the stage eating and content.

The aural intrigue of the solo equalled the visual appeal in *My Dream Kitchen*, positioning Glennie as an unhinged, inept and frustrated chef and simultaneously a virtuosic performer; in the moments of theatre, she transitioned from percussionist to sound creator. *My Dream Kitchen* was an embodied performance installation wherein Bates invited the (female) soloist to pose a potent musical question – is a woman's place really in the kitchen? Regardless of the pantomimic integration of costume and set decoration, the repurposing of the kitchen as a site of solo performance made an important statement. There were no male forces present on the stage; the kitchen was no longer a private space; the idea that women are naturally suited to domestic life was forcefully rebuked. All of these elements speak to the power of the female figure, free to operate at the centre of both domestic and professional life, and more importantly as a public figure in a leadership role.

In more recent times, Glennie has once again reinterpreted the adage that "a woman's place is in the home", with a number of short improvisations on her kitchen sink, microwave and kitchen corner (all available via the Evelyn Glennie YouTube channel). *The Sounds of my Kitchen Sink* reimagines the domestic sphere once again as a multi-percussion installation. Bates brought the kitchen to the concert hall; Glennie brings the audience to her home. There is a marvellous rejection of gender stereotypes and a blurring of private and public (female and male) spheres in each respect. The kitchen becomes a multi-percussion instrument, with domesticity replaced by creativity, sound exploration, experimentation and performance. Percussion is everywhere, in everything, for everyone.

Dualism Revised: *Castle of the Mad King* (1998) and *Concerto of the Mad Queen* (2000)

Growing interest in the timbres and rhythmic language of percussion in the mid-twentieth century necessitated a steep learning curve for many composers. The birth of literature dedicated specifically to the art of percussion in the 1960s was an important development, reflecting the discipline-specific complexities of nomenclature, style, technique and instrumentation (requiring publications extending beyond standard orchestration treatises). Many of the most significant texts were written by performers. Blades contributed two seminal works, the concise *Orchestral Percussion Techniques* (1961) and the expansive *Percussion Instruments and Their History* (1970; reprinted in 2021 with Foreword and a new chapter on solo percussion by Glennie). Reginald Smith Brindle's *Contemporary Percussion* (1970) followed a similar path, examining techniques, timbres, histories and the inadequacy of traditional notational systems.

This final point resonates throughout subsequent percussion manuals. In orchestral scores of the past, standard nomenclature was sufficient to denote the relatively simple roles played by timpani and auxiliary percussion. As the complexity of parts evolved, composers needed to provide greater clarity on their vision for percussionists. The graphic notation adopted in early solo percussion repertoire offered a potential solution, but one largely unsuited to specific and detailed directives. The advent of the percussionist–composer has been an important means of advancing understanding and scoring methodologies for the discipline, ensuring that works are legible, exciting, challenging and practical. Glennie has worked with various percussionist–composers during the commissioning process (including Marta Ptaszyńska and Másson).

One recurring collaboration is with the Serbian artist Nebojša Jovan Živković, an accomplished and respected solo and chamber performer. Živković generally composes using an extended score, whereby additional staffs are inserted when clarity is needed on notation for instruments played simultaneously. In two of his four commissions to date, Živković cast Glennie as both the king and queen of multi-percussion. *The Castle of the Mad King* (1998) is a solo multi-percussion work, positioning the male protagonist alone in his world of sound rooms; *Concerto of the Mad Queen* (2000) presents the female namesake as powerful and dominant, asserting control over the orchestra. Whilst the gender of the programmatic character is fixed, that of the performer is determinedly fluid. The works are paired because their instrumentation is almost identical; Živković created a king and queen to establish a connection rather than a dichotomy.

It is worth noting, however, that the connotations of madness in each instance are historically gendered. In both medical and cultural histories, the concept of female madness has oftentimes been linked directly to behaviours or practices which are deemed to be socially transgressive – those which contravene the conventions of gender performance. Extensive

The Issue of Gender   117

research is not required to find several centuries' worth of medical texts discussing psychiatric conditions associated specifically with women; the term "hysteria" is one example, derived from the Greek word meaning "of the womb or uterus". There is reference to this in the opening directives for *Concerto of the Mad Queen*, where the soloist is instructed to "interrupt the trumpets with her hysteric solo on the Uchiwa-Daikos [Japanese single-headed frame drums of various sizes] and earth-plates".[26] Otherwise, there are no obvious notational implications that gender is of concern in the compositional design.

The Castle of the Mad King premiered in a theatrical manner, with Glennie and Živković providing two separate concerts on the same day (2 October 1998) in Stockholm. The role of the king therefore immediately belonged to both male and female performers. The madness of the king was presented musically through a series of introspective and eccentric soundscapes: "Behind the walls, the listener discovers the chamber of rage, the chamber of torture, the chamber of joy, the chamber of longing, the chamber of laughter, and those chambers in which it is almost forbidden to enter."[27] Scored for a large multi-percussion set-up positioned as three walls around the performer, the only pitched sonorities are provided by a low octave of crotales. Metal (cymbals, gongs, metal pipes, thunder sheet, wind chime, crotales and earth plates), skin (five tom-toms, split drum, log drum, Uchiwa-Daikos and bass drum) and wood (bamboo wind chime, wood blocks, rainstick) timbres are explored, often initially as solo entities; the most technically complex and musically exciting moments occur where these sound worlds overlap and interact (generally aligned with space for improvisation).

There are few stereotypically masculine traits in evidence; though the final movement has moments of exuberance, the first two (marked "Tranquillo") are generally focused on allowing sounds to resonate and decay to haunting effect. Following a series of sustained gong strikes (played in darkness), the opening on Uchiwa-Daikos is scored as a percussion melody, with the performer moving fluidly between drums as the stage is illuminated. There are no bar lines in this introduction, which is based on alternations of quaver and triplet figurations that consciously avoid any repeated motifs. Crotales gradually enter the soundscape, once again eschewing any clear sense of pattern or defined melody; the focus is on timbre. Small cymbal

---

[26]   Steve Weiss Music (n.d.) *Zivkovic-Concerto #1 for Perc. And Orch. (Concerto of the Mad Queen) – Product Information* (online). Available from: https://www.steveweissmusic.com/product/26025/multi-percussion-accompaniment#full-description (accessed 15 March 2023).

[27]   Ira Produnov (1998) The Castle of the Mad King, *Percussive Notes*, 35 (5), p. 66.

crashes lead to silence. There is an energizing unpredictability where the ear becomes keenly focused and expectant; as each new sound is added, the focus remains on intermittent strikes and the avoidance of clear patterns. This is less about the rhythmic identity of percussion and more about its timbral language. In the closing stages, a dialogue between metal and skin emphasizes speed but not volume.

It is an introspective work; the drama is witnessed in the many movements of the performer and in the energy of anticipating sound. The programmatic title is realized more in the castle of sounds than in the gender of the protagonist. Unlike many commissions which are conceived specifically with Glennie's performance style in mind, *Castle of the Mad King* almost immediately became part of the solo percussion canon, connected in particular to its composer (who recorded it in 2000 on the BIS label). In addition to the 1998 premiere, Glennie gave twenty performances of *Castle of the Mad King* in 1999 and a further two in 2001, before moving on to new repertoire and commissions. To some extent Živković remains the "king" of the composition, and subsequent interpretations posted on YouTube invariably feature a male protagonist. The gender of the performer continues to impact reception, evinced in reviews of Živković which include the term "masculine" in multiple instances; Glennie's performances of *Castle of the Mad King* are instead defined as "electrifying" and "hypnotic".[28]

Continuing to explore madness through the catharsis of solo percussion performance, *Concerto of the Mad Queen* centralized a female figure (in programmatic terms). Živković scores the concerto as a single movement with three distinct sections, with a fluid duration generally not exceeding sixteen minutes; the first and third are frenetic, physical and relentless. Surrounded by instruments, in a configuration almost identical to *Castle of the Mad King*, the soloist is tasked with an exhausting series of ostinati, overlapping rhythmic motifs and colliding timbres, performed with an intensity only briefly alleviated by a vibraphone solo in the middle section. Written by a percussionist (and thereby exploring techniques, positions and combinations which offer motivating challenges), the work is perhaps most enjoyable from the perspective of the performer; the sustained intensity is a challenge to the listener. There is an abiding ferocity in the scoring, an intentionally dramatic duel between soloist and orchestra, wherein multi-percussion emerges as dominant.

Entering with a *crescendo* tam-tam roll and an uneven quaver figuration played *ff* on earth plates, the soloist is a forceful presence from the

---

[28] *Reviews and Concert Critics* (online). Available from: https://zivkovic.de/reviews-concert-critics/ (accessed 15 March 2023).

The Issue of Gender   119

beginning. The madness of the queen is an entirely more intense proposition; noise is an unapologetic feature of the soloist's role, often embedded in the complexities of the notation, but also accommodated in performance directives including "get mad immediately!" at bar 59 (which is improvised). In many ways the concerto feels like a percussion solo with orchestral accompaniment; the most exciting interplay is reserved for interactions between the orchestral percussion section and soloist. It is less concerned with gendered frames of madness than with the emancipation of the percussionist, who is invited to unleash with a sense of wildness the cacophony and physicality of their domain.

As with the solo work, the concerto remained part of Glennie's repertory for three years (ten performances from 2000 to 2002), and has since been interpreted by subsequent performers, including Živković. Unifying both the masculine and feminine stereotypes drawn from centuries of Western culture, the solo multi-percussionist is a potent connective between male and female, mind and body. Živković was not concerned with establishing difference; his central focus was in fact to forge a sense of connection. The king and queen are not dichotomous; their percussive voices are fundamentally the same. For the composer, gender was not relevant to the experience of percussion, and the commissions are not representative of any dualist interpretation of performance. In many ways this case study seeks to problematize the ways in which the gender of the performer and/or the programmatic character can impact reception. Speaking of his collaboration with Glennie, Živković states this with clarity: "I have never thought of her as woman first ... She is an extraordinary HUMAN and MUSICIAN and PLAYER above all ... She has the stage presence of a magician, energy of a tiger and musicality of the nightingale.[29]

The Powerful Female: *Conjurer* (2007–2008)

> When asked to compose a percussion concerto, my only reaction was horror. All I could see were problems. While I love using a percussion battery in my orchestral writing, the very thing that makes it the perfect accent to other orchestral sonorities makes it unsatisfactory when it takes the spotlight in a concerto.[30]

---

[29] E-mail correspondence with Nebojša Jovan Živković, 25 March 2023. Capitalization in original.

[30] John Corigliano (2007) *Conjurer: Concerto for Percussionist and String Orchestra (with optional brass)*, New York: Schirmer, p. 4.

It is not easy to write for solo multi-percussion; the endless number of instruments, limitless range of techniques, conflation of gesture and sound, balance, and issues of notation all contribute to a challenging remit for the composer. Corigliano is not alone in his hesitation; various commissioned composers share similar misgivings about the task of meeting the needs of a virtuosic percussionist and sound creator. Richard Rodney Bennett, in preparing initial ideas for his *Percussion Concerto* (1990), notes: "I decided in this work to concentrate mostly on unpitched percussion ... This limitation imposed very considerable compositional problems, but the challenge was stimulating."[31] Jonathan Harvey, whose commissioned *Percussion Concerto* premiered in 1997, was similarly honest about his experience: "This is the first time I've written for solo percussion, and my first response was that it was very difficult. I don't like the idea of building an enormous percussion edifice for each performance. I prefer to exploit Evelyn's virtuosity with the mallets."[32]

One must remember that it is not easy to play solo multi-percussion either. Though the premise is simple (to strike, scrape or shake an object), the reality of creating musical meaning from any number of timbres using any number of techniques is prohibitively difficult. Glennie requested a commission from Corigliano for at least a decade before *Conjurer*, but the composer had one fundamental problem in this respect: "Evelyn Glennie asked me for many years to write a percussion concerto, and I love her playing, but I really didn't like percussion concertos."[33] Glennie's persistence reflects the main impetus for all commissions – an interest in hearing how a composer she admires channels their style into writing for multi-percussion:

> Just basically I'm a fan of his music. Always with a composer, the main thing is to feel something from the music, and with John I have always found him very exciting as a composer ... There's always substance there; there's always a surprise there. I just felt he could do something really interesting and I'm glad I did actually.[34]

---

[31] Richard Rodney Bennett (1990) *Percussion Concerto*. London: Novello and Co. (World).

[32] Jonathan Harvey quoted in Ian Pillow (1997) Hard Heart, Soft Stroke, *Independent* (online), 24 July 1997. Available from: http://www.independent.co.uk/arts-entertainment/msuic/hard-heart-soft-stroke-1252392.html (accessed 17 August 2017).

[33] John Corigliano in The Cleveland Orchestra (2021) *John Corigliano: Crafting Conjurer* (video online), 6 May 2021. Available from: https://www.youtube.com/watch?v=92uPUONtanY (accessed 18 March 2023).

[34] Interview with Glennie, 27 June 2023.

Corigliano is a revered and prolific contemporary composer, with numerous accolades (including five Grammy Awards, an Academy Award and the Pulitzer Prize). Associated primarily with large-scale orchestral forms, Corigliano has also been successful in writing for stage and film. His reluctance therefore pertained specifically to the medium. Glennie, joined in the effort by conductor Marin Alsop and six US orchestras, collectively persuaded Corigliano to embrace the challenge. For the composer, there were two central obstacles: firstly, the diversity of multi-percussion made it difficult to distinguish the soloist from the orchestra, and secondly there was little scope for lyricism or melody in the solo part. To address the first, he reversed the paradigm of a single voice dominating the ensemble by making the orchestra homogenous (using only strings in the first two movements, with optional brass in the third), allowing the role of multi-percussion to be immediately foregrounded. To further heighten this distinction, each of the three movements focused on one aspect of percussive language (wood, metal and skin respectively). The second issue was alleviated in the middle movement, where the vibraphone is struck with mallets (to acknowledge the natural decay of each note) and bowed (to prolong the sounds) in order to craft a sustained melodic journey. The resultant concerto (an epic and challenging tour-de-force with a duration of approximately thirty-five minutes) has become one of Glennie's most successful commissions in terms of its performance legacy, for both Glennie and many subsequent percussionists. Glennie's association with *Conjurer* is nonetheless enduring; her role in commissioning the work is one obvious mode of connection, as is the fact that she was the first to meet the challenges of Corigliano's third solution in writing for percussion – to place considerable onus on the skills of the performer. Each movement begins with an extended improvisation (and the work also ends in the same manner), thereby allocating the multi-percussionist amplified responsibility for conjuring magic from their instruments. The evocative title (with suggestions of a mystical, powerful and intriguing character) was finalized as a direct result of Glennie's first performance:

> Originally called "Triple Play" for its three movements featuring wood, metal, and skin instruments, the title evolved into "Conjurer" after the first performance. "The conjurer is the soloist," explained Corigliano during a backstage interview in Dallas, "and the pieces of wood, metal, and skin are objects that she brings to life through hitting, stroking or bowing. They become magical."[35]

---

[35] Lauren Vogel Weiss (2008) Evelyn Glennie, *Percussive Notes*, 46 (4), August 2008, pp. 18–19.

In a seminar on the compositional process, Corigliano's discussion of his early sketches (including a fascinating intensity mapping of the concerto), indicate that the movements were originally called "Clatter", "Shimmer" and "Thunder".[36] These terms were replaced in the published score with the simpler "Wood", "Metal" and "Skin", but the atmospheric allusions of Corigliano's initial creative plan are retained in the soundscape. Even though Glennie served as the inspiration for the work's name, Corigliano avoids gendering the protagonist, avoiding the more frightening imagery and histories associated with the terms "witch" or "sorceress"; even magic has been subjected to gender dichotomies in both fiction and reality.

Following twenty performances by Glennie in 2008 (with more in later years), from 2009 onwards the concerto has proven popular with other percussionists; Morris Palter was the first successor (with the Fairbanks Symphony Orchestra). The list of subsequent conjurers is impressive, with numerous performances by Martin Grubinger, whose biography opens by describing him as "possibly the best multi-percussionist of the world",[37] and UK solo percussionist Colin Currie in 2018. All post-Glennie conjurers to date are male.

Regardless of the many interpretations which have ensued (this being the primary aim of commissioning), the original conjurer role was retained for posterity on a 2013 CD release, resulting in a 2014 Grammy Award for Glennie (in the category of Best Classical Instrumental Solo). In terms of female representation (music and multi-percussion) this marks a seminal moment. The Grammy Awards have suffered backlash in recent decades due to the relative absence of female names in both recipient and nominee lists. The Best Classical Instrumental Solo (which has undergone several minor name changes) was initiated in 1959; a female did not receive the award until 1976 (Alicia de Larrocha for Ravel's *Piano Concerto for the Left Hand*). It was almost twenty years before the next female awardee in 1994, Anne-Sophie Mutter. Of the sixty-five Best Classical Solo Grammy recipients to date, fourteen are women.

In response to issues of representation in all categories, the Recording Academy, presenter of the Grammy Awards, launched a survey (initiated in 2018 with Berklee and Arizona State University) to appraise the experiences of women and gender-expansive people in the music industry (with the

---

[36] John Corigliano (2014) *Seminar and conversation with Michael Stern*, Nelson-Atkins Museum of Art (Kansas, Missouri), 30 January 2014 (video online). Available from: https://www.youtube.com/watch?v=X46Pgz8dHrM (accessed 20 March 2023).

[37] *Martin Grubinger Biography* (2019/20), online. Available from: https://www.harrisonparrott.com/artists/martin-grubinger (accessed 26 March 2024).

most recent data released in 2022).[38] Findings to some extent exonerated the Grammys in that gender discrimination was not unique to their institution; the results were a damning indication of the fact that inequalities persist to an alarming degree in all facets of the industry. Glennie was the second percussion Grammy solo winner (and the first female), preceded by Christopher Lamb in 2012 (with Schwantner's *Percussion Concerto*). Given that many other instrumental disciplines have yet to be recognized in this category, two percussion wins is a statement on the importance of this musical language in the twenty-first century (a form of advocacy and representation which transcends gender). Glennie's earlier Grammy award (for Best Chamber Ensemble at the thirty-first Grammy awards) facilitated name-recognition, but the solo win was a more powerful statement of personal success. Winning with *Conjurer* made this point with particular clarity, given that the magic of the work emanates to a large degree from improvisation.

Corigliano specifies the instrumentation for each of the three percussion stations, though there is freedom for the performer in choosing eighteen auxiliary wood instruments or objects to create the hybrid xylophone scored in the first movement (see Fig. 10). Corigliano also provides guidance on rhythmic and melodic motifs for each opening improvisation in order to create an audible relationship between the solo material and the orchestral movement which follows. Improvisations in this context must feel organic and instinctive, balancing freedom with attention to the specifications of the score. Further autonomy is afforded in the later stages of the third movement, though the sense of structural clarity must be retained. From bars 529 to 551 (the last), the directive is to "improvise cadenza on all drums. Keep energy high, and use motives from the written material".[39] Corigliano's commentary on Glennie's interpretation of this section exemplifies the intensity with which she chose to conclude the concerto: "Evelyn goes completely crazy, I must say. It's quite mad – and wonderful."[40]

The album separates the improvised introductions from the movements which follow (with the improvisation at the end remaining part of the third). The confluence of Corigliano's structural rigour and Glennie's response to

---

[38] Erin Barra, Mako Fitts Ward, Lisa M. Anderson, Alaysia M. Brown (2022) *Women in the Mix Study.* Recording Academy, Arizona State University, Berklee Institute for Creative Entrepreneurship.

[39] Corigliano (2007) *Conjurer: Concerto for Percussionist and String Orchestra*, p. 93.

[40] John Corigliano and Mark Damoulakis (2021) *John Corigliano and Mark Damoulakis: Improvisation in Conjurer* (video online), 16 June 2021. Posted by the Cleveland Orchestra. Available from: https://www.youtube.com/watch?v=17fRLBo3IfY (accessed 21 March 2023).

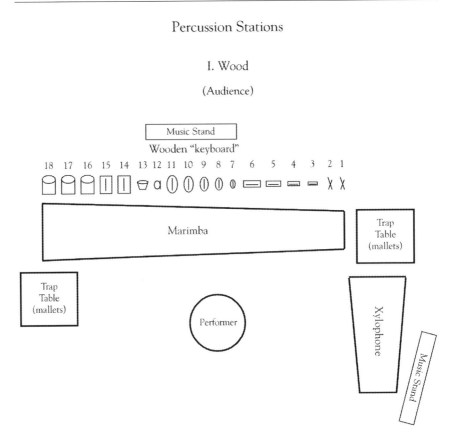

Fig. 10: Percussion station for first movement of *Conjurer*. Permission kindly granted by Wise Music Group.

his vision create a powerful musical narrative which is immediately accessible yet entirely intriguing. Cadenza 1, in the first movement, "Wood", stretches to almost four minutes, beginning with auxiliary instruments and progressing to a cohesive merging of pitched and unpitched wooden sonorities. The solo part is scored across four staves (two for unpitched and two for pitched) and details relative pitches, rhythmic values, placement of rests and pauses (see Ex. 9).

Glennie's attention to Corigliano's dynamics is exacting; pauses are relatively brief, used to heighten anticipation in the space between sounds without disturbing a sense of continuity. The improvisation is playful but not comical, evolving with a sense of purpose and direction as the soloist moves from tentative exploration to more expansive statements across

Ex. 9: Opening of "Wood" cadenza in *Conjurer* (John Corigliano).

multiple instruments. In bar 9 the soloist is asked to *ad. lib* the transition into the first movement; Glennie makes this moment subtle and understated, responding to the *piano* dynamics of the score. The effect is the sense of the solo melting into the orchestral soundscape, as strings maintain the focus on wood timbres with tremolo, "col legno battuto" (striking the strings with the wood of the bow) and "sul ponticello" (bowing near the bridge) effects, and percussive crunches on double-stops. The movement is fast, *staccato* and brittle, an evocation of the rapid decay of wooden percussion instruments and a definitive contrast to the reverberations which characterize the second.

126 *Evelyn Glennie: Sound Creator*

Metal is introduced with a sudden *ffff* strike on tam-tam and tubular bells, answered by a three-bar string melody drawing on musical ideas from movement 1 (and bringing this part of the journey to a close). All of the metal improvisation is to be played loudly, with focus on allowing the notes of the largest instruments to resonate for extended periods. Again, Glennie respects the placement of pauses in the score, but these do not extend beyond the natural decay of notes sounded; there is no hyperbole in the interpretation. The improvisation is disciplined, mindful of its relationship to the second movement and the composer's vision. Evoking metallic sounds in the string orchestra is more difficult than in the "Wood" movement, but Corigliano lightens the texture with *divisi* sections, lengthy note durations and soft dynamics. Rather than linking the ensemble to the sound world of the soloist (as in the first movement), the percussionist instead becomes a string player, bowing the vibraphone from bar 278. The aim of forging a lyrical voice for the solo multi-percussionist is realized to transcendent effect. The melody is simple for both aesthetic and practical reasons; Corigliano uses only white notes for the bowed vibraphone section to ensure complete fluency in the line. Directives earlier in the movement (where glockenspiel also features) include "floating" (bar 212) and "liquid" (bar 237), simple but evocative guidelines for the soloist.

The metallic soundscape fades gently away and the "Skin" improvisation begins in a similarly delicate manner. Again, Corigliano provides an outline for the performer, but there is a heightened degree of freedom, given the instrumental medium. This improvisation is a dialogue between kick drum and talking drum, the latter an instrument of West African origin designed to mimic the patterns and inflections of human speech. An hourglass-shaped body is framed by rope which can be tightened in order to change the pitch (achieved by applying pressure from the upper thighs); played with the fingertips, the voice of the instrument is versatile in terms of timbre, dynamics and resonance. In this instance the soloist conjures life from the drum, reflecting its cultural origins as a mode of communication and connection between words and music. Sustained strings and occasional *glissando* flourishes underpin the "Skin" improvisation from bars 328–334, emerging suddenly and forcefully in bar 335 with a repeated chord to facilitate the soloist's transition from a seated position (with talking drum and kick drum) to the final multi-percussion set-up. In bar 429 an improvised passage connects to the opening sonorities, with four timpani played using the hands or fingertips whilst moving the pedals to alter pitch. The CD recording adds the optional brass section to dramatic effect, culminating in an exciting and goal-oriented movement. It is the responsibility of the conjurer to complete the spell in the closing improvisation; on Corigliano's intensity mapping, this peak is considerably more emphatic than those of earlier movements. From bar 529, Glennie finally releases the power of percussion, layering sounds, moving with speed and establishing polyrhythms; the freedom of improvisation here feels instinctive and exuberant.

There are many factors which have contributed to Glennie's success as a solo multi-percussionist, but her interpretation of *Conjurer* demonstrates that performance in this discipline must revel in extremes in order to connect with the listener. The blurring of dichotomies is applicable in musical terms: loud and soft, tuned and untuned, aggressive and delicate, notated and improvised. This extends to unity of intellect and physicality, masculine and feminine, power and submission, leadership and collaboration. All of these latter features are gendered, but in percussion performance the myths of difference are exploded. The multi-percussionist by necessity performs both genders, but the semiotics of a female musician are particularly potent in this respect, an empowering statement on equality. Every *Conjurer* percussionist is a magician, bringing to life the nuances of timbre, drawing complex and compelling ideas from the simplest of objects, and communicating in a language both ancient and modern.

Reclamation: *The Drum of Orfeo* (2009)

Magic, elements of the supernatural, and the transcendent power of solo multi-percussion are once more referenced in the programmatic narrative of *The Drum of Orfeo*, with the soloist performing the role of the (male) protagonist. The ancient Greek myth of Orpheus, a hero whose musical skills on the kithara (a stringed ancestor of the guitar) enthral all who hear it, remains a compelling and recurring narrative in Western art music. Armed only with the power of music, Orpheus journeys bravely through the Underworld to rescue his beloved Eurydice from the clutches of the afterlife. Sadly, his inability to trust that Eurydice will follow means that he breaks the terms of his agreement with Hades (God of the Underworld) by turning around to look at Eurydice. She is lost forever and Orpheus is killed. There are many ways to interpret and read this enduring tale: it is a celebration of the redemptive and healing power of music; it casts the male at the centre of creativity; it presents the female as victim (twice over). However, it does not glorify patriarchy in the original story, given that Orpheus is unsuccessful in his mission; the music achieves its goal, but the flaws of humanity ultimately lead to failure.

The Baroque period was particularly inspired by the Orpheus myth, with the origins of opera intrinsically connected to this tale. The first three operas ever composed all focused on this protagonist; the most revered of

128 *Evelyn Glennie: Sound Creator*

these is Monteverdi's *Orfeo* (1607), which revised mythology to end with Orpheus rescued and restored to heaven by the God Apollo. Reflecting the patriarchal society in which it was created, Monteverdi's Eurydice remains lost forever in the Underworld.

The Drum of Orfeo, published in 2002 and premiered by Glennie in 2009, is a concerto commission by Marta Ptaszyńska, a Polish percussionist, composer and academic, centred once more on the redemptive power of music (as in the original myth), but reframing gender roles; both composer and premiere performer in this instance were female, and the ill-fated Eurydice was omitted. Positioned ten years after Glennie's first concerto commissions from female composers in 1999, Chen Yi's *Percussion Concerto* and Frangis-Ali Sade's *Silk Road*, gender ratios are particularly unbalanced in this milieu (with such commissions often undertaken in collaboration with particular orchestras and events). To date, ten female composers have written concertos for Glennie; Thea Musgrave has composed two. Ptaszyńska, as a pioneering composer, is an important female role model in this respect; however, she echoes Glennie's own views on the fact that gender has not been relevant to her career experiences:

> I feel I am only and exclusively a composer, with no reference to, or acknowledgement of, gender. Gender has nothing to do with artistic creation, with composing, scientific research, etc. All this is just a state of mind, a so-called specific mental ability, which can be found in different people, both men, women, and children.[41]

Though gender is not viewed by Ptaszyńska as pertinent to the process of composing music, it can nonetheless function as a programmatic source of inspiration. Prior to revising the gender of Orpheus, her 1992 *Ode to Praise All Famous Women* (for orchestra) was a feminist statement made in musical terms. There are also political and historical commentaries in Ptaszyńska's output, including the *Holocaust Memorial Cantata* (1991–1993) and *Polish Letters* (1988), also a cantata. Her works are powerful, complex and ambitious in scope, often featuring extensive roles for percussion (including the expansive 2008 *Street Music* for seventy percussionists). Ptaszyńska has synaesthesia, which in her case provides the capacity to visualize both harmonies and timbres as colours; multi-percussion offers a rich means of exploiting this unique skill. The powerful range of sound colours scored in *Drum of Orfeo* offer the listener an aural painting of what Ptaszyńska

---

[41] Marta Ptaszyńska in Aleksandra Masłowska (2013) *Polish music, especially composition, is doing very well: Interview with Marta Ptaszyńska* (online), 24 June 2013. Available from: https://meakultura.pl/artykul/polska-muzyka-a-zwlaszcza-kompozycja-ma-sie-doskonale-wywiad-z-marta-ptaszynska-598/ (accessed 15 March 2023).

The Issue of Gender   129

sees when she writes, and indications of synesthetic responses are in fact detailed in the work. Lighting cues printed in the conductor's score makes Ptaszyńska's colour palette of sound a visual element of the performance.

Drum of Orfeo begins in darkness, as the solitary sound of the bodhrán (an Irish frame drum) is heard backstage; as the soloist enters, the stage is bathed in white light (bar 2) for four bars, presenting the character of Orpheus with clarity. Ptaszyńska sees yellow from bar 6 when the odaiko drum (a Japanese bass drum) begins, gradually joined by tam-tam, cymbals, triangle and sarna bells. The sounds of the harp, cimbalom and celesta in the orchestra augment the range of percussive sonorities. Red lighting begins at bar 43, aurally realized as a more intense series of solo flourishes transitioning from odaiko to marimba and tom-toms. In bar 105, the score directive is "blueish", a hazy atmosphere intensified by the haunting resonance of temple bells and Thai gong. The white light which heralds the original appearance of Orpheus returns in bar 143, with the solo part centred on Tiger gong and crotales. The mood changes to green lighting from bar 171, aligned with the tempo directive "molto dramatico e appassionato"; metallic sonorities dominate. The stage is a bright white for ten bars (from bar 195), metamorphosing to red as the bodhrán (associated with Orpheus) segues to tom-toms and cymbal. Moving towards the finale, the white light of Orpheus returns as multiple percussion instruments coalesce (returning to many of the musical and timbral ideas featured in the yellow section). *Drum of Orfeo* ends with a haunting blue, as the music of the opening returns on solo bodhrán following a "lento misterioso" directive. Synaesthesia is much more complex than symbolism; there is no direct correlation between the colours which Ptaszyńska sees and the percussive sonorities relative to each. However, the transitioning of light as the work progresses is a dramatic and theatrical iteration of the experience of the composer. It provides some sense of what it means to visualize sound as colour.

Ptaszyńska and Glennie began exchanging faxes and emails on the project in 2008, and a shared sense of energy, excitement and ambition resonates throughout the creative process. In a democratic interaction, aspirational concepts were combined with more pragmatic considerations (most often when acknowledging the requirements of the co-commissioning Łódź Philharmonic Orchestra, instrument availability and hall size). As ever, Glennie's guidelines to the composer were determinedly broad, framed always as suggestions rather than directives. In addition to seeking "a really virtuosic, accessible fireworks type piece full of description", Glennie was keen to commission a work with both musical and theatrical appeal: "I would like the piece to be as tailor made as possible and very unusual. The thought of theatre in a concerto context is very exciting and I always find it useful when I'm made into a character … These images are essential to me musically."[42] Ptaszyńska responded to this remit by casting the solo multi-percussionist as Orpheus journeying through various worlds (and beyond), exploring instruments drawn from a diverse cultural palette in order to exemplify the universality of music. Theatricality is embedded in the drama of seeing and hearing so many sounds, in specific movements and gestures (as in the opening where solo percussion is heard offstage before the performer slowly enters), in lighting directives and in the task of bringing the character of Orpheus to life. The programme notes are clear on the confluence of music and drama in the solo part: "The work combines the features of a classical virtuosic concerto with elements of theatre. The percussionist is not only the performer of a musical part, but is also an actor who plays a role on the stage."[43]

From the earliest stages of planning, Ptaszyńska envisaged a huge and eclectic solo multi-percussion set-up (initially conceived for eighty instruments). Glennie's response to the concept was enthusiastic, demonstrating a willingness to develop proficiencies on new instruments if required and providing details of her own collection for use in the work. The final scoring reduced the arsenal considerably, but maintains the culturally rich objectives of early sketches with the inclusion of the bodhrán (associated with traditional Irish music), the odaiko (a large Japanese barrel drum originally functioning as a call to battle), the Chinese dagu drum (a ceremonial bass drum), Japanese temple bells (found more often in Buddhist temples and used as a call to prayer), sarna bells (small Indian bells attached by lengths of rope with a tag summarizing their history) and the Hau Chi Tiger gong (linked to Chinese Shamanism and martial arts). In this case, Orpheus uses the power of percussion as a transcendent connective between cultures, musical worlds, soloist and orchestra. There are strong links in the histories of these instruments to spirituality, healing, strength and communication. Though challenging to source, Ptaszyńska's vision demanded accuracy in this respect, unifying numerous cultures, sound colours and techniques in the concerto. Supported by a range of more conventional instruments (including marimba, tom-toms, cymbals and triangle) the soloist transitions between five multi-percussion stations positioned around the stage. The intention is to provide both visual and aural intrigue.

Drum of Orfeo begins with a solo improvisation on bodhrán seguing to odaiko drum, immediately connecting two musical and metaphorical

---

[42] Evelyn Glennie (1998) Fax correspondence with Marta Ptaszyńska, kindly provided by The Evelyn Glennie Collection.

[43] *Marta Ptaszyńska: Selected Works Catalogue* (2013) PWM Editions, 27 March 2013, kindly provided by the composer (March 2023).

worlds. Whereas Corigliano asked the soloist to conjure life in improvisations with clear musical scaffolding and structure, Ptaszyńska advocates for much greater creative freedom. As is generally the case with Glennie's rehearsal scores, the most detailed performance notes are written at the beginning, with more pragmatic details (emphasizing bar lines, counts or conductor cues) the focus of subsequent annotations. In advance of the opening cadenza, Glennie establishes the mood of the concerto, writing several notes: "Everything on high drama. Personal drama – Greek tragedy/drama. Deep impression."; "Tell a story through the drum. Dramatic entrance."; "Setting tone of concerto. Haunting, dramatic, atmospheric gestures". These cues are not augmented with specific musical references; the focus is on becoming the character as the concerto begins. In most instances, the frequent cadenza and shorter *ad lib.* moments are left entirely to the discretion of the performer (see Ex. 10).

Ex. 10: Balance between specificity and freedom in *Drum of Orfeo* (Marta Ptaszyńska).

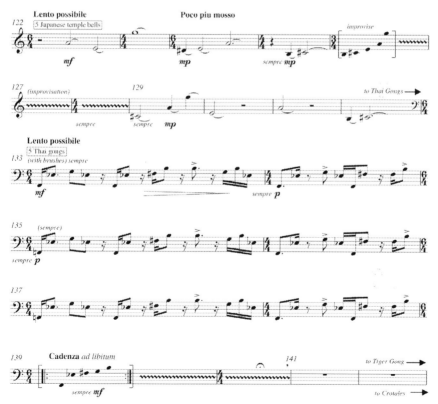

The narrative arc of the work is largely placed in the hands of the soloist; the orchestra plays an entirely secondary role, with few moments of melodic or rhythmic continuity. In the preface, Ptaszyńska is clear that this amplified interpretation of the hierarchical relationship between soloist and ensemble was intentional: "The most perfect place for the performance of the work would be a stage with orchestra located in the orchestra pit. But, if this is not possible, the orchestra can be put on stage ... and be surrounded by the percussion instruments."[44] Whilst many commissioned scores are immediately appealing in terms of the ways in which the language of percussion is harnessed, *Drum of Orfeo* is an entirely different proposition. The work is filled with changing time signatures, forty-two tempo directives, a wide range of dynamics and frequent transitions between instruments. It would be easy for the concerto to become a disparate series of ideas in the hands of the wrong performer; the soloist must literally use the power of their musical skills to make the journey feel coherent and organic. The role of Orpheus is prohibitively difficult in both musical and dramatic terms.

In March 2023 Glennie reprised her role as Orpheus in a Warsaw concert celebrating Ptaszyńska's eightieth birthday. Though the score has been available to purchase from PWM Editions since 2002, Glennie remains the only (professional and public) performer of the work to date. The practicalities of sourcing the instruments is one potential reason for this, as is the fact that Ptaszyńska conceived the work as virtuosic in both musical and theatrical terms; there are pragmatic and aesthetic obstacles for the soloist in this respect. Whilst some commissions reflect the skills of the solo multi-percussionist in general terms, several are written with Glennie's particular performance style and interests in mind; *Drum of Orfeo* is one such example, envisioning Glennie as dramatist, virtuoso and sound creator. This process of writing for a performer is intrinsic to Ptaszyńska's creative approach:

> I write for the particular performer. I include a personality in the piece – his or her personality – and that will stay in the music. Then another performer can play it, but that will be more human. It's not for the instrument, which does not have any feelings. It's just that instrument. But it should be for the person. That's what I have in mind.[45]

---

[44] Marta Ptaszyńska (2009) *Drum of Orfeo: Concerto for Percussion and Orchestra.* Kraków: PWM Editions.

[45] Marta Ptaszyńska and Bruce Duffie (1988 and 1997) *Composer/Percussionist Marta Ptaszyńska: Two Conversations with Bruce Duffie* (online). Available from: http://www.bruceduffie.com/ptaszynska.html (accessed 22 March 2023).

The Issue of Gender 133

Commissioned works which integrate theatricality, movement and gesture (featuring characterization and/or improvisation) become inextricably linked to Glennie in ways that more conventional works do not. The blank canvas of any premiere performance allows the soloist to be the first to give life to new ideas; when this is successfully achieved, their name becomes synonymous with the composition. Most often, this is dependent upon positive reception of the live performance combined with a subsequent recording to crystallize the interpretation for posterity. The fact that a recording of *Drum of Orfeo* does not yet exist is not unusual, given that concertos pose a wide range of problems in both logistical and financial terms. As seen in the extensive work required to convince BMG to facilitate Glennie's vision for *Shadow Behind the Iron Sun* (her most successful album to date), women in the creative industries are required to navigate multiple professional identities. It is not enough to be a respected performer; Glennie must also be effective as a businesswoman and entrepreneur. Her vigilance in terms of ensuring that only high-quality recordings are associated with her name requires leadership and control of the Glennie brand.

This issue was raised specifically in relation to a possible recording of the March 2023 performance of *Drum of Orfeo*; live events have been captured in this way before (Ho's *The Shaman* being one such example), but only as a result of extensive and precise planning. Though a recording of *Drum of Orfeo* would unquestionably have positioned Glennie as the definitive Orpheus of the title, it needed to be achieved on her terms:

> It really doesn't work because your mind-set is towards the audience; it's towards that live performance. With that live performance there's a different kind of execution, you know, you're physically just more giving ... I do prefer when we have dedicated studio time, when people are in a different mind-set and you're really executing your sound towards that microphone.[46]

Demonstrating leadership skills is in itself an influential form of role modelling, as is the fundamental right to say no. Whilst the early stage of her career was typified by a willingness to seize every opportunity, Glennie has since asserted the right to make empowered decisions:

> [In my forties] the diary was so overloaded with concerts and things that I got to the point where the last thing I wanted to do was to play. It was just too much basically ... I found that I just needed to back

---

[46] Interview with Glennie, 10 March 2023.

off … From that point on, it's been a case of really thinking about the projects you want to be involved with.[47]

Given the excitement and energy of the concerto, there is every possibility that subsequent performers will adopt the title role (and recordings will follow). For now, the male hero is reframed as a female heroine, and the mystical sonorities of the kithara are instead replaced by the spiritual origins of percussion.

Beyond the Discipline: "Women in Power" Fashion Show (2019)

Glennie's prominence as a pioneering solo multi-percussionist has unquestionably demonstrated new creative trajectories for the next generation of performer. In this role, the female body is foregrounded, serving as a wordless act of social disruption. The perceived distraction of the body in classical music is not a problem of the past. Blind auditions for orchestras, initiated as a direct result of a discrimination case in the 1960s (against the New York Philharmonic), are now institutionalized. Even then, gender barriers remain. Feminist musical commentary frequently references the experience of trombonist Abbie Conant, who was told after a successful blind audition for the Munich Philharmonic Orchestra in 1987: "You know the problem, Abbie. We need a man for solo trombone."[48] The Vienna Philharmonic did not admit female musicians until 1997; their 2023 roster of orchestral percussionists remains all-male. Responses to Marin Alsop's 2013 appearance as the first female conductor of the BBC Proms included a comment from conductor Vasily Petrenko that: "A cute girl on a podium means that musicians think about other things."[49] Issues with accuracy of translation may have resulted in a more controversial statement than was perhaps intended in this instance, but the underlying problem remains: the female body is at best intriguing and at worst denounced.

---

[47] Musical U: Evelyn Glennie in Christopher Sutton (2019) *The Musicality Podcast: How to Truly Listen, with Evelyn Glennie* (video online), 26 February 2019. Available from: https://www.youtube.com/watch?v=HrgXUEF1Fjo (accessed 17 March 2023)

[48] Abbie Conant in interview with Amy Smart (2013) Female Trombonist Fought Battle Against Orchestra Sexism, *Times Colonist*,Vancouver (online), 17 September 2013. Available from: https://www.timescolonist.com/entertainment/music/female-trombonist-fought-battle-against-orchestra-sexism-1.628198 (accessed 14 June 2019).

[49] Vasily Petrenko quoted in Fiona Maddocks (2013) Marin Alsop, Conductor of Last Night of the Proms, on Sexism in Classical Music, *Guardian* (online), 6 September 2013. Available from: https://www.theguardian.com/music/2013/sep/06/marin-alsop-proms-classical-sexist (accessed 14 June 2019).

Solo female performers are in a position of power which allows them to refute negative stereotypes both within and beyond the sphere of music; distance from the patriarchal structure of the orchestra is advantageous. Whilst Glennie spent the early part of her career carefully avoiding intersectional issues of gender and disability in order to foreground multi-percussion, recent decades demonstrate a more active role in these respects. In relation to gender, Glennie has started to speak more openly about the experiences of being a female in the creative industries. She has participated in the International Women's Day Conference at the University of Aberdeen (2014), a Musician's Union Panel on the gender pay gap in music (2019) and an event hosted by the Open University entitled Women Leading Equality, Diversity and Inclusion in Music Education and the Music Industries (2021). In all instances, Glennie has broadened discourse beyond the gender divide, focusing instead on the larger imperatives of inclusion and access. This is connected directly to her own experiences, where othering has related primarily to her disability (as a profoundly deaf musician); to some extent, this seems to have distracted attention from the fact that she is also a woman:

> In my situation as a solo percussionist, whereby the career of a full-time solo percussionist had not existed before, it wasn't actually the gender aspect that was the challenge or the issue ... In a way, the fact that I was a woman percussion player was kind of way down the list. It really wasn't talked about so much at all.[50]

Addressing issues of exclusion in relation to gender in contemporary music seems like a natural progression, but her high profile as a prominent female performer can resonate beyond this into other facets of the creative industries. The "Women in Power" fashion show offers one such example; though connections between fashion and music might at first seem tenuous, both reflect the fact that professional women are judged on the basis of image and appearance. Just as music can make profound statements in the absence of words, so too can fashion.

Costume and visual appeal are intrinsically linked to Glennie's professional identity, given the importance of marketing her brand and professional identity; she is not alone in this respect. In a chronology of the interrelationships between fashion and classical music, journalist Claire

---

[50] Evelyn Glennie (2021) *Women Leading Equality, Diversity and Inclusion in Music Education and the Music Industries.* Panel discussion hosted by the Open University, June 2021.

Jackson cites numerous examples.[51] These include Mozart's signature scarlet jacket, Stravinsky's collaborations with Chanel, and the more recent mini-dresses and high heels of pianist Yuja Wang. Following considerable critique of the male gaze, it has become increasingly difficult to discuss visual appeal in discourse on female performers. But the ambivalent relationship between empowerment and attire predates this age of cancel culture, linked to second-wave feminist views on clothing as a mode of patriarchal control and metaphor for subjugation. Protests by women at the Miss America Pageant of 1968 were indicative of the rejection of fashion and its assumed association with female objectification; women's magazines and bras were described in this instance as "instruments of oppression".[52]

Both fashion and the body were reclaimed in the third wave, with clothing becoming a relevant means of self-realization. No longer perceived as disguise or artifice, woman was freed to embrace the body as an expressive articulation of identity. With more female designers, a broader range of apparel options, and the co-existence of femininity and feminism, clothing became a relevant medium for expression and empowerment. Glennie's own extensive repository of costumes (part of The Evelyn Glennie Collection) reflects the symbolic value of her concert attire as visual accents to her musical language.

Edeline Lee's Autumn/Winter fashion show on 15 March 2019 was preceded by a series of three-minute talks given by thirty-four prominent women working in a diverse range of industries and research domains, the last of which was given by Glennie (see Table 4).

Titled "Women in Power", all contributors were dressed in black garments (designed by Lee), a visual statement focusing attention on the message, and not the female body through which it was delivered. The concept for Lee's show, and the inspiration for the fashion collection, was Professor Mary Beard's feminist manifesto *Women and Power* (2017). Beard asserts that paradigm shifts are neither definitive nor stable; the concept of women in positions of power remains an emergent and contested transition. From the impetus of Beard's manifesto, Lee aimed to create a collection and show which acknowledged the importance of the female perspective and experience whilst also sharing Beard's sentiment that progress in all domains is often incremental. The show was opened by Beard, who established and

---

[51] Claire Jackson (2021) *Classical Music's Enduring Relationship with Fashion* (online), 25 January 2021 (originally published in *BBC Music Magazine* June 2020). Available from: https://www.classical-music.com/features/articles/classical-musics-enduring-relationship-with-fashion/ (accessed 23 March 2023).

[52] Elizabeth Groeneveld (2009) "Be a Feminist or Just Dress Like One", *BUST*, Fashion and Feminism as Lifestyle, *Journal of Gender Studies*, 18 (2), p. 181.

Table 4: Speakers at the "Women in Power" fashion show.

Name of Speaker	Profession
Professor Dame Mary Beard	Classicist, Professor of Classics at University of Cambridge
Brita Schmidt	Executive Director of Women for Women International
Professor Dame Jane Francis	Director of the British Antarctic Survey
Sally Gunnell OBE	Olympic Gold Medallist in Track and Field
Dr Suzy Lishman CBE	Histopathologist and former President of the Royal College of Pathologists
Patricia Rosario OBE, FRCM	Soprano and Professor of Singing at the Royal College of Music
Professor Anne Marie Rafferty CBE, FRCN	Professor of Nursing Policy at King's College London, President of the Royal College of Nursing
Pauline Fowler	Family Lawyer and Founding Partner at Hughes Fowler Carruthers
Laurence Benaïm	Journalist, Biographer and Officier des Artes et des Lettres
Clarissa Ward	Chief International Correspondent for CNN
Isabella Macpherson	Co-Founder of Platform Presents
Tammy Smulders	President of Wednesday London
Reni Eddo-Lodge	Journalist and Author
Dr Marta Weiss	Senior Curator of Photographs at the Victoria and Albert Museum
Francesca Findlater	CEO of Bounce Back Foundation
Anne Sebba	Author and Biographer
Baroness Jane Bonham-Carter of Yarnbury	Politician and Liberal Democrat Member of the House of Lords
Beatrix Ong MBE	Designer, Author, Philanthropist
Dr Priyanki Joshi	Biochemist at the University of Cambridge
Lynne Franks OBE	WiseWoman, Changemaker, Activist and Influencer
Professor Dame Wendy Hall DBE	Computer Scientist and Executive Director of the Web Science Institute
Dame Helena Morrissey DBE	Head of Personal Investing at L&G and Founder of 30% Club
Dr Zoe Whitley	Curator, International Art at Tate Modern and Curator Attached to British Pavilion, Venice Biennale 2019

138   *Evelyn Glennie: Sound Creator*

Table 4 *continued*

Name of Speaker	Profession
Jane Rapley OBE	Professor Emerita CSM, Former Head of Central St. Martins, Pro Vice Chancellor of UAL
Carmel McConnell MBE	Author, Activist and Founder of Magic Breakfast
Grace Savage	Singer, Songwriter and UK Beatbox Champion
Gaylene Gould	Broadcaster and Head of Cinema and Events, British Film Institute
Jacqueline Perry QC	Barrister, Queen's Council at 2 Temple Gardens
Shahira Fahmy	Actor and Architect
Alison Wenham OBE	Founding Chairman of Worldwide Independent Music Industry Network
Emily Orton	Co-Founder of Darktrace
Reverend Dr Christina Beardsley	Church of England Priest and Retired Hospital Chaplain
Professor Dame Amanda Gay Fisher	Cell Biologist, Director of the Medical Research Council at Imperial College London
Dame Evelyn Glennie CH, DBE	Solo Percussionist

voiced the conundrum of women in power today: "I wonder why it is that we don't see women as powerful or even hear women's voices as authoritative, even when they're expert and knowledgeable."[53]

Each speaker interpreted the theme of women and power from their own frame of reference. Dr Suzy Lishman (histopathologist and former president of the Royal College of Pathologists) opted to read a transcript from a pathology exam; Professor Dame Jane Francis (director of the British Antarctic Survey) talked about current efforts to address climate change; Clarissa Ward (chief international correspondent for CNN) relived the experience of reporting from Aleppo. Some women chose to highlight experiences of gender discrimination in various professions. In a summary of female trailblazers in the discipline of law, Pauline Fowler detailed the interview process for a post: "More than one interviewer asked me if I had a family; one asked if I cried easily. That was what we were up against."[54]

[53]   *Edeline Lee at AW19 at London Fashion Week* (2019), video online. Available from: https://www.youtube.com/watch?v=UTMxA7G_6p0 (accessed 15 March 2019).

[54]   Ibid.

The Issue of Gender   139

Professor Dame Wendy Hall recounted the experience of being told that medicine was not a career for women and Professor Dame Amanda Gay Fisher used her time to reflect on the fact that the contribution made by women in science is often not acknowledged. Glennie was one of three participants providing a diverse representation of women in the music industry, with Patricia Rosario, soprano and Professor of Singing, and Grace Savage, singer, songwriter and UK Beatbox Champion. Both Rosario and Savage performed during their three minutes; Glennie opted instead to speak. Closing the presentation, Glennie provided an honest but ultimately optimistic vision for the future: "Together, we have that opportunity to make a difference through the art of listening."[55] Events such as the "Women in Power" fashion show are indicative of the increasing relevance of interdisciplinary collaborations in contemporary culture. Blending fashion, history, performance, and personal experience, the show demonstrated how empowerment can be facilitated and encouraged through creativity. Glennie's inclusion in the powerful opening testimonials reflects the fact that her success in music has segued to contributing to broader societal and cultural changes; in such contexts, Glennie foregrounds the identity of expert listener.

Glennie as Entrepreneur and Brand

Both Edeline Lee and Mary Beard later featured as guests on The Evelyn Glennie Podcast (launched in 2020). The emphasis of this project is on open-ended conversations which explore a range of issues associated with both professional and personal experiences. Though not intended as a commentary on gender, many female guests on the series have much to say on their efforts to promote greater inclusion in a wide range of industries and disciplines. These include, in episode 1, YolanDa Brown, whose primary professional identity of saxophonist now extends to broadcasting, writing and restaurant and venue investment. Nicola Benedetti speaks to Glennie in episode 10, sharing her work as a solo violinist but also as founder of The Benedetti Foundation, a charity with the vision of providing access to music for all. Sally Gunnell (episode 25) contributes insights into the challenges and rewards of excelling in sport; she is the only female athlete to hold World, Olympic, European and Commonwealth Gold medals at the same time. Gunnell is also an active advocate for positive ageing. Beard features in episode 7 and Lee is the guest for episode 12. With Beard, challenges and opportunities for women in leadership roles and the public

---

[55]   Ibid.

sphere is the central focus. Glennie's discussion with Lee references the experience of "Women in Power", allowing each to share their thoughts on the intersections between music and design, women and fashion, success and empowerment.

As with many of the speakers featured in the Edeline Lee fashion show, Glennie's professional portfolio is diverse. The podcast is an important manifestation of Glennie's ongoing professional evolution. Whilst still retaining focus on the concept of expert listening, it is an entrepreneurial venture into relatively new terrain; Glennie reverses the more typical structure of media engagement, transitioning from interview subject to interviewer. As Glennie has recognized from the earliest stages of her career, success in the contemporary industries and arts is dependent upon the ability to diversify, collaborate and experiment:

> We are in the music business, so each person has to realize that they are a business person. Now that doesn't mean that that individual has to be good at business, but just have a pool of people or a person or something – a team – that can deal with the various aspects of what they want to deal with ... As far as being an entrepreneur, I mean, not everybody is like that.[56]

Glennie makes an important distinction between business acumen and entrepreneurship, suggesting that the former is a necessity and the latter a vocation. Engaging with the business of the music industry is an essential part of working as a professional performer today; as stated by Glennie, "you are basically a business person and your product is music."[57]

Despite ongoing debates concerning the gender pay gap and the relatively poor representation of females in certain professional domains, contemporary society is now familiar with prominent businesswomen and industry leaders. Glennie is successful in business and has consolidated income from performances and recordings with sponsorship from a wide range of percussion companies including Sabian (with whom she developed Glennie's Garbage Cymbals), Promark (designing and promoting Glennie ranges of sticks and mallets), Aluphone, Grover Pro Percussion and Adams. She has extended her potential to promote and sell merchandise as a representative for products and services unrelated to the percussion profession, including Rolex watches and the Toyota Prius. Her website launched in 2002, and Glennie continues to use technology and social media to promote her

---

[56] Interview with Glennie, 3 May 2019.
[57] Charlotte Higgins (2000) Drum Machine, *Guardian* (online), 18 July 2000. Available from: https://www.theguardian.com/culture/2000/jul/18/artsfeatures.proms2000 (accessed 17 August 2019).

business and brand; she is an active presence on Facebook, Instagram and X (formerly Twitter).

Establishing a definition for entrepreneurship as distinct from business (a division noted by Glennie) is potentially problematic. At the core of entrepreneurial ventures is the importance of innovation, yet this is also an intrinsic aspect of any business model. Identifying opportunities and taking risks are key features of the entrepreneur; yet these too are present, at least to some extent, in business contexts. Entrepreneurship is distinguished best by the ability to see and pursue paths that others do not; it is a spirit of adventure and curiosity based on instinct and vision. To employ a metaphor, business is scored notation and entrepreneurship is free improvisation; these facets of Glennie's professional identity are not separate:

> It's very much trial and error, a journey, an exploration – there isn't instant gratification. You have to peek around this corner and that one and then you find yourself going in completely different directions. In the meantime, you're building your arsenal of tools for creativity. You can't just click on a button and get experience. It takes years and years and years and times where you fall flat on your face, and you pick yourself up and say, "Ooh, I learned from that." You have to experience that. I don't believe in shortcuts.[58]

Despite the particularities of definition, one aspect of entrepreneurship has remained stable: in the history of innovation, most entrepreneurs have been male. Many of the personal and behavioural characteristics associated with entrepreneurs remain connected to stereotypically masculine traits. The resultant cultural conditioning has ramifications for women in the music industry, an environment which is particularly susceptible to social, cultural and economic shifts. Add to this the fact that the physicality of instrumental performance means that a lifelong career is unlikely and it becomes clear that musicians may need to be more aware than other professionals of expanding and diversifying beyond a single career trajectory. The timeline of Glennie's entrepreneurial ventures indicate that her primary efforts focused almost exclusively on establishing and sustaining a career as a solo percussionist. This is unquestionably her most significant achievement as an entrepreneur – identifying, pursuing and creating a career path which did not yet exist. This required a gruelling schedule of touring, performing and recording, consolidated and developed by commissioning new works for solo percussion. Once Glennie's position as a full-time solo percussionist was established, she opted to expand her

---

[58] Evelyn Glennie in Esther Fellows (2008) Dame Evelyn Glennie: Percussion's "First" Lady, *The American Music Teacher*, 57 (6), p. 18.

142   *Evelyn Glennie: Sound Creator*

brand and business in directions which moved beyond the boundaries of a performance career. It is clear that Glennie sought out passion projects, choosing arenas of business and commerce that were personally relevant or significant. The 1998 release of her own tartan, The Rhythms of Evelyn, is one such example that reflects her Scottish heritage to commercially viable effect. In the shop section of Glennie's website, a wide range of products are available for purchase (and this has been the case since it was established in 2002). These include books, scores and CDs but also extend to a jewellery collection. Glennie is responsible for all jewellery designs and has collaborated with a number of manufacturers for several ranges, including Ortak and Filipa Malho (see Fig. 11).

The intersection between music and business is evident in Glennie's jewellery, which often features percussion symbols; the design for Fig. 11 is based on the opening bar of Glennie's early marimba composition *A Little Prayer*. Although this pursuit reflects the creative and innovative aspects of her performing career, it is an entrepreneurial venture independent from her work as a musician. In addition to producing and designing for

No. 20 pendant
18" No. 40 heavy snake chain
Engraved, oxidized and polished silver
'A Little Prayer' pendant

Fig. 11: Prototype sketch for pendant (in collaboration with Ortak).

commerce, Glennie has also channelled personal skills and experiences in order to extend her portfolio of professional services. Glennie is defined in recent biographies as concert musician, speaker and presenter, consultant, masterclass leader and composer. Whilst many of these are directly related to her role as a multi-percussionist, speaking and presenting engagements often move beyond this sphere. A lucrative market, motivational seminars are an opportunity for Glennie to apply the principles of expert listening in the contexts of business and public life. More recently, The Evelyn Glennie Podcast embraces the concept of expert listening as separate from the idiom of performance. These informal discussions involve numerous musicians but also extend to actors (including Griff Rhys Jones and Riz Ahmed), comedians (Bill Bailey), athletes (Sally Gunnell) and journalists (Jon Snow). The art of expert listening is a transferable skill which Glennie has commodified to great effect.

In her fifth decade as a professional musician, Glennie now has the opportunity to challenge another paradigm – the perceived association between ageing and decline. Glennie is not afraid to age; her silver hair has been a trademark of her image from her mid-forties, a small but substantial acceptance of the process of growing older. Whilst the profession of virtuosic solo multi-percussionist is unlikely to be lifelong, the parameters of sound creation and expert listening are not bound by physical agility; there are no restrictions that age can impose on these identities. Diversification, eclecticism and entrepreneurship have future-proofed Glennie's career.

In music, as in all facets of Western society, ageing is gendered. The UK Labour Party established a Commission on Older Women in 2012, with politician Yvette Cooper stating that "a toxic combination of sexism and ageism is causing problems for this generation."[59] When the male gaze turns away from the ageing female, this sense of invisibility is combined with more universal ageist assumptions on diminishing intellectual capacity and physical skills. High-profile women are tasked with challenging all of these ageist stereotypes. In her forties, Glennie made a conscious decision to accept only projects and performances that she wanted to be involved in; she no longer needed the validation of the public to the same extent. Nonetheless, Glennie is cognizant of the fact that audience attitudes change as musicians age; the sight of an attractive young performer generates a different frisson to the presence of a mature female musician:

---

[59] Yvette Cooper in Jane Martinson and Jo Adetunji (2012) Generation of Women Hit by "Toxic Combination of Ageism and Sexism", *Guardian* (online), 29 September 2012. Available from: https://www.theguardian.com/world/2012/sep/29/generation-women-toxic-ageism-sexism (accessed 25 March 2023).

It's very interesting because I think the relationship with an audience, or your awareness of the relationship, changes over time. I remember when I first started out playing, you really felt the audience absolutely behind you, because they were seeing a young musician, and audiences love young musicians. They just love to feel as though they're supporting and being part of that journey, and I definitely felt that ... Now, you can just feel an audience because they don't know how long you're actually going to be going on for so they're like, "Oh well, we'll give her a nice reception because we may not see her again!" So it's a slightly different sort of situation.[60]

Whilst Glennie has certainly not become invisible in her fifties, her touring schedule has become considerably less intense, with the sudden hiatus imposed by COVID-19 presenting further opportunities for streamlining and planning. In particular, it reaffirmed her view on the necessity of diversity and entrepreneurship in the career of any professional musician: "The past ten months [of lockdown] have shown us that we can't just have a plan A. We need a plan B, a plan C and possibly a plan D because if this pandemic can happen now, it can well happen in the future. We need to be prepared for that, both psychologically and skill-wise."[61] Post-COVID, Glennie's diary remains filled with engagements, but the schedules of today are increasingly varied. Public concerts, recording sessions and media events continue, but are augmented with a wider range of speaking and philanthropic activities. As Glennie ages, she is finding new ways to engage with the listener. Her next metamorphosis is perhaps emerging, as The Evelyn Glennie Foundation begins its mission to promote social listening. Music-making and access will be part of its remit, but there is a larger interest in exploring the ways in which the transferable skills of the musician might be applied in new contexts. Empowerment and role modelling, two recurring terms in feminist literature, apply equally to the experience of ageing in the public sphere. Just as it is important to see women succeed and lead in the creative industries, it is correspondingly important to see them age and mature. Experience is itself a valuable commodity.

[60] Interview with Glennie, 27 June 2023.
[61] Evelyn Glennie in Hannah Nepilova (2021) Evelyn Glennie: How Do You Listen Through Technology?, *The Financial Times* (online), 7 January 2021. Available from: https://www.ft.com/content/0678c546-2683-4db8-9b49-e2073d28db0e (accessed 2 April 2021).

Concluding Thoughts

Glennie's mission to integrate multi-percussion into the cultural consciousness means that the narrative of her evolution is voiced primarily by the general media. This has been positive in terms of allowing the discipline to reach a large audience demographic but has also proven negative in narrowing the frame in which her work is understood and in the invasive blurring of lines between personal and professional identity. It is interesting to note that Glennie has been subjected to considerable scrutiny and appraisal based on the fact that she is a deaf performer to a much greater extent than any commentary centred on the fact that she is female; sexism has proven less problematic than the gaze of ableist culture. In some ways, this has been advantageous; subsequent generations of solo multi-percussionists accept without challenge the fact that the most famous proponent of their discipline is a woman. Glennie's ability to balance musical creativity and business, public profile and personal life, image and integrity unquestionably provides a relevant case study to musicians and innovators of all genders. However, to women in the creative industries, her contribution is particularly important. Though Glennie does not acknowledge gender discrimination as a significant issue in her career, she emerged at a time when the gatekeepers of the music industry were male, and she was required to challenge the status quo in multiple ways in order to fulfil her ambitions. As solo multi-percussion has asserted its right to be at the centre of contemporary culture, so too has the female performer.

4

"I'm not a deaf musician. I'm a musician who happens to be deaf."

Inclusion

An extract of a 1988 interview with Glennie for the BBC1 programme *The Garden Party* is preserved for posterity on YouTube.[1] In an uncomfortable and demeaning line of questioning, the interviewer seems intent only on discussing the fact that Glennie is deaf. Glennie is calm and polite in her responses, graciously deflecting the title of "musical curiosity" and negotiating a comparison with Beethoven's anguished Heiligenstadt Testament in which deafness is described as "the greatest despair". In a fifteen-minute segment, Glennie's work as a virtuosic and pioneering solo multi-percussionist is diminished and almost ignored. It is little wonder that for so long Glennie preferred not to discuss deafness, given its prominence as a fascination bordering on fetish for many media commentators; *The Garden Party* is far from unique in its perspective. It has taken several decades to progress beyond the discomfiting tone of this 1988 interview, moving from reductive assumptions about deafness towards the holistic remit of expert listening. This transition has not been straightforward, and it has taken time and patience to reframe discourse: "In the early years, where it was just all about deaf, deaf, deafness, and deaf musician and this and that, which I just got so fed up about basically, to the point where I didn't want to talk about it at all."[2]

For many years, the byline of the Evelyn Glennie website has been "to teach the world to listen". In 2023, this mission was passed to The Evelyn Glennie Foundation, a charity centred on listening as a means of promoting

---

[1] VHS Bits (2019) *1988 Evelyn Glennie Interview – BBC1 "The Garden Party"* (video online), 11 November 2019. Available from: https://www.youtube.com/watch?v=7E3_BXgPdas (accessed 29 March 2023).

[2] Interview with Glennie, 3 May 2019.

social and cultural inclusion. Glennie firstly reconceptualized deafness through actions, with music performance an empowering means of demonstrating and promoting the multi-sensory nature of listening; this transferable skill has since extended her remit to other philanthropic initiatives. As stated in her TED talk: "My aim is to teach the world to listen. That's my only real aim in life."[3] Discussion of Glennie's processes of listening are important but are best considered in the larger frame of inclusion, mirroring her own advocacy work which extends beyond disability activism into a range of contexts including education, age, socio-economic structures and wildlife preservation. To teach the world to listen is not a vocation based only on validating and modelling deaf hearing; it is a much larger and more ambitious statement of intent related to Glennie's roles as sound creator, innovator and philanthropist.

In 1835 Liszt stated that "a great work, a grand religious and social MISSION stands imposed upon artists".[4] Virtuosic performers have always captured the attention of the general public, making music an invigorating and inspiring personal and communal experience. Glennie's work in the domain of solo percussion performance, consolidated and supported by a mission statement "to teach the world to listen", is an expansion of Liszt's vision. Glennie's work invites us to listen actively – to the ever-shifting timbral soundscape of solo percussion performance, to the outcomes of collaboration, improvisation, and sound creation. In harnessing this skill to address specific social justice issues connected to inclusion, accessibility and equality, Glennie also advocates for ethical listening.

This chapter will consider how Glennie has challenged othering in both musical and extra-musical initiatives. It will begin by considering perceptions of percussion as the other of the orchestra, a peripheral presence which has since evolved into a medium with the capacity to serve as a connective thread between epochs, cultures and genres. Deafness will be discussed in terms of what it means to truly listen, chronicling changing attitudes towards difference and the claiming of disability. Glennie's philanthropic work in collaboration with various charitable initiatives will also merit attention.

---

[3] TED (2003; published 2007) *How to Truly Listen: Evelyn Glennie* (video online). Available from: https://www.youtube.com/watch?v=IU3V6zNER4g (accessed 3 January 2018).

[4] Franz Liszt (1835) On the Situation of Artists and Their Condition in Society (Final Instalment), *Gazette Musicale de Paris*, 11 October 1835, in Christopher H. Gibbs and Dana Gooley, eds. (2006), *Franz Liszt and His World*. Princeton: Princeton University Press, p. 298.

Inclusion: Percussion and Art Music

As with all facets of Glennie's professional identity, and all modes of diversification in her career, activism began with advocating for the potentialities of percussion. A medium denigrated and undervalued for much of the history of Western art music, this first mission was a challenge to many existing stereotypes and assumptions. Percussion began at a disadvantage in art music, expressed in orchestration manuals of the late nineteenth and early twentieth centuries, which shared three common views: the timpani (and timpanist) were musically superior to their peers; the absence of melody and harmony in unpitched instruments meant that they were of negligible musical value; noise and effects were the main contributions made by this section. Berlioz delineated this hierarchy concisely: "The first comprises instruments of fixed sound, and musically appreciable; the second includes those of which the less musical product can be ranked only among noises destined to produce special effects."[5] Almost one hundred years later, Frank Steward Howes in *Full Orchestra* was less diplomatic in his terminology: "Of this motley company the only instrument of serious and permanent musical value ... is the set of kettle-drums."[6]

By the late Romantic period, the orchestra boasted a relatively large range of percussive sounds, but perceptions of these instruments as exotica drawn from non-Western cultures retained negative Eurocentric connotations which persisted well into the twentieth century; they were deemed both musically and culturally inferior. Though various iterations of these instruments have been ascribed different names based on time and place, timpani or kettle-drums originated in the Middle East, the bass drum is a descendent of the Turkish drum, the triangle is drawn from Egyptian music and the tambourine is found in artefacts from a number of global sources. Only the snare drum can claim Western origins, derived from the tabor of the Middle Ages. When avant-garde and experimental composers emancipated and celebrated the diversity of percussion, the introduction of new instruments (both invented and discovered) did not automatically solve this implicit xenophobia in Western art music.

If viewed idealistically, solo multi-percussion serves as a contemporary refutation of past ideologies, a statement on the diversity and universality of new music, a hybrid and global soundscape exemplifying a utopia of integration. In reality, this intention is only realized when composer and performer remain vigilant in ensuring that the trope of the exotic does not

[5] Hector Berlioz (1844) *A Treatise on Modern Instrumentation and Orchestration*, trans. Mary Cowden Clarke. London: Novello, p. 198.

[6] Frank Stewart Howes (1942) *Full Orchestra*. London: Secker and Warburg, p. 58.

Inclusion 149

persist. One means of enacting change is by devoting time and attention to studying practices beyond the West, taking more than instruments from the rich history of the discipline. Key figures in this respect include John Cage, who subsumed the processes and philosophies of the East into his work, Steve Reich, who immersed himself in a number of music-making communities (including Ghanian drumming and Balinese gamelan), and the extensive studies of various members of the Nexus Percussion Ensemble. Glennie's formative years included lessons with Keiko Abe on Eastern methodologies; she spent time in Brazil in 1992, exploring the cultural practices and musical techniques associated with samba; she has studied with Japanese taiko drummers; she has taken lessons in the bodhrán with Irish traditional musicians. Glennie's commissions conflate instruments from multiple cultures and the composer list demonstrates a wide range of national identities, all of which contributes to fostering a democratic interaction between instruments and communities of music-making. A varied confluence of ideas, techniques and instruments permeate her recording releases and commissions. The task is to fully integrate new sonorities into the instrumental palette so that there are no dividing lines, no negative attitudes towards difference and no cultural appropriation.

Inclusion involves the removal of hierarchical structures. In art music, this began as a gradual rebalancing of the status of melody and harmony in relation to rhythm and timbre, transitioning to a larger series of changes in perceptions of tuned versus untuned percussion and Western versus non-Western practices. If multi-percussion is to present a musical statement on inclusion, inter-cultural exchanges must also be reciprocal. The contemporary performer can certainly look outward, but they must also be ready to contribute their own experiences, practices and knowledge in so doing. Percussion instruments travel well; so too must the ideas of the percussionist. Whilst this often means adding new sounds and styles to art music, the process can be applied in reverse, with conventional orchestral percussion instruments instead introduced into alternative ensemble configurations. Richard Causton's *Concerto for Solo Percussion and Gamelan* (a 2001 commission) is one such example, with the soloist focused on integrating xylophone, wood blocks and cymbals into the gamelan ensemble. Yiu-Kwong Chung's *Concerto for Solo Percussion and Chinese Traditional Orchestra* (2009) juxtaposes snare drum, marimba and eleven drums of various sizes with Chinese instruments, divided into bowed strings, plucked strings, wind and percussion.

Chung's concerto premiered at the twenty-first Summer Deaflympics in Taipei in 2009 with each of the three movements inspired by an extract from the works of Sonia Huang, a partially deaf Taiwanese poet.[7] The Deaf-lympics event is a successor to the International Silent Games, first held in Paris in 1924 "at a time when societies everywhere viewed deaf people as intellectually inferior, linguistically impoverished and often treated as out-casts".[8] This sobering summary by the International Olympic Committee is a reminder of how negative stereotypes have perpetuated processes of othering in any number of cultural and social contexts; music and sport offer two sites where inclusive practices can be modelled. Chung's concerto is the opening work on Glennie's *Ecstatic Drumbeat* (released in 2012) and was also part of a documentary based on her tour with the Taipei Chi-nese Orchestra (2012) titled *Onward to Europe: Integrating the East and West*. The documentary follows the orchestra on their first European tour, performing in three cities (Manchester, Hanover and Paris). Extracts of the concerto's first and third movements are featured, part of a varied pro-gramme which includes repertoire by Oscar-winning composer Tan Dun, homages to the Taiwanese Pei-Kuan style of opera and an atmospheric ensemble piece based on Japanese haiku. Glennie (the only Western artist featured on the European tour) is one of several high-profile Western per-formers to have collaborated with the Taipei Chinese Orchestra, part of a larger effort by Chung (general director since 2007) to ensure that Chinese music is subsumed into what he describes as the "global village".[9]

The percussion section of the orchestra exemplifies Chung's interest in the fluid intersections between Eastern and Western sonorities, combining traditional Chinese instruments with those derived from the symphony orchestra (including timpani). As evinced in the documentary, the sec-tion is expansive, requiring all of the rear-stage space. The percussionists (mostly female) use a range of emphatic, choreographed arm gestures to denote important musical moments. Whilst the language of the traditional Chinese orchestra offers a new melodic, harmonic and timbral palette (in the context of concerto writing), the sounds and sights of the percussion section feels directly connected to the performative language of Western multi-percussionists.

The concerto is scored in three movements, with the solo percussionist positioned at a different set-up for each. The first and third are the most

---

[7] Yiu-Kwong Chung (2018) Programme Notes in *Percussion Concerto No.3 for Solo Percussion and Orchestra* (a later transcription of the work for symphony orchestra). New York: Universal Edition.

[8] *Deaflympics: History* (online). Available from: https://www.deaflympics.com/icsd/history (accessed 30 March 2023).

[9] *Onward to Europe, Integrating the East and West* (2012), DVD, Taiwan: Taipei Chi-nese Orchestra.

Inclusion 151

striking in terms of connecting Chinese traditions and Western practice in the writing, with the marimba of the second movement already a medium shared across cultures. The first movement is focused on contrast, with the pervasive sound of snare drum and tenor drum interacting with the ensemble. Based on Huang's poem titled *Lament of the Moon*, which is focused on the experiences of feeling isolated in a soundless world, Chung's scoring uses the abrasive snare drum "to sound out her inner battle cry".[10] There is an emphasis on difference in the opening: delicate harp, solo violin and vibraphone in the orchestral percussion section emerge first, joined by the string section in a beautiful *legato* melody focused on conjunct movement. Snare drum enters quietly with a march-like figuration, but this sense of clarity is almost immediately challenged by intermittent rests. Rolls (open and crushed) remain generally quiet but again any sense of balance is interrupted by sudden and brief *crescendo* entries. At its softest, the snare drum becomes part of the ensemble, but oftentimes enters as an opposing force. Snare drum dominates, but both drums are featured at moments where the momentum of soloist and ensemble builds (reflected in faster tempi and louder dynamics). At these points, fragments of melody emerge, but rhythm is the focus for all instruments. There are few moments of rest for the soloist (as is the case in all movements). Before the opening melody returns in the final stages, brief snare drum flourishes are answered almost tentatively by solo instruments. The two forces interact and gradually the movement fades to silence ending with a snare drum *diminuendo*.

In the final movement, there is a sense of unity; twelve drums merge with both the orchestral percussion section and the larger ensemble; here there is no division between style or sound. The triumphant finale is a reminder of the fact that the drum is universal, common to cultural practices throughout the world for thousands of years; Chung's scoring incorporates concert bass drum (a Western descendent of the Turkish drum), pedal bass drum (developed in the early twentieth century), four tom-toms (Chinese origin), a small roto-tom (a late twentieth-century invention which can be tuned to precise pitches), two bongos (most often traced to Cuba) and three congas (intrinsic to Latin folk music but most likely derived from African instruments). Inspired by Huang's poem *Heading For*, this third movement is celebratory and exultant in tone. It opens with a notated multi-drum cadenza, joined at the end of bar 7 with higher-register string and wind instruments playing sustained notes. The most active role as the music moves towards the first melodic theme in bar 14 is for the orchestral timpanist, emphasizing short rhythmic fragments of the solo line. Melodies inspired by Chinese

[10] Ibid., liner notes.

folk music are a resounding feature, and *tutti* orchestra presents a unified and impressive sound. *Heading For* was written by Huang specifically for the Deaflympics event, and Chung also references this focal point in the scoring: "What seems like a theme for the Olympics appears ... and finally the piece ends with a fanfare coda."[11] In this instance, the solo part does not contradict the musical language of the ensemble; all are driving together towards an exultant finale.

Chung transcribed the concerto in 2018 for a performance in the same year by the Taipei Symphony Orchestra. The soloist in this instance was Yin-Chun Chen. There is a lovely symbolism in the cultural transference of a Western soloist premiering the original version for Chinese orchestra and a Chinese performer introducing the symphonic interpretation of the work. Chung's concerto is a particularly powerful and overt confluence of cultures, but less dramatic assertions are also found in Glennie's solo commissions. Roberto Sierra scores for guiro in his *Fifty for Fifty* commission, titled *Guira y Guiro*, an homage to his own origins and those of the guiro (both of Puerto Rican heritage). Chinese-American violinist and composer Chen Yi writes for a small pair of Chinese cymbals in the 2015 *Colours of Naobo* (also part of the *Fifty for Fifty* project). In a composition lasting less than two minutes, Yi explores six different techniques and sonic properties of these ancient instruments (known as *xiaocha* or *chaguo*).

Percussion is a confluence of sounds and techniques which also extends to a convergence of cultures, both conscious and incidental. The solo multi-percussionist at times foregrounds instruments and practices from beyond the West, and at others subsumes them into a larger soundscape which eludes cultural or genre categorization. The oft-cited phrase "East meets West" is in itself reductive, perpetuating a clear dichotomy that oversimplifies the diversity of musical heritages between and within countries. However, it is a useful way of illustrating the historically insular nature of Western culture. It is a reminder of the time wasted in ignoring or demeaning the music of other communities in Western art music, which (with the notable exception of orchestral percussion) was largely ignored until the early twentieth century. As a sound collector, the multi-percussionist is responsible for connecting potentially disparate instruments into a holistic and unified entity; there are no cultural barriers in this effort. The medium changes as the world changes.

---

[11] Ibid.

Deafness and Music

Disability studies is an emergent field in academic discourse, interrogating legacies of exclusion based on misrepresentations of difference. As a direct result of research and advocacy in this interdisciplinary domain, disability has metamorphosed from a medical and physiological identity to a social and cultural construct which is claimed rather than assigned. This transition has taken place during Glennie's lifetime, and dialogue on the subject of deafness in her experience is a representative case study of changing attitudes towards difference. Straus summarizes this chronology in his seminal study of music and disability; Glennie's career spans the third and fourth categories (not always in a linear manner):

> 1) Disability as an affliction, permanent and indelible; 2) disability as afflatus (defined as divine inspiration), a mark of transcendent vision; 3) disability as a medical defect, a bodily pathology to be overcome through individual effort; and 4) disability as a personal, cultural, and social identity, to be affirmatively claimed.[12]

The d/Deaf community is one of many which can be claimed in accordance with the fourth category, a complex and multi-faceted cultural construct, and a reminder of the fact that the term "disability" accommodates an expansive range of identities. The differentiation of deaf and Deaf is linked to the claiming of disability. The term "deaf" is a physiological definition and is often linked to the use of lip-reading as the primary form of communication, whereas use of the capitalized term "Deaf" indicates cultural affiliation and is most often associated with communication via sign language.

Exclusion on the basis of disability was the first historical legacy to be challenged in academia and activism, and the relationship between deafness and music is particularly burdened by culturally conditioned stereotypes. In a study of this association, Holmes notes that "deafness has long served as the universally accepted disqualifying impediment to musical engagement and apprehension".[13] One of the most enduring misperceptions is that deafness is part of a dichotomy which definitively divides sound and silence, connected to a second problematic assumption that music is thus irrelevant to people on the d/Deaf spectrum. Such ideologies are derived from longstanding associations between disability and deficit, propagating

---

[12] Joseph N. Straus (2011) *Extraordinary Measures: Disability in Music*. Oxford: Oxford University Press, p. 5.

[13] Jessica Holmes (2017) Expert Listening Beyond the Limits of Hearing: Music and Deafness, *Journal of the American Musicological Society*, 70 (1), p. 172.

the narrow and erroneous view that auditory perception is the only means by which music can be accessed and appreciated.

When considering the relationship between deafness and music, Beethoven is invariably presented as the standard-bearer, a figure whose disability was often romanticized to subscribe to the traditional narrative of overcoming. Glennie has inevitably been subjected to comparisons with Beethoven: "Roll over, Beethoven, and make room in the history books for Evelyn Glennie, who is both profoundly musical and profoundly deaf."[14] In the first decades of her career she was frequently represented as a heroic figure who had bravely transcended the obstacle of disability. Deaf musicians are immediately denoted as extraordinary because their scant representation in the history of music has rendered them exceptional; the fact that Beethoven is aligned with Glennie's work several centuries later is testament to this fact. Celebrating triumph over adversity in instances of any form of difference is an oft-used trope, but contextualizing achievements only in relation to overcoming disability is simplistic and often factually incorrect. Howe's exploration of the one-armed pianist Paul Wittgenstein's performance of disability is one example of the pervasive and problematic nature of the hero narrative:

> As it frequently does in discourse about disabled bodies elsewhere, the trope of "heroic overcoming" returns repeatedly in reviews of Wittgenstein's performances – not to portray his justifiably heroic battle against music culture's constructed normalcy, but to describe (and thus construct) an embodied battle of ability versus disability.[15]

Howe's acknowledgement of the fact that Wittgenstein's main obstacle was societal ignorance resonates with Glennie's experiences. Her 1990 autobiography does not read as a triumph over the adversity of deafness but does acknowledge the ways in which she has had to supersede the misperceptions and stereotypes appended to her as a result of it – "the negative voices that I had to overcome".[16]

As discussed comprehensively in *Good Vibrations*, Glennie has been profoundly deaf from the age of twelve. In medical terms, this means that the ears can access sounds in excess of 95 decibels (dB). Treatments for hearing loss vary between individuals, depending on the physiology of their condition and also on personal choice. Glennie used hearing aids in the early stages of her diagnosis, but found that these were problematic for musical

---

[14] Pamela Sommers (1994) A Different Drummer, *Washington Post*, 5 March 1994.

[15] Blake Howe (2010) Paul Wittgenstein and the Performance of Disability, *The Journal of Musicology*, 27 (2), p. 140.

[16] Glennie (1990) *Good Vibrations*, p. 5.

Inclusion   155

engagement: "Everything became this wall of sound that I couldn't control."[17] She has also experimented with the haptic vest, an invention designed to send soundwaves directly through the skin of the torso. Glennie found the vest similarly distracting, an impediment to the relationship needed between performer and instrument, and a distortion of where sounds are naturally experienced through the body. Guidelines provided by Eastern Kentucky University are helpful in indicating the fact that profound deafness does not negate auditory perception. In a section on musical instruments, findings indicate that all woodwind and brass instruments can surpass 95dB, as can *tutti* orchestra, timpani and bass drum.[18] Glennie's preference is for the deep resonance and vibration of the lower registers: "The low sounds are by far the more amazing experiences. All the high sounds are quite nauseating because they're all in the upper part of the body."[19]

In addition to experiencing sounds through the ears, Glennie accesses sensations through the body, with sight also an important means of ensuring accuracy. This multi-sensory approach is not unique to profoundly deaf musicians; the process of listening is always subjective, and musicians invariably use multiple modes of engagement both with their instruments and with the audience in the moment of performance. When the discussion shifts from deafness towards listening, difference applies to all in this respect; sensory experiences are inherently personal. Hearing does not equate to listening, and deafness does not equate to silence. This now obvious statement was not so clear to the media or to music institutions even in the later decades of the twentieth century. The only real dichotomy which merits attention is the division between public perception and self-perception in relation to Glennie's deafness.

Glennie and Deafness: Public Perception

In a 1982 letter to friends and mentors Ezra and Ann Rachlin (the former a conductor and pianist and the latter founder of The Beethoven Fund for Deaf Children), Glennie describes her response to a query from Her Majesty's Inspector for Schools on how she experiences sound. Predating

---

[17]   Evelyn Glennie (2021) *Evelyn Glennie at the EA Festival* (video online), 26 August 2021. Available from: https://www.youtube.com/watch?v=cnx9eyS9E28&t=1766s (accessed 23 April 2023).

[18]   EKU Health and Safety PDF (online). Available from: https://www.eku.edu/musicprogram/wp-content/uploads/sites/59/2023/09/ekuhealthandsafety.pdf (accessed 26 March 2024).

[19]   Artful Narratives Media (2022) *Dame Evelyn Glennie Talks Percussion, Profound Deafness, and Learning How to Listen* (video online), 3 October 2022. Available from: https://www.youtube.com/watch?v=gfrz_MUOln4 (accessed 10 April 2023).

Good Vibrations considerably (Glennie was aged seventeen at this point) the correspondence is interesting for several reasons: it is a reminder of the fact that her success as a solo performer is part of a larger support network; it indicates that questions about her listening processes began at an early stage; it references the many medical and administrative appointments required to pursue her ambitions to perform. Glennie describes hearing lower sounds through the legs and hips and higher sounds in the throat and chest, proceeding to explain how she addresses the practicalities of tuning timpani. Justifying her ability to engage with music seems to be what the school inspector requires, which Glennie provides in a direct and pragmatic manner. She also ends the letter with a larger statement on inclusion: "People are convinced that music doesn't mean a thing to a deaf person but it is the most important subject to them whether they are interested or not – the satisfaction of feeling something and being able to communicate through music is so important."[20]

As Glennie began to realize her intentions to become a solo performer, the necessity of justifying her ability to make music segued to another equally exclusionary mode of interpreting disability: the narrative of overcoming. This idealized and largely hypothetical reading of difference is a particularly problematic societal construct to evade. Glennie, like many other public figures with disabilities, has sought to avoid being subsumed into this trope, described succinctly by Stella Young as "inspiration porn".[21] Virtuosity, in itself a form of difference, garners further public intrigue when combined with the persona of a deaf performer working in new musical terrains. At the start of Glennie's career, accommodating interest in the confluence of these fascinations was largely unavoidable; as the most visible proponent of the discipline, Glennie was subjected to heightened scrutiny. Focus on deafness dominated reception of her work in the general media, often depicting Glennie as a romanticized heroine. A 1991 article in the *Los Angeles Times* with the headline "Percussionist Plays From her Heart" unquestionably sought to perpetuate this mystique: "'There's a sound there,' she says, pointing to her heart, 'rather than here, in the ears.'"[22] Table 5 provides examples of the foregrounding of deafness in response to Glennie's work.

[20] Evelyn Glennie (1982) Correspondence with Ezra and Ann Rachlin, 25 August 1982. Kindly provided by The Evelyn Glennie Collection.

[21] Stella Young, cited in Holmes (2017) Expert Listening Beyond the Limits of Hearing, p. 183.

[22] John Henken (1991) Percussionist Plays from Her Heart: Hearing Loss Hasn't Slowed Evelyn Glennie, *Los Angeles Times* (online), 13 September 1991. Available from: http://articles.latimes.com/1991-09-13/entertainment/ca-2291_1_hearing-loss (accessed 1 May 2019).

Table 5: Headlines referencing deafness.

Date	Source	Article Title
28 November 1991	*Waterloo Record*	Sounds of Silence: Applause Falls on Deaf Ears for Percussion Virtuoso
13 September 1991	*Los Angeles Times* (John Henken)	Percussionist Plays From Her Heart: Hearing Loss Hasn't Slowed Evelyn Glennie
4 October 1995	*Toronto Star* (Peter Goddard)	Deafness Made Evelyn Glennie the Champion of Percussionists
7 October 1995	*The Globe and Mail*, Canada (Tamara Bernstein)	Deaf Scottish Percussionist Sets a Musical Fire with TSO
13 October 1995	*Star Tribune* (Michael Anthony)	Deaf Percussionist Hears World Masterfully
29 April 1996	*The Independent* (Michael Church)	Home on the Range; Evelyn Glennie, the Western World's Only Deaf Solo Percussionist, Will Hit Anything in Sight – Even the Kitchen Sink
26 November 1996	*The Ottawa Citizen* (Steven Mazey)	Evelyn Glennie Percussion Virtuoso Feels the Music She Can't Hear
6 April 1997	*Hartlort Courant* (Steve Metcalf)	Despite Deafness, Glennie Sets Pace as Percussionist
16 February 1998	*Star Tribune* (David Stablers)	Glennie Wants to Be Seen as a Musician First, Not as Deaf
17 May 2000	*New York Post* (Barbara Hoffman)	World-Beater: Deafness Doesn't Stop Solo Percussionist Evelyn Glennie
3 December 2001	*The Telegraph* (Roger Highfield)	Deaf Musician Learns to Thrive on Good Vibrations
11 March 2006	*Pantagraph* (Dan Craft)	If You Could Hear What Evelyn Feels
1 March 2011	*The Globe and Mail*, Canada (Robert Everett-Green)	Dame Evelyn Glennie, the Deaf Percussionist Who Listens with Her Whole Body
2 March 2011	*The Globe and Mail*, Canada (Robert Everett-Green)	For a Deaf Percussionist with Room to Improvise, the Audience Helps Fill in the Blanks
6 August 2015	*The Times* (Damian Whitworth)	From the "Nobel Prize" of music to her own Prom: Despite being deaf, Evelyn Glennie has become the world's leading solo percussionist and at 50 she's busier than ever

158   *Evelyn Glennie: Sound Creator*

Table 5 *continued*

Date	Source	Article Title
21 January 2017	*The Times* (Kenny Farquharson)	"It's not whether you hear or don't hear. It's whether you pay attention": Deaf from 12, Dame Evelyn Glennie taught herself to listen. She tells Kenny Farquharson it's a trait we all need now
24 January 2017	*The Scotsman* (Alison Campsie)	Deaf Musician Evelyn Glennie on Finding New Ways of Listening
29 June 2017	*Lichfield Mercury* (Jenny Amphlett)	Percussionist reveals that being deaf has made her become better listener

A courteous and engaged interview subject, Glennie consistently demonstrated efforts to extend discourse into more meaningful conversations about percussion and performance. Speaking in 1996 she stated: "I suppose I am very touchy about my deafness. It is quite a private thing and it is not easy to put into words the process I have to go through to perform or digest music ... I do get annoyed when that is all people want to talk about."[23] Glennie views the process of listening (for anyone) as a personal, subjective, unique and ultimately private experience, essentially too complex to describe in words. In a 2001 interview for the *New York Times* under the heading "Call Her a Musician, Pure and Simple", she is clear on this division between public and private identity: "I understand what the media are going through. But at the end of the day, my feeling is that I'm hired by an orchestra or an organization to perform, and the performance is what has to be written about."[24]

One of the first priorities of disability studies has been that of reclamation, identifying and acknowledging seminal figures in history who were excluded or ignored by society. The history of disability has been one of silencing, where belief systems are constructed by those without lived experience. In many ways, Glennie's growing frustration at invasive media questioning was a response to the continuation of this narrative. Interviewers ascribed attributes, made assumptions, and over-reached in their appraisal of the role that deafness played in Glennie's life; almost without noticing, they rendered her voiceless. Post-2000, there was a growing sense

[23]   Lester Middlehurst (1996) Hearing Again Would be a Real Handicap. *Daily Mail*, 20 January 1996.
[24]   James R. Oestreich (2001) Call Her a Musician, Pure and Simple, *The New York Times*, section 2, 30 September 2001.

of frustration in response to this enduring and obstinate mode of discrimination: "I have never in my entire life felt disadvantaged and I don't feel any frustration when being with other individuals who may have a disability. I don't believe there is such a thing as a disability unless we all agree that we ALL have some form of disability."[25]

The head archivist of The Evelyn Glennie Collection, Caroline Thompson, who has now catalogued hundreds of reviews, interviews and commentaries, is witness to the volume of invasive and one-dimensional appraisals of Glennie in her early career:

> The only thing that gets to me in what I read is the rather irritating emphasis on the deafness, rather than on what is actually critical in the archive, which is Evelyn's career which has developed percussion to the point where it's an accepted solo instrument. For me that's the critical thing; the deafness is an added layer, and Evelyn has worked very hard within the deaf community and done wonderful things, but really the amazing thing is how she's developed percussion. So it is a bit irritating when so many of the articles hammer on the deaf thing instead of thinking "this is amazing".[26]

In alignment with growing activism, positive representation, and the evolution of disability studies in numerous interdisciplinary contexts, the public narrative is shifting, a transition also noted by Thompson as Glennie's timeline is assembled. This has created more constructive fora in which Glennie can articulate views on both deafness and expert listening in her own terms. The press release announcing Glennie as recipient of the Polar Music Prize (2015), reflects the impact of this increasing advocacy and empowerment, noting that she has "widened our understanding of what music is and shown us that listening is only partly to do with our ears."[27] Glennie has, after decades of being subjected to biased and stereotyped scrutiny, claimed her disability in recent years in a way which resonates with her own understanding of its role in shaping her identity. Deafness is not relevant; the importance of listening is.

---

[25] Cyril Agnes Walters (2003) *Music Development and Hearing Impairment: A Case Study of Evelyn Glennie*, MA thesis, University of Cape Town, p. 43.

[26] Interview with Caroline Thompson, 27 June 2023.

[27] Cited in Damian Whitworth (2015) From the "Nobel Prize" of Music to Her Own Prom, *The Times*, 6 August 2015.

Glennie and Deafness: Self-Perception

> I've in a way always been associated with deaf organisations really from the word go and I think what's changed is how I talk about that … I am a sound creator so I want to talk about listening, and so that has developed, which has now enabled me to talk about deafness in a more holistic way and I think a more personal way as well, without it being "freaky".[28]

Glennie's listening processes are her own; she has never wanted to be perceived as a de facto spokesperson or representative for the d/Deaf experience, which is too vast to be defined by one individual (regardless of how prominent or successful they might be). At times, this has been misconstrued as an effort to separate herself from the d/Deaf community. The fact is that Glennie's career began at a time when the general public were still consumed by the hero narrative in relation to disability; even at her most vocal, the realities of her experiences would likely not have been heard. Whilst associations with events celebrating the claiming of disability seem to be relatively recent features of her public profile, Glennie's collaborations with d/Deaf communities has been consistent throughout her career.

Her association with The Beethoven Fund (providing musical experiences to children with hearing impairments) began when she was sixteen, followed by patronage of d/Deaf empowerment organisations including The Elizabeth Foundation, Cued Speech, the Royal National Institute for Deaf People and Audio Visibility. In addition to these partnerships, Glennie has publically and directly discussed deafness (in her own terms), at several points. Such statements differ from interviews, in that Glennie is in control of how the narrative is framed. The most notable of these efforts are *Good Vibrations* (1990), "Hearing Essay" (2003), the TED Talk "How to Truly Listen" (2003) and *Touch the Sound* (2004). These are the signposts in defining Glennie's self-identity as a musician who happens to be deaf.

Good Vibrations is an early autobiography, published when Glennie was twenty-four. One of the main motivations in writing this memoir was to address public interest in the idea of a deaf virtuoso: "My motive has been simply to set on record the story of how I came to be a musician despite the apparently major disability of being profoundly deaf."[29] Glennie's use of the term "apparently" is featured elsewhere in the introduction, and is indicative of the fact that her attitude towards deafness differs considerably from the broader cultural consciousness at the time of the book's

---

[28] Interview with Glennie, 3 May 2019.
[29] Glennie (1990) *Good Vibrations*, p. xi.

publication (1990): "I hope that *Good Vibrations* will show that it is possible to succeed with one's ambitions, despite apparently almost insurmountable obstacles."[30]

The exploration of Glennie's diagnosis, use of hearing aids, issues with dated and discriminatory education systems, and methods of learning to listen in an embodied way are unquestionably detailed enough to have eliminated the need for further public scrutiny of her deafness. She is specific about various medical appointments and treatments but seeks to redirect the narrative instead towards significant career achievements and "firsts". In a caption beside an early newspaper article titled "Amazing Evelyn: Deaf – But She Makes Music!", Glennie recalls the adage that "All publicity is good publicity." As the book progresses, however, mentions of deafness are conspicuously absent; as Glennie perfects her listening process it is no longer a relevant consideration. Glennie is clear about the need to educate the public in this respect:

> I had another photo session and an interview with Valerie Ward. The feature was very well written, but it inevitably concentrated on my deafness rather than my music, and it was about this time that I really began to think about publicity and to determine that my work as a percussionist must be the focus of attention rather than my hearing.[31]

The openness and tangible energy of *Good Vibrations* contrasts starkly with Glennie's "Hearing Essay", a short and direct public statement originally written in 1993 (co-authored by Greg Malcagni), and undergoing various minor amendments in subsequent years. Written only three years after her autobiography, the essay was a personal response to ongoing scrutiny and fascination with her status as a deaf performer. The "Hearing Essay" was a definitive declaration of Glennie's desire to end discussion of the matter, a direct rebuttal of the heroine narrative and the associated exaggerations of the role that deafness had played in her career development:

> Unfortunately, my deafness makes good headlines. I have learnt from childhood that if I refuse to discuss my deafness with the media they will just make it up. The several hundred articles and reviews written about me every year add up to a total of many thousands … More than 90% are so inaccurate that you would be forgiven for thinking that it is impossible for me to be a musician.[32]

---

[30] Ibid., p. xi.

[31] Ibid., p. 124.

[32] Evelyn Glennie (2003; revised 2015) *Hearing Essay* (online). Available from: https://www.evelyn.co.uk/hearing-essay/ (accessed 20 September 2019).

162   *Evelyn Glennie: Sound Creator*

As with *Good Vibrations*, Glennie's intention in the "Hearing Essay" was to promote more holistic engagement with her work:

> I hope that the audience will be stimulated by what I have to say (through the language of music) and will therefore leave the concert hall feeling entertained. If the audience is instead only wondering how a deaf musician can play percussion then I have failed as a musician.[33]

Glennie's frustration was palpable and directly addresses the negative experience of being othered: "This essay is designed to set the record straight and allow people to enjoy the experience of being entertained by an ever evolving musician rather than some freak or miracle of nature."[34] In general, the "Hearing Essay" suggests that Glennie continued to feel silenced. Though brief, this statement is important because it departed from the composed and accommodating persona invariably presented in both print and television. It was a frustrated and honest reaction to enduring stereotypes which sensationalized and misrepresented difference. The closing statement is one which merited repetition throughout the early decades of Glennie's career: "Please enjoy the music and forget the rest."[35]

The essay remains on the Evelyn Glennie website, consolidated since 2019 with a press pack which addresses two questions on the same subject ("When did you start going deaf?" and "Do you wear hearing aids?"). Glennie's request to "forget the rest" has never fully been accepted by media or academia; even when contextualized as expert listening, the risk still exists that Glennie's larger contribution to contemporary music will always be viewed from this perspective. The focus on listening must co-exist with the art of performance and sound creation; otherwise the process of othering continues.

In 2003, the same topic was revisited in the TED Talk "How to Truly Listen", which has been viewed over 2.4 million times on YouTube since it was posted in 2007. The 2003 TED theme was Rebirth, and Glennie's short lecture–demonstration interpreted this through the lens of her early career experiences, transitioning from aspirational amateur to professional percussionist. Success and failure merit attention in TED Talks, the intention being that speakers are honest about the realities of their journey. For Glennie, this meant placing the focus on her admission to the Royal Academy of Music. An opening discussion on translation versus interpretation (in reading music) is a metaphor for how Glennie differentiates between hearing and listening; the challenges faced in her early career relate directly to

[33]   Ibid.
[34]   Ibid.
[35]   Ibid.

this distinction. Glennie is clearly proud of her achievements in changing the admissions process for music institutions in the UK. She acknowledges that deafness has never been a personal obstacle, but that external perceptions unquestionably had the potential to negatively impact her career trajectory. The resultant modifications apply not only to people on the d/Deaf spectrum, but to every potential applicant.

The TED Talk is centred on empowerment, embracing difference, and acknowledging the individual lived experience of every musician. Glennie is definitively positioned as an expert listener, but also as a virtuosic solo multi-percussionist, innovator and pioneer. For some, the talk was representative of a definitive claiming of disability, but it repeated the same narrative initiated by Glennie in *Good Vibrations*; the experience has not changed, but the attitudes of the public have allowed for less invasive and discriminatory engagement. A 2018 internet search for "Evelyn Glennie TED Talk" was accompanied by a number of other queries related to this topic, the first of which was "Is Evelyn Glennie really deaf?" In one sense, this is a testimony to the fact that deafness has not impeded Glennie's success and reputation as a virtuosic musician. On the other hand, it may be a sad indication of a society more willing to doubt the validity of a disability than to accommodate difference. However, progress is more evident in recent years. The same search in 2023 elicits a first question which reflects more thoughtful engagement: "What are the main points about Evelyn Glennie?"

Touch the Sound (2004) combined the three central facets of Glennie's professional identity eloquently; there was no diminution of the musical experience. Riedelsheimer pitched the idea to Glennie as a documentary about sound, and she was initially reluctant to participate, concerned that deafness would supersede her work as a performer: "At first I declined because I said I'm absolutely not interested in having yet another film about me and my hearing situation."[36] Having developed a positive shared vision on the content and arc of the documentary, Glennie did explain her listening processes, but in direct relation to her practice as a musician: "Hearing is a form of touch, something that's so hard to describe because in a way, you know, something that comes, sound that comes to you, you know. You can feel as though you can literally, sort of, almost reach out to that sound and feel that sound."[37]

---

[36] Evelyn Glennie in interview with Dave Birnbaum (2021) *Teach the World to Listen* (podcast), 16 August 2021. Available from: https://podcast.davebirnbaum.com/teach-the-world-to-listen (accessed 23 April 2023).

[37] Glennie in Riedelsheimer (2004) *Touch the Sound* (DVD).

It is clear that Glennie finds it difficult to explain in words how she listens; there is hesitancy and concentration in attempting to provide clarity, but there is a sense that the performance event (which does not require explanation) is the most potent means of doing so. In the documentary, each discussion of hearing, listening and deafness is aligned with music-making which clearly demonstrates resonance, vibration and bodily connection. Later in the film, Glennie outlines why she tires of questions about deafness:

> If someone asks me "Oh well, how do you hear that?", then I simply say "I really don't know, but I just basically hear that through my body, through opening myself up. How do you hear that?" "Oh well I hear it through the ears." "You know, well, what do you mean through the ears? What are you actually hearing?" So when you try to bounce the question back to a so-called "hearing person", they simply do not know how to answer these questions, so therefore why should I be put in that position? That is just slightly upsetting.[38]

This statement echoes an earlier comment in the "Hearing Essay": "I remember one occasion when, uncharacteristically, I became upset with a reporter for constantly asking questions only about my deafness. I said 'If you want to know about deafness, you should interview an audiologist. My specialty is music."[39]

Returning to the narrative already provided in *Good Vibrations*, Glennie recounts the gradual process of losing her hearing in *Touch the Sound*. Before beginning secondary school aged eleven, she had an appointment in which the doctor stated that hearing aids would be essential, music-making would cease and attendance at a school for the deaf would be compulsory. Once more, the silencing of persons with disabilities is evident: "Thirty minutes before, I could do whatever I wanted to do, but then thirty minutes later apparently the medical profession tells you that you can't do something."[40] Glennie's public outreach in discussing deafness is a case in point on the difference between hearing and listening. The exhaustive detail in *Good Vibrations*, the honest frustration of the "Hearing Essay", and the patient repetition in *Touch the Sound* all provide clear information, but the continued fascination suggests that the public were not listening.

In many ways, Glennie was right in seeking not to discuss the subject; in the domain of live performance, all questions are rendered redundant; it is clear that Glennie listens intently, accurately and holistically. In a 2011 case

---

[38] Ibid.
[39] Glennie (2003; revised 2015) *Hearing Essay.*
[40] Glennie in Riedelsheimer (2004) *Touch the Sound* (DVD).

study of Glennie, Straus defines the holistic and multi-sensory nature of listening as "deaf hearing", a means of approaching communication which has implications extending beyond the d/Deaf community:

> Let us then imagine a deaf listener as one who engages the visual, the tactile, and the kinaesthetic in apprehending music: deaf hearing involves seeing, feeling, and moving to music. Of course deaf listeners can learn to hear "normally", and hearing listeners can learn deaf hearing; these are modes of apprehension, not essential attributes of bodies.[41]

Glennie favours instead the term "expert listening", which serves as a broader definition for the multi-faceted nature of musical and social engagement. Glennie has consistently claimed disability in terms of refuting any sense that deafness or difference equates to disadvantage. The reluctance to discuss her hearing is connected instead to an unwillingness to subscribe to the narrative of overcoming or to the suggestion that deafness is responsible for her many achievements. As she says to Straus: "I have not succeeded in spite of my deafness or because of it. Deafness is simply an irrelevant part of the equation."[42]

In early interviews, Glennie was increasingly troubled by what she determined to be an unnecessarily fetishized interest in her deafness, referencing several times her desire not to be positioned as a "freak". Externally imposed assumptions about the experience of listening for a profoundly deaf performer distracted from the primary objective of validating solo multi-percussion. But over time, Glennie has chosen to use music as the best means of modelling expert listening, replacing the ambiguity of words with the clarity of performance. Deafness is not loss; it is difference: "So is hearing loss ever an advantage? In my situation, it's an advantage because it allows me to put my stamp on the interpretation of the music. I don't rely on recordings to know how a piece should go ... So, everything I do is entirely mine."[43]

It would be entirely possible to appraise Glennie's work as a solo multi-percussionist without addressing deafness. Glennie lip-reads and speaks with clarity; her practice of playing barefoot is one adopted by multiple hearing musicians in various genres; the use of gesture and embodied engagement is intrinsic to the art of performance. But to do so would also restrict discussion of Glennie's work as an expert listener, a term which resonates both within and beyond her work as a musician. To define Glennie

[41] Straus (2011) *Extraordinary Measures: Disability in Music*, p. 169.
[42] Ibid., p. 147.
[43] Ibid., p. 148.

166   Evelyn Glennie: Sound Creator

as a deaf musician is reductive and imposed by external forces; the identity of expert listener is claimed and embraced as intrinsic to her practices as performer, sound creator, communicator and philanthropist. An interview with Disability Talk in 2017 is a useful summary of Glennie's position on deaf identity, once more elucidating the consistent points made throughout her career: "As a profoundly deaf person I prefer to determine my own level of disability rather than others determining or categorizing me."[44]

The Spectrum of Listening: *The Deaf and Loud Symphonic Experience* (2018)

The first *Deaf and Loud Symphonic Experience* took place in Detroit on 16 December 2018. A confluence of deaf and hearing musicians fusing Classical, hip-hop and Motown genres performing on a stage designed to facilitate multi-sensory engagement, the event represented a determinedly diverse and inclusive musical experience. Glennie's involvement in the project began as a result of her interest in the work of Sean Forbes, a Deaf rapper who uses American Sign Language (ASL) to make hip-hop accessible to the d/Deaf community. Forbes began his musical career by producing ASL cover versions, starting with Eminem's "Lose Yourself", and released his first original track "I'm Deaf" in 2010. Founder of D-PAN (the Deaf Professional Arts Network, established in 2006), Forbes is focused on validating the use of ASL in contemporary culture and in promoting more public intersections between the Deaf community and musical experiences. Forbes and long-term collaborator Jake Bass, a musician and producer, had already discussed the potential of working with a chamber ensemble in a confluence of musical styles. Glennie phoned Forbes in 2015 after reading a profile on his work, and the project subsequently evolved into a much larger collaboration with the Detroit Symphony Orchestra. The *Deaf and Loud Symphonic Experience* was the culmination of a shared vision to make musical spaces inclusive for all types of listeners.

Forbes is a proud representative of Deaf culture and has created an art form which merges music, rap and ASL. Though Glennie does not use the capitalized term (and in fact has never included reference to deafness in marketing, programmes or self-promotion), there are other parallels between the two. Both have created lucrative and pioneering careers in the music industry; both have embraced the ways in which d/Deafness has promoted

---

[44] *Dame Evelyn Glennie Speaks with Disability Talk* (2017), online. Available from: https://disabilitytalk.co.uk/2017/09/28/dame-evelyn-glennie-speaks-disabilitytalk/ (accessed 1 September 2019).

more diverse modes of listening; both are visually compelling performers. Glennie's style is associated with gesture and theatricality, whilst Forbes has created a mesmerizing and fast-paced visual art form which functions as both a language and musical response to pulse and rhythm:

> Forbes' mesmerizing, rapid-fire signing has an impulse all its own that's compelling to watch even if you don't know what it means. His hands switch from ballistic spasms to soft curves, from smooth laminar arcs to short, sharp chops, within the span of a single verse, ranging over a rich landscape of tones.[45]

Glennie is an oralist who communicates primarily through speech and lip-reading; her work is most often received and created with hearing musicians. For some members of the Deaf community, Glennie is therefore not associated directly with Deaf culture. Every d/Deaf experience is distinct, and this impacts the ways in which each person chooses to communicate and to listen. In a BBC documentary discussing *Deaf and Loud*, Forbes and Glennie are clear about their differing approaches. Forbes states: "In several songs I mention being deaf. I mention my proudness of being deaf … I'm proud to be a deaf person and I think all deaf people should have a sense of pride."[46] Contrastingly, Glennie notes: "I think in my case I don't feel that really, simply because I was a deafened person, so I was not born deaf. And I think that makes a difference really." This is a valid point often overlooked in relation to Glennie's experiences, but one which she has mentioned previously in a number of interviews. In 2002, she notes: "It's difficult for me to take a position on the oral versus signing controversy, because I'm a deafened person – and not somebody who was born deaf. For me, that is where the controversy stops."[47]

The Detroit Symphony Orchestra and the Deaf Professional Arts Network were intent on providing a musical experience relevant to the full spectrum of listening. *Deaf and Loud* was not a convergence of the deaf and Deaf worlds; its ambitions were much larger and more inclusive. For Glennie, it represented a celebration of diversity which transcended disability activism:

---

[45] Alex Stone (2015) Deaf Rapper Sean Forbes Makes Himself Joyfully Heard on the Hip-Hop Scene, *Washington Post* (online), 25 January 2015. Available from: https://www.washingtonpost.com/entertainment/music/deaf-rapper-sean-forbes-makes-himself-joyfully-heard-on-the-hip-hop-scene/2015/01/25/15943fdc-a0f4-11e4-9f89-561284a573f8_story.html (accessed 27 September 2019).

[46] BBC See Hear *When Evelyn Met Sean* (video online). Available from: https://www.facebook.com/bbcseehear/videos/1139039246148146/ (accessed 25 September 2019).

[47] Evelyn Glennie in Jim Reisler (2014) *Voices of the Oral Deaf: Fourteen Role Models Speak Out*. London: Mc Farland and Company, p. 48.

I think that sometimes people just want to put you in a box. But through my experience as a musician, who also happens to be deaf, I've been able to challenge this. I've learnt that inclusion is so important, and we shouldn't assume that different people with the same label will have the same experience. Someone shouldn't need to have a sensory loss to make us think about how we communicate with them.[48]

Forbes, Glennie and Mandy Harvey (an American songwriter and singer associated with pop and jazz styles), all of whom are d/Deaf, were featured soloists. But the music sought to extend beyond d/Deaf culture, into the merging of other identities pertaining to genres, repertoire and audience demographic. The finale of Eminem's "Lose Yourself" combined all musicians, with Glennie providing accompaniment on marimba, vibraphone and Aluphone. In many ways, this offered a tangible statement on the point which Glennie has tried to make throughout her career: in the moment of musical performance, d/Deafness is not relevant. Rhythm and sound are vibrational; their resonance is always multi-sensory. Forbes used sign language and voice, with the words captioned throughout; these were the only indications that the performance was connected in any way to the d/Deaf community. Glennie has been faced with so many questions on deafness, hearing and listening, but all such queries are addressed with clarity in the moment of performance: "'Deaf' is just a label, it's just a word, that's all it is."[49]

Glennie has always been conscious of the fact that she makes music designed to reach every listener, in whatever capacity they experience sound. For Forbes, this event marked a significant means of signifying that ASL hip-hop can do the same. Despite the fact that Forbes represents the next generation of Deaf culture, he is still dealing with societal misconceptions on the significance of his art. An article discussing the rise of d/Deaf hip-hop in 2013 evokes many of the sentiments which served to potentially narrow Glennie's remit in the early stages of her own career: "To the majority of the hearing world, these artists register only as heart-warming stories of determination, not music you want to bump to in your jeep with the top down."[50]

---

[48] Evelyn Glennie (2019) *I'm a Grammy Award Winning Musician and I'm Deaf* (online), 28 May 2019. Available from: https://www.evelyn.co.uk/im-a-grammy-award-winning-musician-and-im-deaf/ (accessed 2 June 2020).

[49] Evelyn Glennie in Kate Ginn (2002) The Stubborn Virtuoso, *Daily Mail*, 19 June 2002, p. 24.

[50] Dave Peisner (2013) *Deaf Jams: The Surprising, Conflicted, Thriving World of Hearing-Impaired Rappers* (online), 29 October 2013. Available from: https://www.spin.com/2013/10/deaf-jams-hearing-impaired-rappers/ (accessed 1 September 2019).

The *Deaf and Loud Symphonic Experience* was a particularly assertive statement on inclusion, but the reality is that every musical performance should be viewed in similar terms. Live music is exciting because it is innately multi-sensory; d/Deaf and hearing audiences engage with the visual appeal of the event; all bodies respond to the emanating vibrations; all react subjectively to the musical moment. Deafness can so easily be read into everything that Glennie does as a performer, and in the early stages of her career, this is exactly what happened. Now defined instead as an expert listener, it is important to avoid doing the same under more politically correct terminology. Whilst some may view *Deaf and Loud* as a public statement claiming disability (given that the term d/Deaf is so prominently featured for the event), this is not necessary for Glennie, who has always embraced this facet of her identity as an attribute. In much the same way that Forbes is proud to identify as Deaf, Glennie is equally proud to self-identify as an expert listener; though the terms are different, the sense of empowerment in each instance is the same.

Inclusion: Education

Glennie's primary mission has been to validate, diversify and sustain the profession of solo multi-percussionist. Through the medium of live performance, she has energized and engaged audiences in various contexts, reaching new listeners and disseminating new music as an intrinsic feature of her programming. In addition to forging her own successful career, it has always been Glennie's intention that many solo multi-percussionists will follow; she has promoted both her own work and the art of percussion. The BBC Young Musician of the Year Competition, initiated in 1978, introduced the solo percussion category in 1994 as a direct result of Glennie's intervention:

> I was really frustrated that percussion was not included in the BBC Young Musician of the Year competition, so I bombarded the director with letters, and he eventually allowed me to give him a 30-minute recital – at my own expense – to prove there was enough repertoire available to include percussion in the competition.[51]

---

[51] Evelyn Glennie in Emily Gunton (2021) Drumming Up Future Talent: Dame Evelyn Glennie, *Music Teacher* (online), 1 July 2021. Available from: https://www.music-teachermagazine.co.uk/features/article/drumming-up-future-talent-dame-evelyn-glennie (accessed 14 April 2023).

This competition has since launched the careers of a number of British percussionists including Colin Currie (finalist in 1994) and Adrian Spillett (the first percussionist to win, in 1998).

Many of Glennie's compositions are pedagogical in nature, including *Perpetual Motion* (2015), a collection of short works for solo piano (subsequently arranged for marimba) and the recently published *Hal Leonard Glockenspiel Method* (2022), designed specifically for beginners. Yet what will remain her most enduring contribution to the evolution of music education are Glennie's commissions, over two hundred works offering percussionists a wide range of styles, configurations and opportunities to develop their skills. These commissions include works by seminal figures in contemporary music (including Harrison Birtwistle and Iannis Xenakis) but also promote emerging composers at the early stages of their career. These include Bertram Wee, who composed a percussion duet for Glennie in 2014 (*Trench Songs with Crossfire*) and subsequently a work for Aluphone (*Dithyrambs*), which premiered at the BBC Proms in 2015 whilst Wee was still an undergraduate at the Royal College of Music. Many of Glennie's commissions are now recognized features of recital and concert repertoire. In terms of concertos, *Veni, Veni Emmanuel* (James MacMillan) and *Der Gerette Alberich* (Christopher Rouse) have been interpreted by numerous soloists, as evinced in the many performances uploaded to YouTube; Elliott Gaston-Ross included Heath's *African Sunrise/Manhattan Rave* in his recital for the BBC Young Musician of the Year competition in 2014. In relation to solo works, Másson's *Prim* for snare drum and Michael Gordon's *XY*, premiered by Steven Schick, are widely performed in percussion recitals.

Advocating for the future of solo multi-percussion was Glennie's first objective, but this has since segued into a larger mission to ensure that music education is an inclusive, diverse and accessible creative space for all. Glennie speaks fondly of her childhood and early musical development in *Good Vibrations*. Music lessons started in primary school, with weekly sessions comprising vocal training, theory and recorder ensemble. Glennie received piano lessons with a private tutor and also started clarinet aged ten before choosing percussion in secondary school; opportunities even in a relatively remote rural area were plentiful and inexpensive. Without access to these resources, Glennie's ambitions would never have been realized. Inclusion in music education (for students at all stages) has become a significant issue in her work as patron and advocate, seeking to ensure that the opportunities from which she derived so much benefit are valued and maintained.

Inclusion 171

On multiple occasions Glennie describes musical engagement as healing or curative, stating in a 2003 interview that "music is a form of medicine and has a huge impact",[52] and noting in her TED Talk that "music really is our daily medicine". These sentiments are the driving force behind her work as patron and campaigner for music education initiatives. In an age of austerity, amplified by the COVID-19 crisis, the arts have invariably been the first to suffer in UK schools and universities; even before this, standards of music education have often been directly dependent upon the political and economic agendas of the government. Students today face issues with cost, provision, quality and consistency in terms of accessing instrumental tuition and opportunities to perform. Glennie did not have to address these obstacles; the first difficulty in this respect was based not on resources but on discrimination, when Glennie was initially rejected from the Royal Academy of Music (on the basis that she was a deaf musician):

> I think really the main challenge was not so much to do with my professional career but literally just getting into the academy and just changing the mind-set there. It really just took one person on the panel to say, "Well, hold on a second. We can't start picking and choosing like this just because someone might be deaf or blind or this and that." So I think that if that was still a decline from them I don't know where or what I would be today; I would be a very different person.[53]

Aged sixteen, this first form of education activism instigated systemic changes to the college admissions process, an achievement which Glennie remains particularly proud of.

Glennie started primary school in 1970, secondary school in 1977, and the Royal Academy of Music in 1982. Her timeline of musical development therefore predates the changes imposed by Margaret Thatcher's government when the National Curriculum was introduced in 1988 by the Education Secretary Kenneth Baker. Though multiple issues have contributed to an increasingly unfair distribution of music education resources in the UK, the National Curriculum is unquestionably responsible for undermining the value of the subject and narrowing its creative remit. A determined effort to eschew what was perceived by the Conservative government as liberal pedagogy, the National Curriculum offered a much more prescriptive (and assessment-based) approach to education for UK children aged five to sixteen. Originally, it was envisaged that all ten subjects (including

---

[52] Evelyn Glennie (2003) Great Scot or Great Human Being: It Doesn't Matter as Long as They're Giving Back to the Next Generation Says Evelyn Glennie, *Sunday Mail* (Glasgow), 22 June 2003, p. 42.

[53] Interview with Glennie, 3 May 2019.

music) would be taught until the age of sixteen; only three years after the curriculum was implemented, this was amended. Art and music would no longer be compulsory after the age of fourteen, a telling indication of the fact that creative subjects were undervalued.

The design of any music curriculum is problematic, given the diverse nature of the subject, and debates concerning content, style and modes of assessment for music were particularly vitriolic in developing the National Curriculum. The Music Working Group (including composer Pierre Boulez and conductor Simon Rattle) advocated for increased emphasis on performance, creativity and a diverse range of musical genres. This was tempered by members of the National Curriculum Council who ultimately drafted a syllabus centred primarily on the Western art canon, theory and history.[54] Glennie contributed to this discussion, firmly advocating for the vision of the Music Working Group: "A great opportunity has been missed ... There is now too much emphasis on academic requirements."[55] Confident in using her prominent public profile to make a contribution to the issue, Glennie's emergent interest in activism was greatly undermined only one year later. In 1993 Glennie resigned her membership of the Arts Council Music Advisory Panel in protest against cuts to funding for London orchestras, refusing to associate her name with such decisions, and openly frustrated that they were made without adequate consultation:

> I am not disillusioned, I am angry. I felt cheated, that I had been used as a patsy to give the Arts Council some credibility. I was totally against stopping the funding and I was never party to that decision ... This whole episode has taught me a lesson. I will be very wary about lending my name or joining something like that again.[56]

This negative experience changed Glennie's views on how her professional identity could be abused. Though Glennie continued to serve as patron and ambassador for a significant number of music charities in intervening years, she did not again assert her position publically on national issues until 2002, when Glennie, Sir James Galway, Julian Lloyd Webber and composer Michael Kamen formed a consortium to once more highlight problems with the music education system in the UK. A letter

---

[54] Vic Gammon (1999) Cultural Politics of the English National Curriculum for Music, 1991–1992, *Journal of Educational Administration and History*, 31 (2).

[55] Evelyn Glennie in ibid., p. 143.

[56] Evelyn Glennie in Jan Moir (1993) Women: Good Vibrations, Public Lives: Evelyn Glennie, Catapulted into the Media Spotlight by her Protest Resignation from the Arts Council Last Week, *Guardian*, 8 December 1993.

Inclusion 173

to Culture Secretary Tessa Jowell and Education Secretary Charles Clarke outlined their concerns:

> As four musicians who have forged successful international careers in the music industry, for which we owe a tremendous amount to the music education we received, we are writing to raise our grave concern about the increasing marginalisation of music, particularly classical, in primary and secondary schools.[57]

A report from the same year by the Qualifications and Curriculum Authority indicated that only 8–9 per cent of students were opting to study music at GCSE level, supporting the consortium's assertion that the school system was failing. A resultant meeting with Education Secretary Charles Clarke allowed the musicians to express their frustrations, and all four were actively involved in promoting their views via the general media. At this time, Glennie was clear about the fact that activism in music education was not necessarily an essential aspect of her career, but it was an issue that she was passionate about: "I don't have to be involved in education. As long as I have enough concerts in the diary I could say, 'Thank you very much, I'm fine.' But that's not what it's about, it's much, much more than that."[58]

Eighteen months after the open letter, in 2004, the UK government published its Music Manifesto, but the consortium opted not to support the proposed amendments because they were not consolidated with appropriate funding allocations. As Webber stated: "This document is a masterpiece of talk and waffle. It's not going to help the people we want to help."[59] Financial support for music was not a priority at any level of the education system. Whilst issues around the Music Manifesto continued, Glennie returned her honorary degree from Exeter University in response to the decision to close their music department. In an open letter to the *Guardian* Glennie stated:

> As an honorary doctor of Exeter University and a supporter of music education rights, I am outraged at news of the possible closure of its music department ... To show my disgust, I will be returning my honorary doctorate and no longer offering my support to the establishment.[60]

---

[57] James Morrison (2002) Education: Classical Stars Rail at Musical "Illiteracy", *Independent on Sunday*, 1 December 2002.

[58] Evelyn Glennie (2003) Great Scot or Great Human Being.

[59] Julian Lloyd Webber in Nicholas Pyke (2004) Top Musicians Attack Master Plan for Schools, *Independent on Sunday*, 4 July 2004.

[60] Evelyn Glennie (2004) Letter: Save Music at Exeter, *Guardian*, 10 December 2004.

174   *Evelyn Glennie: Sound Creator*

At all levels, the 1990s and 2000s witnessed debilitating spending cuts for music education. Exeter University's rationale for closing its department was representative of the perception of the arts as less valuable to industry and society. The money in this case was instead diverted towards larger and more successful departments. Cuts to instrumental tuition and reduced access to specialist disciplines, including percussion, in schools were problems which operated in parallel to the restrictive nature of the National Curriculum. Glennie continued to advocate in this respect with a number of initiatives. In 2009, she contributed to The Charter for Instrumental Music in Scotland, a plan to provide tuition to every child in the country. Again, the curative potential of music, and the right to access this art were central to her views: "From the womb to the grave, we crave music. Music is the primary source of communication crossing all boundaries. Music teaches us everything we need to survive in life as we pass through this world – please do not cut this lifeline."[61]

Glennie has since added her support to similar efforts in Scotland, including Let the Children Play (2013) and Save Our Strings (2018). In 2021 she became a Sistema patron, and in 2022 participated in their Big Noise project with an online workshop streamed to several Scottish towns and cities. Such community projects are now fundamental to education provision, given that the instrumental tuition available to Glennie's generation is no longer offered to the same extent. El Sistema originated in Venezuela in 1975 as a social and pedagogical initiative designed to provide orchestral performance opportunities for children from deprived socio-economic backgrounds; similar needs exist in Western countries as a result of social inequalities and the marginalization of music education. Proposed budget restrictions to Sistema Scotland in Torry, Aberdeen, in February 2023 are indicative of the fact that the arts continue to be undermined and underfunded. With another of the four Big Noise projects in Tayside already cut, Glennie is involved in fighting to save it: "I find it exasperating that we are still having to talk about the benefits of music participation and plead for funding for transformational projects like this."[62] Glennie has always advocated for the value and importance of percussion in contemporary music, but there is now a broader need to speak on behalf of all facets of music

---

[61] Evelyn Glennie in Fiona MacLeod (2009) Glennie Calls for Every Scots Child to be Given "Lifeline" Education in Music, *Scotsman*, 23 December 2009.

[62] Evelyn Glennie in Calum Petrie (2023) *World-Renowned Musician Adds Voice to Calls to Save Big Noise Torry* (online), 27 February 2023. Available from: https://www.pressandjournal.co.uk/fp/education/5443255/dame-evelyn-glennie-big-noise-torry/?fbclid=IwAR2I_j9GFs2WGS8b9YRRWgxmNG-YFHxcK-miICFoANjJvG-maaWpUPHCBU3Y (accessed 13 April 2023).

education. It is no longer about facilitating opportunities for percussion; it is about ensuring that music remains an accessible and inclusive space for all. The Evelyn Glennie Foundation, established in 2023, positions this mission as the first of its charitable objectives:

> To advance the education of the general public, in particular by supporting the development and application of curricula and practices that enhance communication skills and cognitive development including through workshops and training sessions in active listening, through the use of music.[63]

Transition, change and evolution are all associated with creativity and innovation; pedagogy is no different. The problems with ongoing amendments are that these decisions are most often made by those with no direct experience; the trend has favoured demise rather than growth. As with the silencing of persons with disabilities, the silencing of music is a form of exclusion in the UK education system. Collaboration between politicians and industry professionals seems to be the most logical way of alleviating this disparity, but with the exception of Glennie's ill-fated Arts Council membership, it seems that independent charities have instead been tasked with the role. Glennie is keenly aware that the diversification which has been so important in sustaining her career is also a prerequisite for music education; she remains optimistic that change and progress remain possible for the next generation of students:

> I mean, because I'm in the industry I'm constantly being made aware of things that have been cut back, or that's not developing any more, or that's not happening any more, or we can't do this or we can't do that for whatever reason. But at the same time I see this big, big picture whereby you know, although there may be cut backs at school, as regards to the arts, actually a lot is happening at home through individuals ... So just when we think that something is, you know, where there might be doom and gloom in one area, there's always something sprouting up. There has to be this yin and yang all of the time. So I never get too despondent even though I'm fighting for the arts to be in our schools.[64]

---

[63] *The Evelyn Glennie Foundation: Charity Overview* (2023), online. Available from: https://register-of-charities.charitycommission.gov.uk/charity-search/-/charity-details/5193276/full-print (accessed 29 April 2023).

[64] Interview with Glennie, 3 May 2019.

Inclusion: Age

In 2018, the documentary *Love is Listening: Dementia Without Loneliness* was released by Memory Bridge. The film featured several prominent figures involved in outreach work with dementia patients, and followed their journeys of engagement and interaction. Glennie was invited to participate in the project in order to explore how her processes of listening might be applied in this context. Michael Verde (founder of Memory Bridge, a charity seeking to address the emotional isolation of people with dementia) explains his rationale for adding Glennie to the project:

> She is the world's premier percussionist, so I knew that she could pay attention in a way that was extraordinary. She hears through vibrations. She goes onstage barefoot, so you can imagine the quality of attention that's involved in tuning in like that. That's what I wanted to learn about: could that kind of attention be invested in people with dementia, and if it was, what difference would it make?[65]

Ageism is a form of discrimination largely absent from public discourse, with the realities of the ageing process an issue that Western society tends to ignore or avoid. The resultant silencing of the older generation is exacerbated further for people with dementia, an inherently isolating condition which results in distance from the intellectual, emotional and physical self.

Glennie's involvement in *Love is Listening* was an important means of highlighting ways in which the arts can serve as a means of alleviating exclusion based on ageism, a practical intervention reflecting her views of music as catharsis. Validating the rights of the older generation, and people with dementia, is also an issue of social justice, particularly in light of the fact that they are often both literally and figuratively excluded. Music therapy and community music initiatives are key to providing care in these environments, but as with the schooling system, availability is inconsistent and unfairly distributed. For *Love is Listening*, Glennie used the simplest of resources to demonstrate that active listening and non-verbal communication are skills that everyone can employ in order to offer dignity and respect to people with dementia.

Many forms of disability (including deafness) are now understood as social and cultural constructs, as personal identities which are claimed rather than assigned. Dementia is more challenging in this respect, given the fact that patients are often unable to advocate for themselves:

---

[65] Michael Verde in N. Ryabova (2018) *Love is Listening: Dementia Without Loneliness* (DVD) Memory Bridge.

Dementia discourse has historically been dominated by a highly "medicalised" notion of dementia, as a disease associated only with irreversible decline and deficits where "nothing can be done". However, there has been a recent shift in the discourse. Dementia is increasingly being viewed as having a rights-based dimension.[66]

With increased life expectancy in the developed world, the numbers of people with dementia is also rising; current projections anticipate that over one million people in the UK will be living with the condition by 2025.[67] There is no cure for dementia; palliative care is currently the only available provision. Encouraging the simple act of listening and connection was the central theme of the documentary, intended to remove the stigma of dementia. This is the overarching mission of Memory Bridge, dedicated to removing the "dis-ease" of dementia, seeking to address society's uncomfortable relationship with the realities of the ageing process. The other participants in the documentary are also committed to similar projects. Benjamin Mathes, who assumes the role of narrator throughout, is the founder of Urban Confessional, defined as a "free listening project". Naomi Feil developed Validation, a means of working with elderly people centred on active listening and engagement. Jean Vanier established L'Arche in 1964, a foundation dedicated to providing support networks for people with intellectual disabilities.

Glennie's segment in the film begins at 13'25". She discusses how engaged listening became fundamental when she was beginning to notice issues with auditory perception: "From the age of eight I was finding that sound was becoming slightly more distorted and subconsciously I think I was beginning to pay attention to people more."[68] This simple point is actually very important; we understand how a musician can be framed as an expert listener given that their career depends upon this skill, but it is not always immediately obvious what it means when used beyond the multi-sensory domain of live performance. The fact that Glennie notes she has been paying close attention in order to converse and interact in social settings from the age of eight indicates that active listening has been part of her life since childhood. The sense of being an expert in this respect has therefore been

---

[66] Mental Health Foundation (2015) *Dementia, Rights, and the Social Model of Disability: A New Direction for Policy and Practice?* (online). Available from: http://www.innovationsindementia.org.uk/wp-content/uploads/2018/01/dementia-rights-policy-discussion.pdf (accessed 29 April 2023).

[67] Alzheimer's Society (2023) *How Many People Have Dementia in the UK?* (online). Available from: https://www.alzheimers.org.uk/blog/how-many-people-have-dementia-uk (accessed 15 April 2023).

[68] Glennie in *Love is Listening: Dementia Without Loneliness.*

a process of becoming, of choosing to live and work in a hearing world and in a profession where listening is profoundly significant; it is not a concept derived solely from her work as a professional musician, but a way of life.

There is then a clear logic in applying these skills of concentration, patience, openness and commitment to new social interactions as explored in *Love is Listening*. Glennie brought a frame drum and soft-headed mallet to her meeting with a patient at Willett House Nursing Home (Chislehurst) called Babs. After a few halting attempts at verbal interaction, Babs began to rub her hand vigorously around the drum, and Glennie could immediately respond in kind. Their communication was conducted without words; together they explored the sound, resonance and sensation of both instrument and beater; the frame drum became a link between them. In one instance, Glennie strikes the drum with her hand and physically passed the sound and sensation to Babs by stroking her forearm, with the vibrations of the drum felt and understood more keenly than the audible. Babs was improvising, using gestures which were spontaneous and exploratory. Music-making is instinctive in this short non-verbal conversation, a shared act based on a simple premise: "We can all do this. We don't need fancy instruments; we don't need fancy gear. It's not an expensive situation. All it is, is two people coming together, really opening up themselves, taking time, having the patience to just be together."[69]

In *Love is Listening*, Glennie is an instrumentalist, but also an expert listener. The main point is that music does not need to be complex in order to be valuable; creativity is communication which functions even in the absence of words. The documentary is powerful in its efforts to demonstrate that the multi-faceted nature of listening is a transferable skill which can make a contribution in multiple social contexts. As Glennie passes her fifth decade in the profession of solo performance, she is philosophical about the ways in which ageing will change and expand her own practice; age is not a barrier to engagement: "One thing is sure is the reality that the body will not always be physically able to manipulate the instruments … But that doesn't stop you from being a musician."[70]

[69]   Ibid.
[70]   Talks at Google (2023) *Evelyn Glennie "Listen World"* (video online), 8 December 2023. Available from: https://www.youtube.com/watch?v=MV1kuZSNCF4&t=67s (accessed 29 April 2023).

Inclusion: Social Awareness at the 2012 Olympics

At the London Olympics Opening Ceremony in 2012 Glennie was positioned at the helm of an ensemble of one thousand volunteer drummers, many of whom had never played an instrument before. This striking moment celebrated percussion, acknowledged Glennie's value as a cultural icon in UK music and was a dynamic statement on inclusion. Rhythm in this instance was a force which connected all present; improvised instruments of plastic and metal buckets were the primary medium; Glennie was the representative of her art. Featured in both the opening and closing stages of the ceremony, this global platform was a particularly resonant commentary on Glennie's role as one of the most significant and recognizable proponents of the discipline, presenting multi-percussion to the world.

The focus of any Olympics Opening Ceremony is to celebrate the cultural and social richness of the host nation. In many instances percussion instruments feature prominently: the 2008 Beijing Olympics began with the choreographed movements and rhythms of hundreds of performers in an impressive synchronized display centred on pattern, gesture and pulse; forty-six minutes into the Rio Opening Ceremony (2016), the sounds of samba drums filled the arena as fireworks exploded; a steady 4/4 ostinato on auxiliary percussion instruments provided the heartbeat supporting mimed athletic endeavour as Tokyo 2020 opened. London opted to present a chronology of innovation, all signposted with UK music that is globally resonant.

Glennie worked with the artistic director Danny Boyle from the early stages of planning, and both shared a sense of the socially inclusive statement that could be generated with a diverse and expansive ensemble of volunteer performers. As ever, Glennie also integrated advocacy for the discipline into this vision: "My whole career has been about promoting solo percussion so I was very adamant that I wanted percussion to be at the forefront."[71] Boyle designed a narrative intended to celebrate the achievements of the UK in commercial, industrial, social and cultural terms; the spirit of collaboration was the overarching theme. The title of the ceremony, *Isles of Wonder*, reflects an artistic vision which included "performing cultural work which could also be political work through a meshing of popular culture, historical reference and social commentary".[72] In the narrative

---

[71] Sofia Pasternak (2013) Evelyn Glennie on the Olympics Opening Ceremony, *Tom-Tom Magazine* (online). Available from: https://tomtommag.com/2013/02/evelyn-glennie-on-the-olympics-opening-ceremony/ (accessed 28 August 2019).

[72] Anita Biressi (2013) The London 2012 Olympic Games Opening Ceremony: History Answers Back, *Journal of Popular Television*, 1 (1), p. 117.

180 *Evelyn Glennie: Sound Creator*

of Britain's history, Boyle simultaneously chronicled and emphasized the importance of cultural legacy; art was the universalizing means by which the story could be told.

Glennie was first presented in the third section called *Pandemonium*, a fifteen-minute montage acknowledging Britain as the birthplace of the Industrial Revolution. It was a depiction of power, community and labour, fittingly denoted by a volunteer cast of over 2,500 dancers, drummers and actors. Percussion represented the hard work and shared endeavour of this historical period in a composition by Rich Smith titled "And I Will Kiss". Glennie featured prominently in the live coverage, but it was unfortunate that the commentator for the Olympic Channel introduced her by stating that "rhythm is found in her feet for she's been stone deaf since birth".[73]

A rumbling drum roll announced the beginning of *Pandemonium* as the drummers moved to positions in all sections of the stadium, ensuring that everyone in attendance experienced sound as a multi-sensory event. Glennie opened "And I Will Kiss" with aggressive *forte* strikes on a multi-percussion set-up which included bongos, four tom-toms, a number of bass drums and several suspended cymbals. Joined by a gradually intensifying backing track, the drummers amplified and punctuated the soundscape, using emphatic gestures. There were multiple worlds coalescing in this moment: professional and amateur, sound and vision, acoustic and electronic, participant and audience, attendees and viewers. Glennie functioned as both soloist and musical director, leading a compelling amalgam of music, choreography and action which was inescapably affecting. A series of subtly shifting rhythmic ostinato, a standard role for percussion in both dance music and art music – which meet in this composition – drove the central section of the work (see Ex. 11).

Glennie recalls the visceral sensations of this *tutti*:

> It was very infectious, very moving, a purposeful rhythm, and something that can easily be memorized. Something that the audience can truly feel, as well. It was this indescribable feeling that was physical as well as aural. Something that was quite unique and very raw, indeed.[74]

Percussion was a rousing, collective energy in *Pandemonium*, with the musical community of drummers also representing a larger social statement on inclusion. Participants were drawn from all parts of the UK, converging and communicating through music. This intense dance track was

---

[73] Olympic (2012) *The Complete London 2012 Opening Ceremony* (video online). Available from: https://www.youtube.com/watch?v=4Asoe4de-rI (accessed 14 July 2019).

[74] Pasternak (2013) Evelyn Glennie on the Olympics Opening Ceremony.

Inclusion 181

Ex. 11: "And I Will Kiss" ostinato figurations. Transcription based on recording of the Olympics Opening Ceremony. Original scoring by Rick Smith.

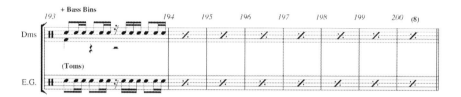

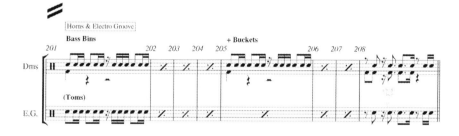

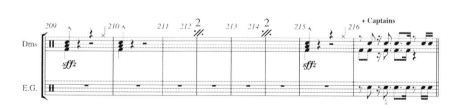

a celebration of the capacity of rhythm to create excitement, anticipation and connection.

Glennie returned at the culminating moment of the ceremony, with the Glennie Concert Aluphone serving as the resonant feature of "Caliban's Dream", a contemplative and inspiring track which accompanied the arrival of the Olympic torch in a section titled *There is a Light that Never Goes Out*. A moment of extraordinary national pride and global interest (generating an estimated four billion viewers), the Aluphone resonated throughout the stadium to a huge worldwide audience, a direct result of Glennie's promotion of the instrument to the creative team. "Caliban's Dream" (composed by the *Underworld* duo Rick Smith and Karl Hyde) featured the Aluphone as the only live instrumental sonority, supported to emotive effect with three solo voices (Elizabeth Roberts, Esme Smith and Alex Trimble) and a stadium filled with the sound of choirs (Dockhead Choir and Only Men Aloud). The atmosphere was dream-like and transcendent, echoing the balance between aspiration and reflection which pervaded the ceremony's narrative. With lyrics drawn from some of Britain's finest poets, the final moments offered a subtle power which was a determined contrast to the energy of earlier sections (such as *Pandemonium*). Glennie was positioned at the side of the stadium as the torch passed, with the image and sound of the Aluphone presented and promoted to the world. Given that *Underworld* (commissioned to write the original music for the event) are associated most frequently with techno and dance genres, it is unsurprising that rhythm functioned as the connective thread which united all parts of the ceremony. Percussion in its myriad forms was a consistent presence.

The Opening Ceremony was unquestionably important for self-promotion, framing Glennie as a key figure in contemporary British music; she shared the stage with an eclectic representation of cultural creativity including the BBC Symphony Orchestra, the Sex Pistols, Mr Bean and Sir Paul McCartney. It also promoted the diverse and inclusive remit of percussion; the volunteer drummers represented every facet of contemporary British society, and instruments used ranged from buckets to tubular bells to drum kits. Rhythm became a collective call for unity, a connective force more potent than any single performer or genre. The ceremony closed with the striking of the world's largest harmonically tuned bell (constructed specifically for the event), a final acknowledgement of the importance of percussive sonorities in the global community and in the history of all nations. Inscribed with a quotation from Shakespeare's *The Tempest*, percussion is celebrated and foregrounded in this hugely significant cultural artefact: "Be not afeard, the isle is full of noises."

Inclusion: Environment – World Elephant Day (2019)

Ecomusicology is an interdisciplinary academic mode of exploring the ways in which music serves as a means of connecting man to the wider world in terms of both culture and nature. An emergent discipline, it arises as a socially aware musicological response to the ways in which the world is changing. Whilst much of this research translates to discourse rather than action, consolidating the role that the arts can play in highlighting issues of social relevance is the central intention of such work. To some extent, Glennie's contribution in alignment with over one hundred international charities to World Elephant Day on 12 August 2019 can be positioned as both commentary and activism. Music was used to create a potent statement on an environmental issue; percussion intersected with the sounds of the elephant's habitat, merging culture and nature; the written word and atmospheric music were combined.

This small yet poignant contribution adheres to Titon's definition of ecomusicology as "the study of music, nature, culture, and the environment at a time of environmental crisis".[75] With increasing globalization, there exists the risk that commercial integration assumes precedence over social connection. Elephant poaching is indicative of a climate where financial gain takes priority; inclusion in this respect pertains to a larger international conversation on our relationship to the natural world. World Elephant Day was first launched on 12 August 2012, an initiative co-founded by filmmaker Patricia Sims and the Elephant Reintroduction Foundation of Thailand. Marked each year by a short documentary release, the confluence of imagery, words and soundscapes are combined to promote awareness of the imperative to protect these animals. Videos are generally accompanied by electronically generated music, as was the case for the 2018 release, which opened with the sound of xylophone and closed with a rousing drum kit pattern. On World Elephant Day in 2019, Glennie released via YouTube an immersive musical soundscape designed to raise awareness of the moral and ecological issues surrounding poaching, bringing the message to life using acoustic sonorities. The video and associated soundtrack opens with the stark question, "Are you listening?", in a small white font set against a plain black background. Composed and performed by Glennie, a range of auxiliary solo percussion instruments created a narrative wherein the listener experienced the fear and volatility of regions affected by elephant poaching. In this way, the remit of solo percussion was expanded beyond the arena of sound creation, seeking to promote and stimulate social engagement:

> Music is our universal way to spread and reinforce a true meaning behind our actions. We realized with the range of instruments available to us, we could replicate real-life scenarios and problems through

---

[75] Jeff Todd Titon (2013) The Nature of Ecomusicology, *Música e Cultura: revista da ABET*, 8 (1), p. 9.

the power of sound, in the hopes to teach the world to listen on a social, educational and environmental level.[76]

The composition eludes genre description, presenting a soundscape with moments of musical clarity juxtaposed with atmospheric effects. Infrequent and irregular drum beats emerge gradually, interspersed with birdsong; beauty co-exists with a growing sense of foreboding. Suddenly, the cry of an elephant emerges at the forefront of the soundscape; this is consolidated with echoes which retreat to the background of the auditory experience. A ripping sound follows, suggesting repetitive activity, emphasized with an increasingly regulated rhythmic pattern. With growing volume and intensity, this moment feels like the inescapable pulse of destruction. The absence of any visual stimulus beyond the question posed at the beginning requires the listener to fully engage in the aural experience. At 1'46" the sound of a gunshot breaks through the increasingly dense texture of drums and birdsong. Shortly thereafter the text changes to state: "100 African Elephants are illegally poached every single day." Receding from this declaration, the sound of a motor vehicle leaving the scene is clearly heard. At 1'58" the text again changes to note: "When you truly listen, you truly understand." Both the composition and its mode of delivery are extremely affective for the listener; the plight of the elephants is unquestionably evoked through the use of a range of auxiliary percussion instruments. The fact that listening is centralized relates both to Glennie's own ethos and to World Elephant Day specifically. She is clear about the potential of music to address such fundamental problems:

> We read so many articles regarding the impact poaching has on wildlife but how does "being" in this scenario make you feel with no other influences? When some of your other senses are hindered, those which remain become extremely powerful, providing you with the ability to emotionally travel to a place you may never have experienced before. Music is our universal way to spread and reinforce true meaning.[77]

The listener becomes witness to the reality of poaching, immersed in the rapid and intense activity where elephants are so suddenly removed from their habitat; percussion is the emotive narrative tool. A behind-the-scenes documentary released on the same day provides a useful detailing of the instrumentation used to create the soundscape. Timpani, snare drum,

---

[76] Evelyn Glennie (2019) *World Elephant Day 2019: Behind the Scenes* (video online). Available from: https://www.evelyn.co.uk/world-elephant-day-2019-behind-the-scenes/ (accessed 1 September 2019).

[77] Ibid.

rainshakers, whistles, rubber gloves, dried paper, thunder sheet and siren were recorded as separate tracks in Glennie's Cambridgeshire studio, and also as improvisations performed over layers of recorded sound. It is clear that the search for the right live effect is key to Glennie; multiple strikes on snare were followed by head shakes and subsequent repetitions; several rainsticks were used to find the correct balance and sonority; hands, feet and mallets were all utilised to conjure different timbres. Acoustic percussion provided the foundation which was then subjected to various post-production effects (including pitch shifts, compression and reverb).

It is also evident that Glennie had contributed time to the project, lending more than her name to World Elephant Day; the act of music-making and composition functioned as a statement of intention and purpose. Glennie addresses multi-sensory and active listening, the moral consciousness and the impetus to make meaningful changes simultaneously in this work. Given the increasing prominence of activism on climate change issues, the voice of the musician in projects such as the World Elephant Day commission offers a means by which art can make a positive and valid contribution in this domain. Inclusion pertains to ensuring that music is part of the discussion, that performance can serve as a call for change, and that environmental issues are resonant for everyone in society.

Inclusion: The Musician in a Time of Crisis

As streets and communal buildings lay empty, the contemporary soundscape of a world dealing with COVID-19 was altered almost beyond recognition. Tolling bells were sounded by special permission, a call to unity and a commemoration of those lost in places such as Boston, Miami, Toronto, Sydney and Devon. They reminded those in isolation of a timeless and ancient practice, of tradition, congregation, sadness and celebration. A single percussive sonority has the power to do this. Sound was a source of intense nostalgia during COVID-19; music assumed a fundamental role in maintaining motivation and connection in a time of unprecedented change. The image of singers on balconies in Italy, clapping families in Mumbai and the beating of pots and pans for NHS staff in the UK were resonant reminders of how access to music-making provided catharsis.

Music was valued by all, yet the professional musician was left extraordinarily vulnerable both during and after the COVID-19 crisis; the world remembered the significance of music, but commerce forgot the people who make it. Limited government assistance and the apparent disregard for the demise of many creative industries made the voice and professional identity of the performing artist a peripheral presence. Prominent figures including Glennie played an important part in drawing attention to this, speaking on behalf of a cultural community which struggled tremendously under the restrictions of lockdown.

Glennie was named President of HELP Musicians in May 2020, at the most tumultuous period in the history of the organization, during the first and most restrictive UK lockdown. The third holder of this role, following Edward Elgar and Maxwell Davies, the appointment served as a powerful indication of Glennie's significance in the history of British music. One of her first initiatives in this role was to write an open letter to the UK government, acting as an advocate for self-employed musicians, composers and educators. She opened with a simple yet profound question: "Are you listening to the musicians?" The financial burden placed on freelance musicians (most of whom were not eligible for the employment furlough scheme) was aligned with a much larger concern: what would the creative industries look like when COVID-19 had passed? Glennie's words were heartfelt, direct and stark. There was no effort to stray from the harsh realities of the situation. Speaking as a representative for the music industry, Glennie articulated the sentiments of a generation faced with an unprecedented loss of creative outlets and opportunities:

> The lack of clarity on when lockdown will be unwound is deeply unsettling – all we know is that ours will be one of the very last sectors to re-open and that only in the final stage of your re-opening roadmap might there be enough work for all the musicians who need it.[78]

Glennie contributed to numerous initiatives designed to maintain the voice of the artist during the course of the pandemic. Charity fundraisers included the 2.6 Music Marathon, the publication of a composition titled "Grace of Silence", to raise funds for freelance musicians, and performing in the online collaboration *Coronavirus the Musical*. As patron and ambassador for numerous charities, Glennie's philanthropic work became particularly intense during this time of upheaval:

> I was inundated with charitable and educational requests (and still am). It became literally a full-time job catering for the many things asked of me which I knew I could not sustain in a way that was meaningful for myself or the organizations. I need to "feel" a situation in order to genuinely engage with it; this was becoming overloaded and far too frequent, so I made a conscious decision to look at each situation carefully rather than be totally reactive to everything that came my way.[79]

---

[78] Open letter posted on Dame Evelyn Glennie Facebook page, 3 July 2020.
[79] Interview with Glennie, 12 October 2020.

Whilst Glennie's professional portfolio has always been diverse, her primary identity is that of solo multi-percussionist; finding a balance between music-making and activism – or identifying ways to combine the two – was fundamental to her work in 2020–2021. With a hectic 2020 tour schedule which included solo concerts, outdoor festivals, concerto premieres and a series of collaborative performances with Trio HLK, all of Glennie's plans to engage with audiences in a live context ceased suddenly and indefinitely with the emergence of COVID-19. Glennie's tour diary from mid-March 2020 (the initiation of the first lockdown) showed ten cancelled UK and international events. From October 2020, a more hopeful move towards postponements was observable, with four events rescheduled rather than cancelled. July 2021 marked Glennie's first live performance since the onset of the pandemic, followed in November 2021 with the delayed premiere of *The Language of Bells*. This collaborative work is a pertinent example of how the creative process was reimagined, sustained and extended during a period when live music was mediated through technology. It is a musical contemplation of an unprecedented historical moment and a statement on the imperative for creative community building.

Glennie, composer Jill Jarman, the Chelys Viol Consort and four vocalists were part of the project, which was conceived and initiated pre-COVID. Merging old and new musical sonorities and compositional processes, Jarman's early intentions were to centralize the communicative power of bells whilst reflecting upon the myriad symbolic meanings of this medium. During the exigencies of lockdown, *The Language of Bells* extended this vision to become a creative artefact of the COVID-19 experience. Given the uncertainty about the reopening of concert halls and performance sites, the most immediate solution to ensuring that the project reached the listener would be to premiere the work online; numerous musicians proceeded in this way during lockdown. Whilst Glennie contributed to a number of online initiatives, she was always clear on her view that this alternative did not offer a meaningful replacement for her touring schedule. Despite the longevity of COVID-19 restrictions, this sentiment did not alter over time. In her keynote address for the Music and Care Conference in March 2021, Glennie maintained this view:

> I felt that I wasn't getting the enjoyment by giving virtual performances. There were too many elements: was the angle of the camera right? Was the sound right – which was never right. There were too many compromises there I felt, and also people were not getting the essence of what's so important when you're with someone.[80]

[80] Evelyn Glennie (2021) Keynote Address: Music Care Conference 2021. Streamed live to delegates 17 March 2021.

188 Evelyn Glennie: Sound Creator

Therefore, *The Language of Bells* required alternative outlets to progress; the premiere would happen when live performance returned, but momentum was sustained in other ways in the interim. *The Language of Bells* became a community, a form of outreach and connection, an interdisciplinary forum, and a shared creative experience. Aligning performance with discourse and pedagogy has always been a fundamental feature of Glennie's work. She is both practitioner and philosopher, a role model advocating for the value, meaning and significance of her art; *The Language of Bells* integrated all of these elements. Connection, collaboration and interaction were the central aspirations of the project, with scheduled workshops, rehearsals and per-formances reimagined as a Creative Café and Living Sound Exhibit (both online). The Creative Café, accessible to the global community via *The Language of Bells* website, offered a means of engagement, reflection and interaction in the absence of face-to-face communication. It invited visitors to contribute to various online conversations at the composer's coffee table, musician's meeting, children's corner, artist's workshop, writer's forum and reminiscing table.

At the composer's coffee table, Jarman invited participants to embrace everyday sounds as music. Contributions included a sound sculpture con-flating bell sonorities, and a composition based on change ringing. The musician's meeting asked listeners to look for bells in unlikely places, an endeavour realised fully in the Living Sound Exhibition, a website section led by Glennie. As an instrument collector, and inventor of new percussive entities, Glennie's interest in timbre was reflected in this online exhibition, which served as an aural gallery of sounds and experiments inspired by bells. Glennie introduced some of the instruments featured in *The Language of Bells*, including bells worn by animals, African bells, tin bells and bicycle bells. These short pedagogical videos echoed outputs on Facebook during lockdown, wherein Glennie demonstrated and discussed a wide range of sound objects including egg shakers, metal log drum, paddle drums, Wasamba shakers and household items re-purposed as musical instruments (including Glennie's kitchen sink). The general public con-tributed to the Living Sound Exhibition with enthusiasm, creating bell-like sonorities with water and wine bottles, egg timers, field recordings, pipes, goblets, pans and bowls. The exhibition removed the boundary between performer and listener, with participants themselves becoming sound cre-ators and percussionists.

Whilst the Creative Café and Living Sound Gallery allowed the audi-ence to interact and engage with the project, *The Language of Bells* also needed more concrete support. In order to proceed, *The Language of Bells* undertook a crowdfunding initiative, asking the general public to

Inclusion 189

participate in both financial and creative terms. The crowdfunding target of 10,000 pounds was reached on 20 March 2021, following twenty-eight days of fundraising; 119 supporters contributed. Again, the sense of creating a democratic and collective emerging musical product was evident in this funding initiative, with donations linked to the opportunity to "own" parts of the composition. These ranged from 40 pounds for four bars of music to 1000 pounds for the last note or the loudest thirty seconds of the piece. With momentum maintained in the absence of live performance, *The Language of Bells* subsequently premiered at the Norfolk and Norwich Festival on 4 November 2021. A summary of the programmatic context of the composition can be read as a metaphor for the COVID-19 experience which shaped the work:

> The programme opens as the day begins, and we feel we are inside the bell, the sound drawing us into a day that starts calmly, with glimpses of monastic church life drifting across the landscape. The day goes well and the bell witnesses dancing, a wedding, and joy. Until, suddenly, the peace is shattered by a panicked alarm. Now the bell's job is to ring out a warning. As the chaos settles a period of calm and reflection follows, with the bell now bringing a feeling of sanctuary and peace. This builds to a cacophonous celebration and the day finally ends as it began, where Eastern and Western influences can be heard in a more meditative vein, drifting off, ready to start a new day with new adventures tomorrow.[81]

The premiere began with the pealing of church bells as the audience entered the venue, an acknowledgement of the traditional art of bell ringing. This juxtaposition of old and new was further reflected in the programming, where the six movements of *The Language of Bells*
were interposed with Renaissance repertoire and a multi-percussion improvisation (see Table 6).

Whilst the timbre of bells was evoked through both voice and viols in *The Language of Bells*, the solo percussion part is the most significant source of resonant effects and sonorities. Scoring included passages for crystal bells, Chinese temple bells, wrist and ankle bells, flower pots, traditional bells, toy bells and blossom bells. In microcosm, the percussionist merged old and new, tradition and innovation; the ancient sounds conjured by the crystal and temple bells coalesced with more recent inventions including bell plates and Aluphone. With emphasis on reverberation, the bell sonorities of the composition (whether traditional or newly invented)

---

[81] *The Language of Bells* (2021), online. Available from: https://www.evelyn.co.uk/evet/the-language-of-bells/ (accessed 4 July 2023).

190   *Evelyn Glennie: Sound Creator*

Table 6: Programme for *The Language of Bells* world premiere.

Composer	Work
Jill Jarman	*The Language of Bells: "Opening Bell Strikes and Chants"*
Jill Jarman	*The Language of Bells: "Awakening Part I"*
Jill Jarman	*The Language of Bells: "Awakening Part II"*
C.F. Abel (1723–1787)	*Prelude*
Evelyn Glennie	*Percussion improvisation*
Orlando Gibbons (1583–1625)	*Magnificat*
Anthony Holborne (1545–1602)	*Suite of Dances*
Michael East (1580–1648)	*Quick, Quick, Away!*
Jill Jarman	*The Language of Bells: "Alarm"*
Evelyn Glennie	*A Little Prayer*
Jill Jarman	*The Language of Bells: "In Celebration of Peace"*
Jill Jarman	*The Language of Bells: "Close of Day Bell Strikes/ Chants"*

functioned as modes of confluence uniting multiple eras, genres, cultures, faiths and rituals, an aural emblem which has accompanied all stages of human development. Art forms were also drawn together in *The Language of Bells*: the text for "Awakening Part I" was based on a poem by Abi Hicks commissioned for the project which used nature imagery to anticipate the "Grand Awakening". The vibraphone in this movement was engaged in word painting (again a reference to the conventions of the Renaissance repertoire which framed *The Language of Bells*); Glennie's annotations directly reference extracts of the poem to denote the role of the instrument. Bars 1 and 2 are "the breath within the breath"; the ornamentation of bar 3 is "the orchestra of birds"; bar 5 realizes "the unfurling leaf"; repeated triplet figurations in bars 10–11 are "wild and free", followed with a fE at the end of bar 12 representing "the sun by morning" (see Ex. 12). Supported by voices which surround the recitation of the poem, the result was a haunting yet hopeful sense of patient expectation. Performance notes at the beginning of the vibraphone score reflect this intention: "The poem is to be recited with a calm, even, soft voice. The second voice is to be shared around the other three voices, creating a 3D effect."

Though the title of the fourth movement invites a powerful musical representation using the volume and resonance of percussion, Jarman instead interpreted "Alarm" as a series of repeated (and often soft) melodic motifs

Ex. 12: Vibraphone in *"Awakening Part I"* from *The Language of Bells* (Jill Jarman).

foregrounding marimba. At a time when the world recovered from the trauma of COVID-19, this more delicate iteration of a warning felt appropriate. Volume and drama were instead reserved for the final movement, which ends with all performers playing bell plates (a triangular metal plate with clappers), culminating in a "celebratory cascade of bells". The sense of a musical language with the capacity to connect and restore the listener was realized on both an aural and visual scale, with the ensemble functioning simultaneously as bell-ringers and percussionists.

From the earliest stages of her career, Glennie has been aware of the fact that her social and cultural role is larger than that of a pioneering performer. First and foremost, the musician is a human being, a member of society, and a part of the local and global community. Whilst COVID-19 presented innumerable challenges, *The Language of Bells* offers one example of music as a form of catharsis. It was a collaborative project which served as a creative artefact reflecting the COVID-19 journey. To this end, it seems particularly appropriate that the resonance and sonority of bells

192 *Evelyn Glennie: Sound Creator*

were the central feature. Transcending time, era, genre, culture, faith and class, the bell symbolizes a sense of community, ritual, celebration and hope. As Glennie states: "Resonance is the connector of all things."[82]

Concluding Thoughts

Inclusion means a willingness to embrace difference and diversity as attributes; it demands an effort to promote integration and equality in any number of contexts. Contemporary society must always address this issue; practices, conventions and behaviours of the past need to be viewed from new perspectives as society evolves and progresses. The art of performance can contribute much to these larger discussions, heightened in the discipline of solo multi-percussion, which has already fostered inclusive creative spaces within and beyond art music. All musical experiences are part of a reciprocal relationship between creator, performer and listener. The social responsibility of the artist is rooted in the fundamental fact that music-making, engagement and participation are parts of an interactive and dynamic communal ecosystem; the ethics of community are also the ethics of music.

It is overly simplistic to reduce Glennie's contributions to inclusive practices in relation only to her experiences as a deaf performer. Glennie has supported social inclusion on many more levels, using the foundations of holistic and engaged listening to promote discourse in relation to ageism, environmental issues, class and education provision. The overarching message in Glennie's philanthropic work is that difference is not disadvantage; though this can be applied in the context of disability rights it is also equally relevant in relation to many other issues of injustice and discrimination in contemporary society, including gender stereotyping. Centralizing the curative and productive impact of music-making has resonance in relation not only to improving the status of the arts in society but in creating a world where inclusion is applied in all contexts. Glennie's identity as sound creator has transcended the boundaries of conventional performance contexts to position music as a form of cultural commentary, adding a new dimension to the potential applications of solo percussion, and re-evaluating the role of the artist in contemporary society. She has subsequently expanded the relevance of collaboration, creativity and experimentation into a range of philanthropic contexts. The connective message in all instances is the fact that active listening allows people to recognize that difference is an attribute, not a disadvantage; the instrumental democracy of multi-percussion serves as a metaphor for this conviction.

[82] Interview with Glennie, 12 October 2020.

5

"I hope the seeds I have sown will be taken up by those who follow me."

Legacy: A Series of New Beginnings

Often, the legacy of a person is considered posthumously; the term is associated with the details of a last will and testament and implies the process of reflecting on a completed journey. Given the length of Glennie's career, she is in the relatively unique position of curating her own legacy whilst simultaneously continuing to evolve and diversify; The Evelyn Glennie Collection is collating the physical artefacts of a life in music even as The Evelyn Glennie Foundation plans for the future, continuing Glennie's mission to teach the world to listen (see Fig. 12).

Glennie's legacy is multi-faceted, retained for posterity in the commissions, recordings, images and awards that represent more than five decades

Fig. 12: The Evelyn Glennie Foundation (established 2023).

in the industry. Her presence in the cultural zeitgeist is preserved in eclectic and diverse creative outputs that foreground the role of multi-percussion as a fluid and expansive mode of musical communication. In much the same way that silence is a potent connective between receiving and anticipating sound, many of Glennie's most significant contributions are found in the spaces between recordings, awards and scores. Live performances are destined to be lost to time, powerful precisely because they serve as singular and transient experiences which will never be repeated in the same way again. Even if captured as recordings, the frisson and connection of embodied engagement is changed; the energy of the live event can only truly happen once:

> I never try to remember what I played beforehand, which mallets I used, or anything like that. It is all about what is happening right *now* in this space. That is what I relate to. Once it's done, it's done. Once recordings are made, they're over. There's no referring back to them, for interpretation or sound or anything. The performance is done in that space of time, with that particular frame of mind at that moment. Then I move on. That gives me the feeling, as a performer, that every piece of music that I play is like a new piece of music.[1]

Western art music history is a narrative of the composer, whose creative artefacts are distilled with clarity on the written score. In the absence of equally definitive evidence, performers are either relegated to footnotes or instead assume an almost mythological status. Sometimes, it is both. Liszt was condemned by many critics as a self-indulgent showman even while concert halls were filled to capacity for his recitals. Paganini was assumed to have made a deal with the devil to heighten his skills, imbuing his violin performances with an almost mystical energy. Even with Glennie's extensive discography, she too has generated various myths as a virtuosic performer: the extraordinary skills of the virtuoso imprinted with triumph over deafness, the assumption that other senses are heightened in the absence of auditory perception, incredulity at the physical prowess of a petite and softly spoken female performer, and fascination with the transition of the orchestral other from rear to centre-stage. Given that multi-percussion is an evolution based on collection and expansion, these myths are accommodated in the narrative of the discipline. They are also challenged, reframed and changed over time. There is little question that

---

[1]   Evelyn Glennie in Ian Brennan (2023) *Evelyn Glennie: "Sound can be the most subtle thing, but the body does need to slow down in order to connect with it"* (online). Available from: https://tapeop.com/interviews/154/evelyn-glennie/ (accessed 8 May 2023).

Glennie seeks to surprise, enthral, mystify and confound in the moment of live performance. The feeling of spontaneity, presence and freedom intrinsic to Glennie's style might feel like a form of magic, but it is the culmination of extraordinary commitment and relentless effort; the virtuosic performer is made, not born.

Galton, one of the first academics to explore the concept of genius, observes that musical virtuosity can only be ascribed to those who have "ability combined with zeal and with capacity for hard labour".[2] It is also important to remember that virtuosity means more than skill, technique, stage presence and charisma. A passion and vocation, for Glennie it is the opportunity to tell a story through sound, to make a profound connection, to avoid categorization or stasis, to embrace challenge, to take risks and to experiment. In order to reach the listener, the performer must foster an ongoing sense of curiosity and enthusiasm for their art. For Glennie, this is given voice in the many commissions and premieres which align the creative vision of the composer with the interpretation of the performer. She has also searched for more definitive experiences of being present in the moment of performance, acquiescing to the unpredictability of improvisation. As with any performer, she thinks of the needs of the audience, but is also keen to continue her own personal journey of discovery.

Glennie's legacy as a performer will supersede her career in physical artefacts, but it will also resonate elsewhere – in the interdisciplinary and post-genre directions of contemporary music, in the balance between musicianship and entrepreneurship, and in the intersection of performing and listening. A legacy provides the recordings and scores, but it is perhaps more important to retain the ethos which made all of them possible, the attitude of curiosity and the spirit of adventurism which brought them to fruition. Glennie's contribution to the evolution of solo multi-percussion begins with performance but extends to the professional identities of sound creator and expert listener, roles which are determinedly open to evolution, metamorphosis and innovation. These paths are intentionally undefined and therefore essentially limitless in terms of scope and duration. This chapter will consider the confluence of past and present from a number of perspectives, examining works and projects which reference legacy, history and innovation simultaneously. It is both a conclusion and an introduction, given that Glennie's work continues to evolve and diversify.

---

[2] Francis Galton (1892) *Hereditary Genius: An Inquiry Into Its Laws and Consequences.* London: Macmillan, p. 33.

Classic Literature Meets Multi-Percussion: *Troilus and Cressida* (2018)

Glennie's work as a composer offers a defined and timeless means of providing the next generation of performer and listener with documents intended to invite subsequent interpretations and experiences. Many of her publications are pedagogical in nature or provide accessible repertoire for recital performance, whilst more lucrative engagements for media and the film industry support and consolidate the voice of multi-percussion in the larger cultural zeitgeist. Glennie's 2018 collaboration with the Royal Shakespeare Company (RSC) posited a new opportunity, integrating percussive sonorities into the established milieu of classic literature. Old meets new in the soundscapes which elucidate Glennie's reading of the words, sentiments and imagery of Shakespeare as part of an interdisciplinary interpretation of *Troilus and Cressida*:

> This is my first time writing for theatre. It's a whole other world. It's as though one is in a time capsule. It's also another way of thinking musically due to the many other elements associated with this medium, such as the spoken word, movement, set, lighting, costumes and so on. It has been a fantastic experience and a huge learning curve.[3]

Much intellectual energy has been expended in analysis and discussion of *Troilus and Cressida*, first published in 1609. It does not subscribe to the conventions of Shakespearian comedy or tragedy and therefore occupies an uneasy space between the two in a sometimes confusing alignment of humour and despair. It is history, legend and fiction, a love story set against the tumult of war. There is no agreed thematic construct, with various positions adopted in this respect: is it about time? Politics? Love? The futility of enmity? In many ways, it seems best to approach *Troilus and Cressida* from the same perspective that one is invited to engage with any solo multi-percussion performance, accepting the unpredictability and diversity of the narrative trajectory. As noted by Shakespearian scholar J.C. Oates, "the play is a classic monument to ambiguity".[4] Whilst not yet classic, the same point could be made about the eclectic sphere of multi-percussion. Artistic director Greg Doran dedicated this 2018 production to his predecessor John Barton, a hugely significant figure in the early development of the

---

[3] Evelyn Glennie (2018) Music Interview – Dame Evelyn Glennie, *Yorkshire Evening Post*, 2 November 2018.

[4] J.C. Oates (1966) The Ambiguity of Troilus and Cressida, *Shakespeare Quarterly*, 17 (2), p. 150.

Royal Shakespeare Company, who first staged the work in 1960. Doran's production notes embrace the uncertainties of the work:

> Is it comical? Tragical? Historical? Mythical? Political? Formal? Naturalistic? Psychological? Metaphysical? What should the general tone be? Cynical? Romantic? Obscene? Homeric? Medieval? Elizabethan? A bit of each? Intellectual? Poetic? Absurdist? In fact, it's a mixture of all these: that's Shakespeare's point. He paints a picture of life in which all these extremes exist.[5]

The Royal Shakespeare Company commission music for every production, with an archive of over four hundred scores ranging from those intended to emulate the sounds of Elizabethan theatre to more experimental compositions designed to complement innovations in scenography and style. For Doran, live music in *Troilus and Cressida* offered the possibility of bringing clarity to the meanings embedded in the text whilst also creating layers of connection in the spaces between dialogue. The score, by Glennie and co-composer/sound engineer Dave Price, served as a sonic thread and became a non-verbal character. To some extent, the contemporary sonorities of multi-percussion evoked the Greek chorus, passing comment on the moods and actions taking place centre-stage. Glennie and Price composed the score during the rehearsal period, participating in acting workshops, watching scenery and costume designs evolve, and engaging in many conversations with the director about the potential meaning of words, actions and events. The music was intended to offer an organic and direct response to the convergence of theatrical elements:

> Once he [Doran] started acting the scenes out, I was just like a fly on the wall, and it was really interesting. I was just writing down some ideas, and Dave was writing down a few ideas, and we did a few sessions here [Cambridgeshire office] and recorded all sorts of bits. That was how we began building the score and then obviously talking to Greg, talking to the crew and meeting the actors and actresses was amazing. They really saw the score being built during the whole process.[6]

The central source of antagonism in *Troilus and Cressida* is between the Trojans and the Greeks, with the play beginning seven years into the siege of Troy. These two factions were represented by contrasting musical worlds. At times, their respective sonorities coalesced and merged in beautiful synchronicity; in times of conflict, they were separate and opposing

---

[5] Royal Shakespeare Company (2018) Programme, *Troilus and Cressida*.
[6] Interview with Glennie, 27 June 2023.

forces. As geographies, relationships and events changed, these timbral leitmotifs distinguished levels of interaction, conflict and resolution: "The Trojans' world is more refined, with larger phrases that are more sophisticated, harmonic, and organised. The Greeks' world has harder sounds, is more 'bitty', more chaotic and less refined."[7]

The Trojan world is often melodic, featuring vibraphone and Aluphone; it is resonant and shimmering (as in "Cressida's Theme", Ex. 13). As the aggressors, the music of the Greeks is appropriately powerful, with auxiliary percussion and abrasive timbres the defining features. "Greek Sennet" opens with a multi-drum pattern supported by deep timpani; distorted electric guitar fosters this sense of intensity and the interlude ends with an unsettling, wavering male voice.

This RSC production centralized the role of music by bringing it into the frame; musicians are often part of the action in these productions, but the visual appeal of percussion in terms of instrumentation and gesture make their role particularly prominent. Positioned on balconies overlooking the action and later moving on-stage to perform, the four percussionists were part of the world of the play. Actors also became musicians, creating sounds by striking props and by their movements between intentionally resonant platforms; the stage was a living percussion instrument: "We want people to think that they are literally 'in' a percussion instrument, you know. They're not just creating the percussive sounds, but they are the instrument; they are the sound."[8]

The first RSC score to centralize multi-percussion, this innovation was accompanied by two other firsts: casting the play with an equal gender ratio (matched in the percussion section with Sarah Chatt, Miriam Kitchener, Tim Farmer and Kevin Waterman) and featuring the first d/Deaf actor in a main-stage production. Charlotte Arrowsmith, in the role of prophet Cassandra, signed the words of Shakespeare to charismatic effect.

The music merged onstage percussion with a backing track, the result of several improvised sessions at Glennie's Cambridgeshire studio captured by Price. Glennie features on the recording but did not perform in the theatre. Offstage, the ensemble was augmented by keyboard, singer, wind player (including the double-reed duduk of Armenian origin) and electric

---

[7] Evelyn Glennie (2018) Percussionist Evelyn Glennie: Listen – Immersive Sound Opens Up Amazing Theatrical Possibilities, *The Stage* (online), 19 October 2015. Available from: https://www.thestage.co.uk/opinion/percussionist-evelyn-glennie-listen--immersive-sound-opens-up-amazing-theatrical-possibilities (accessed 11 May 2023).

[8] Evelyn Glennie (2018) *Sounds of War* (video). Documentary screened during interval of live screening, 14 November 2018.

Ex. 13: "Cressida's Theme" from *Troilus and Cressida* (Evelyn Glennie and Dave Price).

guitar. Percussive sonorities dominated throughout, and their presence was intrinsic to the scenography. Hanging metallic installations (including the largest of three Barimbulums made for the performance) hovered above an extensive range of instruments, pipes, metal barrels, wooden boxes and exhaust pipes. The multi-percussion stations were literal walls of sound and metaphorical representations of division and siege. Scoring was unapologetically noisy and chaotic in many instances, fitting the battles and adversity of the narrative, but also reflecting Glennie's interest in embodied listening: "It's important for me that many of the sounds in *Troilus and Cressida* are felt throughout the whole body, which is why the types of live sounds played and the many pre-recorded sounds we made from my home are extreme in dynamics and frequency range."[9]

Whilst never equal to the experience of being present in the Stratford-upon-Avon theatre, the decision to screen the performance live on 14 November 2018 is indicative of efforts by the RSC to ensure that Shakespeare is accessible to all. Likewise, the pre-show advertising demonstrated outreach in various educational initiatives including tours, school presentations and an interactive website. As the sounds of the expectant audience in Stratford reverberated throughout the space, the sense of anticipation was shared. The prologue was delivered as Helen descended in a metal globe, accompanied by the scraping and striking of cymbals underlain by sustained vocal tones and haunting bells. This delicate calm was interrupted by aggressive drums and intermittent reverberations as Troilus and Pandarus entered the stage. As Troilus bemoaned his weakness for battle as a consequence of the softness of love, the drums acquiesced to a repetitive bongo rhythm and the striking of a bell; the sensations of war and love co-exist in the score. Mirroring Troilus' vacillations between valour and submission, there was a jarring juxtaposition between delicacy and foreboding in the music. This sense of unease, of two sides opposed, is integral to the music of the play.

Responding to the directive "sound alarum", a harsh whistle and blaring horn follow the exit of Pandarus; this entry felt invasive, intruding on the ponderings of Troilus and heightening his sense of inner conflict. He answered the percussionists "Peace, you ungracious clamours! Peace, rude sounds!" As his Trojan friend Aeneas entered there was a fleetingly beautiful moment of warm bells and flute, but as their dialogue continued (and the news became bleak) there was an increasing sense of insistence; wailing guitar, beating drums, deeper and more resonant vibrations accompanied their discussion.

---

[9]   Glennie (2018) Percussionist Evelyn Glennie: Listen – Immersive Sound Opens Up Amazing Theatrical Possibilities.

The music is more than sound effects, often rippling beneath the spoken word and subtly colouring the subtext (to intimate danger or to reflect latent emotion). Interludes emerged as almost inaudible vibrations which gradually intensified with added layers of sound; they were an energy and a presence before they became a musical structure. Abrupt silences and jarring entries were also key to maintaining a sense of anticipation when the music was juxtaposed with dialogue, with the eye drawn as much to the preparations and movements of the percussionists as to events onstage. At times, Glennie and Price responded directly to events, with sonorities for secondary textual directives such as "alarums" or "sound a retreat" provided. The waterphone called the audience to attention for the entry of Ajax and Thersites in Act 2 Scene 1, and chaotic multi-timbral stumbles accompanied their ongoing scuffle, the music amplifying the energy of their movements. The later battle was also appropriately noisy and literal in evoking the sounds of war, ominously anticipated by a soft timpani roll. When Cassandra entered in Act 2 Scene 2, filled with anxiety and a sense of frantic fear, she repeatedly signed "Cry, Trojans, cry!" Her foreboding warning was articulated by repeated drum patterns and rattling metal wherein it felt as though the space (and the world of the play) was literally coming apart. Anticipating the attack of the Greek army, abrasive sonorities again denoted this external threat.

Though some moments demanded the symbolism of alarms or distant noises, there was a conscious effort to avoid the obvious; Shakespeare's references to trumpets and music were not always realized in the scoring:

> It's interesting when you read a play because the initial reaction is to read the words and think how you can then put that into sound and that's often quite an obvious thing to do so if you read something like "the trumpets are now sounding" or whatever, you imagine [trumpet effect from Glennie]. That's the last thing we want to do, so how else can we create that feeling of a trumpet?[10]

In response to Pandarus asking "What music is this?" in Act 3 Scene 1, the score answered with a rebellious squealing guitar entry. Instead of creating the beautiful music to which Shakespeare's characters allude, Glennie and Price anticipated the subsequent efforts of Pandarus. His comical song (delivered with musical ineptitude but wholehearted passion) was accompanied by a playful melody reminiscent of carousel music featuring kalimba, Aluphone and the vibrations of small instruments on a large timpani head.

---

[10] Glennie (2018) *Sounds of War*.

In many instances, there were multiple timbres converging from different parts of the theatre – on balconies, offstage and through speakers. When a single instrument was foregrounded, it therefore served as a call to pay close attention. As Ulysses spoke in Act 1 Scene 3, two percussionists played the Aluphone, an aurally and visually beautiful moment as they *crescendo* and *accelerando* to sudden silence when he says "Take but degree away, untune that string, and hark what discord follows." Again, the temptation to follow this statement with cacophony was not considered. The decimations of war, as discussed by Ulysses, instead lent itself to stark silence. Abrasive noises which evoked squeals of anguish accompanied the entrance of a Trojan messenger later in the scene, yet the call from Aeneas "Trumpets blow loud!" was not realized in the music. Bells were the only sonority heard as Pandarus exited in Act 3 Scene 1, arousing the warmth of emotion to follow in the dialogue between Paris and Helen. Again, the audience was offered a clear musical cue to establish the action to come. Metallic sounds were the focal point as props descended from overheard to frame Troilus in a matching visual frame for a brief monologue in Act 3 Scene 2; the symbolism was both visual and audible.

There is little action in *Troilus and Cressida*, with the lens instead focused on relationships between characters and discussion of events which take place beyond the world of the play. To some extent, the percussionists provided movement and energy where it would otherwise not exist; they became the moving frame of war and division which surrounds and informs the narrative trajectory. The collective momentum of the four percussionists who moved dynamically throughout the performance space was reflective of the collaborative energy between Price and Glennie during the compositional process. In the intermission documentary *Sounds of War*, Price notes that free improvisation was the starting point: "Quite often she'll start playing and absolutely brilliant material will sort of emerge from that very naturally in quite an organic way."[11] Much of this improvisation was retained on the backing track.

There was also space for the percussionists to improvise during the performance, selecting their own sounding objects at times and creating their own instinctive effects at others. Freedom to respond to events onstage also extended to the full ensemble; under the exchange between Pandarus and Cressida early in Act 1 Scene 2, percussion, wind and guitar had short sections for improvisation. Given the multi-sensory nature of percussion as a potent onstage presence, each degree of separation removes some of the energy felt keenly in the live experience. Watching the event live in the

[11] Ibid.

cinema retained an element of shared engagement; the subsequent DVD release still allows the viewer to watch the movements and non-speaking roles of the percussionists as they dance, strike and reposition themselves between multi-percussion stations.

The CD is perhaps best suited for those already conversant in the sights and sounds of the original production. A selection of speeches (both with and without music) and a number of instrumental interludes offer evocations of the live performance, but these are somewhat disparate in the absence of the full text and score. Nonetheless, the CD is interesting for another reason: it also includes a number of compositions commissioned for the original 1960 RSC production. Humphrey Searle's interpretation of "Pandarus' Song" is a key means of demonstrating the contrasting aesthetic approaches taken then and now. The cacophony and beauty of multi-percussion is instead replaced by Searle with an ensemble intended to reference the sounds of Renaissance theatre; guitar or lute and recorder accompany a melodically simple and memorable rendition of the love song. Occasional dissonances function as forms of word-painting (for example on the word "cry") but otherwise, the song is pleasant and succinct. The 2018 music represents an aural artefact of a production instead evoking a dystopian world of metal and the detritus of war.

When a collaboration is successful, it feels organic and natural; the 2018 RSC interpretation of *Troilus and Cressida* achieves this. Even in the absence of action in Shakespeare's narrative, the world comes alive in a visceral way. Words, with their intrinsic patterns and rhythms, are already a soundscape; Glennie's score is a manifestation of the latent musicality of Shakespeare's language and imagination.

Music as Historical and Social Commentary: *Gernika 85* (2022)

Glennie has always been associated with "firsts" and this term often precedes descriptions of her professional identity, performances and creative outputs. Commissioning and premiering new music is an enduring feature of her career. Aitor Etxebarria's *Gernika 85* demonstrates the fact that this process proceeds with vigour, being one of seven 2022 commissions; Glennie's list of firsts is not yet retrospective. *Gernika 85* united past and present on multiple levels: it created new paths for percussionists in a canon already populated by many of Glennie's commissions; it recalled the orchestral origins of percussion as militaristic colour whilst exploring new techniques and sounds; its programme was a historical event denoted through contemporary compositional approaches; it was a commentary on war with resonant implications for the current reverberations of conflict.

It was acoustic and electronic, instrumental and vocal, minimalist and expansive, sound and vision, an ambitious commission which once more extended the remit of the multi-percussionist. It was also indicative of Glennie's intention to support emerging artists, aligning an established performer with a young composer creating his first orchestral score.

Historical events written on a page can feel abstract, detached and surreal. Reducing the moments which change humanity to lists and dates rarely possesses affective power. Art has the capacity to make these events visceral, experiential and alive, to revisit history from an emotive perspective. So often, music has served this function to chilling effect: the marches of war in the symphonies of Shostakovich are disturbingly ominous in their insistence and volume; the cannons which fire in Tchaikovsky's *1812 Overture* inspire nationalist fervour far beyond the pride of Russia. Music as a statement on national identity is inherently communal; from anthems to symphonic poems which present soundscapes in honour of people and places, there is a power in this medium to unite and inspire. Glennie's own Scottish heritage is a source of pride, reflected in her commissioned tartan, memories recounted in her autobiography of a childhood speaking the local Celtic dialect, Doric (incorporated into the solo percussion part of the commissioned concerto *Trance o Nicht* by Sally Beamish in 1991), and in the fact that she plays the bagpipes (scored in Stewart Wallace's 1999 commission for solo multi-percussion *The Cheese and the Worms*). Retaining a sense of connection to people and place is often embedded in the identity of the artist.

Etxebarria was born in Guernica and speaks the Basque language; *Gernika 85* is a keenly patriotic work reflecting his heritage as a member of this small but passionate community. Commemorating the eighty-fifth anniversary of the bombing of the region, a controversial air raid conducted as part of the Spanish Civil War, music became a living memory. There has never been agreement on the total number of fatalities suffered as a result of the bombing, but the town was decimated and many lives were lost. Picasso paid tribute in the 1937 painting *Guernica*, created in the months following the catastrophe. His tableau is both stark and complex; multiple figures in various poses and states of agony overlap, but the colour palette is in greyscale. Etxebarria's music, whilst not directly influenced by Picasso, achieved a similar musical effect. At times, the work maintains a minimalist stasis, and at others multiple musical motifs and timbres merge and intersect. It is difficult to present art which articulates the realities of war without resorting to obvious imagery or sound effects. In many ways, the challenge is exacerbated when working with the medium of multi-percussion, whose loud power can so easily become a direct representation of the sonorities of bombing and gunfire. Etxebarria did not conceive the work as a concerto, which immediately alleviated the potential positioning of the percussionist as a symbol of war: "I don't look for something specific where you hear noises to imagine bombs or bunkers. It's more natural. There are very noisy and eccentric parts, but silence is also very important."[12]

In an interview discussing the genesis of *Gernika 85*, the composer notes that much of the inspiration was drawn from ideas for a documentary soundtrack conceived for the eightieth anniversary of the bombing (in collaboration with Glennie). Issues with funding interrupted the project, and Etxebarria subsequently contacted Glennie to reimagine their concept as an orchestral work for the eighty-fifth commemoration. The scope for *Gernika 85* was a more ambitious live successor to the atmospheric sounds and emotions generated in the earlier collaborative sessions. Choir, symphony orchestra, solo percussion, piano and electronics (played by the composer) were framed by witness testimonies (recorded for the Guernica Peace Museum), seen and heard as part of the soundscape. The only words are those of the witnesses, with the choir providing haunting syllabic ostinato patterns and onomatopoetic effects, amplifying experiences shared onscreen or intimated in the music.

The composition was not literal in its narrative, seeking instead to offer aural vignettes of the Guernica region. Divided into four movements, each was characterized by a particular mood and specific percussive sonority. The score has not yet been published (though a performance copy is retained by The Evelyn Glennie Collection) and only the first eight minutes of the premiere are available to view online.[13] *Gernika 85* is indicative of the transitory nature of the live experience, described in media promotion as "an unrepeatable concert".[14] This work is representative of the "spaces between" mentioned in the introduction to this chapter. *Gernika 85* is living art, written not only with one performer in mind but also conceived for a

---

[12] Aitor Etxebarria in Maialen Ferreira (2022) *A symphonic work with testimonies of the victims will pay tribute to Gernika on the 85th anniversary of the bombing* (online), 20 April 2022. Available from: https://www.eldiario.es/euskadi/obra-sinfonica-testimonios-victimas-homenajeara-gernika-85-aniversario-bombardeo_1_8924065.html (accessed 15 May 2023).

[13] https://www.eitb.eus/es/cultura/videos/detalle/8896601/el-compositor-aitor-etxebarria-estrena-gernika-85-proyecto-sinfonico-en-honor-a-victimas-del-bombardeo/ (accessed 15 May 2023).

[14] Aitor Etxebarria (2022) "Aitor Etxebarria Presentación Gernika 85" 85 Aniversario Del Bombardeo De Gernika (online). Available from: https://kulturagernika-lumo.eus/es/evento/gernika-85-aitor-etxebarria/ (accessed 15 May 2023).

single performance; there is a beauty in this transience, a sense that the work is written as a personal contribution to the legacy of Guernica.

In correspondence between Etxebarria and Glennie, the concert aesthetics were discussed in terms of the relationship between spoken word and music, decisions on instrumentation and the inspiration for each of the four movements. *Gernika 85* is not a work which demands the skills of a virtuosic performer, but Glennie lent her name to the project in order to support the composer, and to reflect the positive collaborative experience of their interactions. This again falls into the spaces between, a creative energy which cannot always be explained: "It's this chemistry thing again. We just got on like a house on fire and I really liked Aitor. I don't know what it is about these sorts of situations, but somehow it worked."[15]

The opening minutes are beautiful, calm and warm, beginning with sounds akin to those of an orchestra warming up. The 1937 bombing took place at 6.30 pm, shortly before sunset; the music evokes the gentleness of dusk. Fragments of melody emerge in flute and oboe, joined by French horns; musical ideas become more defined as instruments coalesce. Etxebarria and Glennie are *tacet* in the introduction, with Glennie's first entry a simple yet resonant repetition of timpani strikes on alternate beats. The multi-percussion set-up is symbolic of the lines of battle; nearest to the conductor is a vibraphone; behind this, a single timpani with various small cymbals; two timpani thereafter (where the soloist begins to play at 7'30") and tubular bells at the rear. The movement ends with the first intimation of tumult; erratic and loud rhythms emerge on timpani with a *tutti crescendo* to close the section. In the second movement, Etxebarria pairs abrasive electronic glitches with tubular bells; the latter evokes the church bells in the village of Guernica, whilst the electronic errors intimate a sense of unease. The solo line is scored, but Etxebarria is open to improvisation on tubular bells in live performance (which Glennie adds from bar 41). As with the first movement, there is a gradual *crescendo* throughout. Glennie notes on her score "bells start distant, then closer". The percussion part is atmospheric and emotive rather than technically difficult, with a repeated ostinato pattern focused on D minor and C minor triads.

In the third movement, the percussionist once more performs an ostinato, articulating the rhythm of the *zortziko* – an irregular five-beat dance rhythm associated with the Basque region – from bar 153 to the end. This pattern serves a dual function: it honours the folk music of Guernica, but its insistence and growing intensity intimates the drums of war. Though the snare drum begins *mp*, Glennie's annotation on the mood of the movement

---

[15] Interview with Glennie, 27 June 2023.

(always written at the beginning in rehearsal scores) states "brutal, wild, savage". The final movement is reflective. Once more the soloist performs an ostinato; in this instance, a two-bar sequence of vibraphone octaves is integrated into the solemn and slow finale (from bar 102). Voices enter with haunting sound effects emanating from various parts of the choir from bar 124, and the movement ultimately ends with a sense of hope and peace.

Gernika 85 is representative of a chronology wherein culture has intersected with history in a potent manner, transitioning from the visual response of Picasso to the words of author Bernardo Atxaga (which inspired the earlier documentary project, *Markak*) to the culminating experience of *Gernika 85*. The premiere, preceded earlier in the day by a chamber arrangement performed in front of Picasso's *Guernica*, was unique in every sense; as with every live event, it will never be heard in the same way again, and may never be performed with full resources at any point in the future.

Not all of Glennie's commissions are published; not all are performed. Part of the experimental journey of innovation involves success and failure. Ambition must never acquiesce to practicality; seeing large-scale works performed in the wake of COVID-19 is particularly important, regardless of whether or not such commissions become part of the multi-percussion canon. Employing culture as a form of social activism further strengthens the significance of such work. Music shapes the narrative arc of everyone's life, marking seminal points, combining past, present and future, and commenting on the human condition. Continuing to promote and commission new music is a means of articulating its value and resonance.

The Nobel Prize of Music: Multi-Percussion and a Place in History

Glennie is the recipient of many awards both within and beyond the sphere of music, with acknowledgements of achievements dating from her school days to the present. Attaining recognition and respect as an individual is certainly important in terms of sustaining a career, but establishing multi-percussion as a valid profession and significant cultural presence is the most important by-product of such accolades. As would be expected, Glennie is recognized in the percussion community, with various commendations from the Percussive Arts Society, *Rhythm* magazine, *Drum!* magazine and a Sabian Lifetime Achievement Award (2006). Aligned with these discipline-specific awards, Glennie has brought solo multi-percussion into the larger musical and cultural sphere. Oftentimes these represent further firsts, including the Royal Philharmonic Society Charles Heidsieck Soloist of the Year (1991) – followed a generation later by the second percussion winner (Colin Currie, 2015) – and the Classic FM Red Award for

Fig. 13: Awards received from Her Majesty Queen Elizabeth II.

Outstanding Contribution to Classical Music (2002). Her significance in the larger zeitgeist is exemplified in more general prizes such as Scotswoman of the Decade (1990) and a *Cosmopolitan* Achievement Award (1994), which reflects the ways in which her early intersections with the media helped to create a resonant public profile. Recognized as a Dame Commander of the British Empire in 2007, this honour is the most functional of Glennie's awards, providing a globally recognized title (see Fig. 13 for Royal honours).

The Evelyn Glennie Collection has collated Glennie's various awards and certificates, ranging from music exams to honorary doctorates. Few are displayed, with a narrow glass cabinet offering the most obvious evidence of successes (including two Grammys). A form of cultural power, prizes are important in terms of revenue, public profile and validating creative outputs. But in many ways, awards are more valuable to others than to the recipient, serving as an external reference point for those otherwise unfamiliar with particular artists or works. Glennie accepts accolades graciously but does not view them as summative. Instead, they are a positive impetus to advance further. In person, Glennie has a tendency to be self-deprecating. This does not infer any lack of confidence; she never undermines her own skills or vision as a performer. It is reflected more in the understated ways in which she discusses high-profile performances, seminal events, moments of significance in her career, and notable awards. Rich Harrold of Trio HLK references this modesty in the experience of recording with Glennie: "She's so down to earth, absolutely zero pretention at all. She doesn't really talk about herself at all actually, or what she's up to, unless you press her to do so. And then she just casually mentions that she's performing with the Boston Symphony tomorrow or something."[16]

In terms of mapping the minds of those who have shaped and changed the history of society and culture, the Nobel Prize remains the focal point for human achievement; music is notably absent from this lineage of innovation. Initiated in 1901, the Nobel Prize recognizes excellence in five categories (physics, chemistry, medicine, literature and peace), with a sixth in economic science added in 1969. In 1989, Stig Anderson (most famous for his work with Abba), established the Polar Music Prize; envisioned as the seventh Nobel, the intention was to recognize the capacity of music to change the world. With two recipients per year, the first Polar Music Prize (1992) was awarded to Sir Paul McCartney and the Balkan states (to support and recognize their rich musical traditions). This eclectic pairing is indicative of the determinedly universal aspirations of the prize. From composers to performers associated with many genres, the winners are representative of the rich diversity of contemporary music. In 2015, Glennie and Emmylou Harris joined this lineage. As the first percussion winner, the discipline itself was also acknowledged on the world stage.

The press release announcing the 2015 recipients was presented as a series of musical montages interposed with interviews.[17] Glennie's first words are indicative of an impetus to continue her work: "Music is a never-ending journey of curiosity." She later defines herself as "still a child" in relation to her exploration of percussion. The soundtrack is a non-verbal history of her career evolution, encompassing transcriptions (including Monti's *Czardas*, arranged in 1990), compositions by Glennie (*Light in Darkness* for marimba, 1997) improvisations (Sorbet No. 1 for guiro and Sorbet No. 5 for multiple auxiliary instruments, from the *Drumming* album), collaborations ("My Spine" and "Oxygen", recorded in 1997 with Björk) and commissions (*Concerto for Solo Percussion and Chamber Orchestra* by Richard Rodney Bennett, 1992). Glennie's enthusiasm for experimentation is genuine and engaging; noting that "everything is special", she improvises sounds to represent Sweden (home of both the Nobel and Polar prizes), introduces the Aluphone, displays her first snare drum and strikes various instruments as she passes. The commentary addresses career achievements and firsts, the subject of profound deafness, and Glennie's larger social mission to help

[16] Interview with Richard Harrold, 23 March 2023.
[17] Polar Music Prize (2015) *2015 Laureate Evelyn Glennie: Announcement Video* (video online). Available from: https://www.polarmusicprize.org/laureates/evelyn-glennie (accessed 22 May 2023).

210 *Evelyn Glennie: Sound Creator*

the world to listen. Insights into more personal details enrich the narrative of her professional development. Glennie identifies "a slightly stubborn streak" in her personality, recounting rebellion against the dismissive attitude of her first audiologist, challenging the ableist barriers imposed by the Royal Academy of Music at her first audition and rejecting early requests to position instruments at the rear of the orchestra for concerto premieres.

Given Glennie's prolific performing career, it seems at first strange to see her positioned as a member of the audience for the Polar Music Prize. This awards ceremony has established a precedent whereby the celebratory concert does not involve the participation of recipients (with the exception of their acceptance speech), an interesting means of allowing them to experience the event without the pressures and logistics of performing. Whilst this seems at first incongruous, a potentially unsettling inference that this award informally represents an ending of sorts, Glennie took an entirely different view: "It was great. That, to me, was one of the major things that made it so enjoyable was not having to worry about playing, equipment, all that sort of thing. That was great, really special."[18] In the video press release, there is an honesty about the difficulty of the profession, with Glennie noting that she rarely enjoys her own performances, a fascinating perspective on the fact that the work of a musician never truly feels complete. This also infers a rationale for her views on awards less as defining moments and more as brief opportunities for reflection: "Every type of recognition is a time for you to pause, reflect, just see where the land lies, where you're at with your journey as it were. And it's given me that, sort of drive and confidence to just think just 'ok, just keep going, keep going."[19] With this in mind, there is a logic in the Polar Music Prize offering performers the opportunity to experience one night in the concert hall from a different perspective.

For the 2015 award ceremony percussion was a central sonority throughout. At times it was foregrounded in direct homage to Glennie's work (with performances of Maki Ishii's *13* by Mika Takehara, John Cage's *Credo in Us* by the percussionists of the Philharmonic and a vibraphone medley played by jazz musician Mattias Ståhl), but it was also a consistent presence in the music acknowledging the legacy of Harris. Percussion was focal in all of the orchestral interludes, and opened the ceremony with a snare drum roll anticipating the national anthem, followed by a medley of past winners necessitating drum kit, timpani, vibraphone, tubular bells and congas. The 2014 winner Peter Sellars read a citation for Glennie, which he executed

[18] Interview with Glennie, 27 June 2023.
[19] Polar Music Prize (2015) *2015 Laureate Evelyn Glennie: Announcement Video.*

with passion and clarity (to facilitate lip-reading). His words were powerful and moving, offering a concise appraisal of Glennie's contribution to the evolution of music: "Evelyn took a step forward on behalf of the human race in the most beautiful way. Most music in the world is percussion music and Evelyn brought that into European Western culture in the most exhilarating manner and she defied all odds in doing it."[20]

Glennie's acceptance speech was interposed with close-ups of her two guests (her mother Isobel and her first percussion tutor Ron Forbes). Their attendance was reflective of the theme of Glennie's words, focused on gratitude for those who helped her to succeed on a lifelong journey in sound. The fact that the Polar Music Prize Ceremony presents recipients with a living legacy of predecessors is a form of musical appreciation in keeping with the theme of Glennie's words. This is both beautiful and poignantly nostalgic. The working life of a musician is destined to pass, so there is a sense of finality; but there is also a celebratory reassurance in knowing that music will always live on. The Polar Music Prize offers a montage of a life in music; for Glennie, three distinct but co-existent stages are discernible when reflecting on her work to date. In each, new creative identities are added to those which precede them.

In the first stage of Glennie's career the focus was on attracting attention to solo multi-percussion, with high-profile premieres and ambitiously expansive commissions allowing virtuosity to be foregrounded. The primary goal was to validate the relevance of multi-percussion in the cultural zeitgeist. Glennie became a source of fascination as both an extraordinary musician and a deaf performer. At this stage, Glennie avoided discourse on hearing (as far as was possible), seeking to elude narratives of overcoming or the equally damaging inference that deafness enhanced her public appeal. The second stage pertained to career maturation and the evolution of a more extensive professional identity as sound creator, with Glennie freed to explore eclectic collaborations, improvisation and interdisciplinary projects. With multi-percussion becoming a recognizable and increasingly popular instrumental idiom, attention moved towards more personally rewarding musical projects. The virtuosity of stage one continued to be a defining feature of Glennie's career, but this was now joined by more instinctive and process-focused outputs. Sound creation was characterized as an accessible and inclusive creative space, unburdened with the conventions and complexities of virtuosity. Reflection and consolidation are key to the third stage, wherein the accumulation of prior learning and experiences allowed Glennie to identify as both teacher (in the broadest sense of the

---

[20] Ibid.

term) and expert listener. Music remains central, but passion for sound creation and engaged listening extend to new settings. Glennie's first stage validated multi-percussion; the third stage contextualizes the larger social responsibility of the musician.

Awards are themselves signposts to various stages of an artist's career, and a means of ensuring a place in history. But the very fact that Glennie has received so many is testament to the fact that accolades are never definitive; they highlight achievements but can never hope to fully encompass what it means to live an artistic vocation. Both fame and success are dangerously reductive, acknowledging only the most obvious signs of achievement; the more important legacy is to ensure that subsequent generations continue with the same passion and momentum as their predecessors.

Looking Back and Moving Forward: The Evelyn Glennie Collection

In a section of the interview for the Polar Music Prize laureate announcement, Glennie was asked about her extra-musical passions. She named two, visiting antique shops and metal detecting, and it is not coincidental that both are concerned with searching, finding and accumulating objects. This interest in collecting is a trait shared by many percussionists, often functioning as both professional necessity and personal obsession. The percussionist amasses instruments for use in performance and experimentation, adding their own inventions and prototypes in order to find the right sound for a particular work or creative direction. As a result, they construct both an internal catalogue of favoured timbres and an external world of physical artefacts. Central to The Evelyn Glennie Collection are more than three thousand instruments, inventions and repurposed objects, but these tools of the percussionist are supplemented with many other physical artefacts including newspaper clippings, faxes, correspondence, photos, costumes, diaries, financial documentation, rehearsal recordings, programmes and posters saved for posterity.

The performing artist today creates an archive by default, given the rise of digital marketing, online performances, audience phone recordings and downloadable materials. Collaborations, creative decisions, contracts, programmes and appearances are documented primarily through email and social media, constructing a timeline which can be reassembled with relative ease. Prior to the twenty-first century, this was not the case; programmes and posters retained by Glennie are likely one of only a handful which remain to denote repertoire choices, venues and performance history. As noted by head archivist Caroline Thompson, the rarest resources are particularly special:

Legacy: A Series of New Beginnings   213

The key finds are the ones that you can't get by googling, and that are written in Evelyn's hand: the letters that she wrote that we found in her mum's attic, or the letters that have been written to her that you can read between the lines how it affected her. It really helps to paint the picture of how she managed to go from quite a rural farm in Aberdeenshire to solo percussionist.[21]

Glennie's career spans the evolution from written correspondence to faxes and email, from vinyl and tape to CD and digital download, and from promotional posters to social media advertising. Glennie belongs both to the paper age and the digital sphere; her work simultaneously traces the development of contemporary solo multi-percussion and the changing nature of the music industry. Glennie's habitual collecting is crucial to facilitating a full and accurate history of her career. What is now officially referred to as The Evelyn Glennie Collection originated as a diffuse and largely disorganized selection of artefacts stored at Glennie's childhood and Cambridgeshire homes, studio and office. Glennie has taken an active role in reconstructing her own history, joined by a team of volunteer archivists who have embraced the challenge with energy and rigour. Initiated in 2016, the process has been led throughout by Caroline Thompson. In collaboration with Glennie, their work began with assigning a unique reference number to every document and artefact. For Thompson, the most logical means of creating order from the relative chaos of multiple boxes of material has been to develop a timeline, wherein categorization can be constructed on the basis of Glennie's public engagements and performances. The decision was made to begin with programmes as the focal point, with related materials then added and linked to this primary data set:

A few days of rooting around in boxes to find concert programmes revealed there were also lots of concert publicity items such as flyers, leaflets and concert series brochures, so if our unique reference number for all published concert material were to start with a 'C', it could have a second letter to indicate the type of document. Hence, 'CP' would be the start of a unique reference number for a concert programme and 'CL' would be a concert leaflet and so on. These letters were followed by six numbers to indicate the date of the performance.[22]

Although the laborious system of cataloguing seems mundane, insights into Glennie's performing career and the music industry emerged even at this early stage. Thompson found that programme information was often lacking vital details (such as date, venue or repertoire), and therefore

---

[21]   Interview with Caroline Thompson, 27 June 2023.
[22]   Interview with Caroline Thompson, 9 May 2023.

connections needed to be made with administrative materials linked to each performance. Discussion of contracts, programming, collaborations and concert schedules tended to be more specific in these documents. Even then, the life of a percussionist is established as one which demands flexibility:

> [Contracts] certainly helped to establish the date and location, but the repertoire for recitals often had to change because the instruments provided by organisers in Evelyn's very early career were not necessarily appropriate for the pieces she had planned to play, or the larger instruments she had brought with her could not be carried up the spiral staircase onto the stage and so she had to change to music that fitted with what she had at her disposal.[23]

In terms of further triangulation, Glennie's personal diaries have served as a key means of consolidating final repertoire decisions; journals dating from 1982 are intrinsic to establishing chronological accuracy.

At some point in the future, much of the collection will be digitized in order to provide a repository of primary data for further research and performance. For the moment, preservation of documents is a fundamental concern. As with the cataloguing process, Thompson consulted with various museums and archives in order to ensure the integrity of the paper materials. Acid-free bags and boxes notated where necessary with 2B pencils are the precursor to digitization, though it must be said that the physical artefacts are powerful in their capacity to evoke more visceral responses. There is an excitement in holding original programmes, which may be the only extant version thereof, or to look closely at photographs from Glennie's personal collection, those which elude the precision of marketing imagery. After adding several volunteers to the team, the process continued along several simultaneous paths, with archivists assigned to specific documents such as newspapers, albums, images, media broadcasts and clothing in order to ensure that reference numbers were not duplicated. Over time, Thompson has started to collate this information into spreadsheets linking all available papers and items pertaining to each performance or public event. The COVID-19 lockdowns presented considerable challenges, given the physical nature of the archive, but with Glennie's concert schedule suspended, she took an active role in contributing to documenting her instrument collection (see Fig. 14): "[Glennie] measured each one of the three and a half thousand, writing up a detailed description of what it looked and sounded like, where and how she got it, who made it and where."[24]

[23] Ibid.
[24] Ibid.

Fig. 14: A selection of instruments from The Evelyn Glennie Collection.

Glennie's involvement in the construction of this legacy has been fundamental; she contributes both time and information to elucidate particular performances or experiences. Several of these reflections were shared during the course of lockdown via social media, starting the process of disseminating findings with the public:

> Looking at the past has been more to do with creating "stories" from The Evelyn Glennie Collection rather than as a result of lockdown ... The timing just happened to coincide with the dramatic change in our lives ... Having the time to look back on past experiences has been rewarding and it has highlighted the types of projects that I would now like to let go and those which require continued focus. Although lockdown has brought so much uncertainty, it has also given a lot of clarity in the overall direction of what needs to be done as well as giving me a chance to listen to my body and mind in order to decide what the next part of the journey will be.[25]

---

[25] Interview with Glennie, 12 October 2020.

Whilst lists and chronologies are the essential framework of The Evelyn Glennie Collection, the intention is to bring the data to life in more meaningful ways. Two volunteers are currently translating dates, repertoire and concerts into narratives for each year of Glennie's career; Thompson has initiated tours of the collection at Glennie's Cambridgeshire studio; The Evelyn Glennie Foundation will use the archive for pedagogical and community music initiatives. A section on Glennie's website provides ongoing updates on progress, with blogs from volunteers indicating the persuasive appeal of many artefacts. What is clear from these testimonies are the many ways in which the collection is of potential interest: it is a chronology of Glennie's work and the evolution of contemporary multi-percussion, a history of shifting musical and visual aesthetics, a social and cultural map of each decade, and a source of information on the changing nature of the creative industries.

Physically connecting with the collection is an emotive and enriching experience, even for the archivists who are constantly surrounded by these materials. In an article recounting its foundations, Thompson includes her personal favourite, a 1974 programme featuring eight-year-old Glennie playing Grade 1 piano repertoire.[26] A blog by volunteer Amanda Roberts is equally enthralled by the photos evoking various stages of Glennie's career, which range from rehearsals in a student kitchen to images on the concert platform and alongside various dignitaries.[27] Volunteer Sylvia Cundell MBE contributes an entry which highlights the extent of Glennie's collecting; lanyards and stage passes, ceremonial invitations, exam certificates and quirky items of memorabilia contextualize and enhance understanding of the details and specifics which surround and precede performance at a professional level.[28] It is so easy to view the musician's work only in terms of the finished product as virtuosic performer and recording artist. The Evelyn Glennie Collection allows for a more honest and accurate account of the life of a musician, a journey which requires consistent effort, exhaustive touring, trial and error, small recitals and prestigious contracts, concepts

---

[26] Caroline Thompson (2022) *The Evelyn Glennie Collection – Gathering Momentum* (online), 29 March 2022. Available from: https://www.evelyn.co.uk/the-evelyn-glennie-collection-gathering-momentum/ (accessed 30 May 2023).

[27] Amanda Roberts (2022) *The Evelyn Glennie Collection –Picture This!* (online), 8 June 2022. Available from: https://www.evelyn.co.uk/the-evelyn-glennie-collection-picture-this/ (accessed 31 May 2023).

[28] Sylvia Cundell MBE (2023) *Variety is the Spice of Life ...* (online), 6 April 2023. Available from: https://www.evelyn.co.uk/variety-is-the-spice-of-life/ (accessed 31 May 2023).

which do not always come to fruition, critique and praise, doubt and confidence. For Cundell, this process is evinced in the archive:

> It has been a particular pleasure to work on the honours section of the collection. I was able to catalogue the material relating to the award to Evelyn of the Polar Music Prize in 2015 ... At the opposite end of the spectrum, I also catalogued the certificates and examiner's comments relating to Evelyn's very first music exams as a primary age child in Scotland – it was fascinating to see the wheel of musical achievement come full circle.[29]

A 2020 conversation between Glennie, Thompson and volunteer Rae Maynard is available on YouTube; recorded as COVID-19 restrictions eased, this is in itself a cultural artefact, with all three seated at the required distance of six feet.[30] The curiosity which Glennie maintains as a sound creator is equalled in her response to the various artefacts shown by Thompson and Maynard. The benefits of working with a living subject are also evident, with Glennie recounting personal recollections and reflections on each of the items; for every object, there is a story which Glennie notes "brings back an awful lot of memories". Thompson reads from a 1982 diary, a data set which has been invaluable in constructing the timeline of appearances, and also an important indication of the fact that Glennie's work as a performer considerably predates her rise to prominence at the end of the 1980s. Whilst instruments and scores are discussed, musical experiences are also described in reference to posters, photographs, costumes and jewellery, all creating what Thompson describes as "a social history".

From a musicological perspective, The Evelyn Glennie Collection has much more yet to offer future researchers and pedagogues. Volunteers are not drawn from professional music backgrounds (though Maynard describes herself as a "fan" in the YouTube conversation); whilst a useful means of ensuring objectivity, this means that the last materials to be catalogued are the scores. This process is beginning, with the collection retaining the only extant versions of several commissions and compositions, several of which are handwritten. Once more, it is in the space between notation and performance where the fascinations are found; Glennie's annotations and amendments are important as a means of understanding her processes, practice methodologies and personal rhetoric both prior to and during performance.

---

[29] Ibid.

[30] Evelyn Glennie (2020) *The Evelyn Glennie Collection – Volunteers* (video online), 28 July 2020. Available from: https://www.youtube.com/watch?v=9OMAzQFqiIo (accessed 5 July 2023).

218   *Evelyn Glennie: Sound Creator*

The collection is a rich repository, a life history, but also an expansive time-capsule of the evolution of the music industry over the course of several decades. Physical artefacts are always imbued with memory and meaning; the fact that Glennie is part of the archival process means that an oral history of her experience operates in direct alignment with the process of discovery and categorization: "The advantage is that you have somebody you can ask questions of. I have noticed that in casual conversation if we mention a particular instrument, or a particular piece of music, she will immediately have a story to go with it, without fail."[31]

To End at the Beginning: The Léonie Sonning Music Prize

The Léonie Sonning Music Prize was first presented to Igor Stravinsky in 1959; Denmark's most prestigious musical honour, it annually recognizes the work of a composer, musician, conductor or singer. Winners are associated primarily (though not exclusively) with art music; in 2023 Glennie became the first percussion recipient. As with the ceremony for the Polar Music Prize, musical tribute is paid to the laureate. Samba drummers moved through the outdoor courtyard as guests assembled, with call and response patterns involving all present in the process of making music. Soloists and duets of percussionists were positioned throughout the internal space of the DR Koncerthuset (Copenhagen) as attendees proceeded upstairs. A work by Søren Monrad opened the evening in the first-floor foyer with an ebullient composition for thirty-five percussion students and soloist Morten Friis (part of the Danish electronic percussion group *Safri Duo*). From the beginning, the event was a reverberating and immersive musical homage both to Glennie and to the compelling appeal of multi-percussion. The main concert positioned Glennie centre-stage, performing three works representing both personal and professional successes: her most famous concerto commission (MacMillan's *Veni, Veni Emmanuel*), an experimental, exploratory sound adventure embracing the dual identities of dramatist and virtuoso (Daugherty's *Dreamachine*), and a finale focused on the communicative power of a single auxiliary instrument (Másson's *Concert Piece* or *Konzertstück for Snare Drum and Orchestra*). In receiving the award, Glennie belongs to the history of the discipline, but in this live performance she also remains at the centre of its ongoing evolution.

The timing of this ceremony was fortuitous in terms of shaping the narrative arc of this book, as it reflects several keys themes of discourse. Glennie's early career was defined by the 1992 premiere of *Veni, Veni*

---

[31]   Interview with Caroline Thompson, 27 June 2023.

Emmanuel; diversification, experimentation and improvisation were the means by which new creative trajectories were followed, as evinced in *Dreamachine*; single auxiliary instruments, in the hands of a skilled performer, are now as compelling and musically rich as expansive set-ups or melodic material (with Másson's short work referencing Glennie's fascination with sound creation and more introspective studies of timbre). The programme itself ended at the beginning, with Másson's 1982 composition offering an example of early recital repertoire written in the year when Glennie began her studies at the Royal Academy of Music. All three works are in the relatively unique position of having retained a place in Glennie's programming long after their first performance; they are personally resonant parts of her own canon.

In a chapter called "It So Happens That Ears Have No Eyelids" from a series of philosophical ponderings by French writer Quignard, the author reflects on the inescapable nature of auditory perception. The constant presence of sound, music and noise is posited by Quignard as a fact of life which is not necessarily chosen: "The listener, in music, is not an interlocutor. He is a prey that surrenders himself to the trap."[32] In the digital age, Quignard's vitriol is prescient; music and sound are everywhere in contemporary culture, immediately accessible via digital platforms, pervading the urban environment, and saturating media in all public spaces. Attending a live performance is different because choice is involved; the listener willingly surrenders and acquiesces to the experience. The focus is on embracing the very fact that sound surrounds, immerses and infiltrates every part of our being. Glennie has been positioned in various commissions as narrator, storyteller, conjurer, magician, shaman, goddess and queen, all of which pertain to the fact that the art of multi-percussion has the capacity to shape and control the ubiquitous world of sound. It clasps the confusion that so frustrates Quignard and welcomes the chaos and omnipotence of the auditory to greatest effect in the moment of live performance.

Amidst the echoes of samba drums, the audience in Copenhagen moved upstairs to witness the energy and spectacle of the percussion ensemble. Monrad (Danish percussionist and composer) based his composition on three of Glennie's most resonant statements: "Make the world listen", "Feel the music" and "Hear the silence".[33] Monrad's musical tribute merged many

---

[32] Pascal Quignard (2016) Second Treatise: "It So Happens That Ears Have No Eyelids" from *The Hatred of Music*. Translated from French by Matthew Amos and Fredrik Rönnbäck. New Haven: Yale University Press, p. 73.

[33] *Evelyn Glennie Receives the Léonie Sonning Music Prize 2023* (online). Available from: https://www.sonningmusik.dk/evelyn-glennie/?lang=en (accessed 5 June 2023).

of the most attractive features of this medium. Cymbal crashes held aloft vibrated to silence; a snare drum cadenza demonstrated precision, speed and power; tonal melodies merging a range of percussion instruments alternated with pulsing auxiliary patterns; the full dynamic and timbral spectrum was explored. This was an appropriate prelude, highlighting the chronological predecessor to the solo multi-percussionist, and reflecting Glennie's own career trajectory. Entering the auditorium, the immediate visual appeal of percussion was apparent, with five stations occupying the full down-stage area, and the tubular bells displayed clearly on a platform rear-centre.

In a chapter focused on legacy, it was particularly fitting to witness Glennie reprise the concerto that defined her identity as a professional solo multi-percussionist. As she evolves and ages, performances of such works will become increasingly rare; *Veni, Veni Emmanuel* has featured in Glennie's programming for over thirty years. Again and again, Glennie has returned to the sensations and transformative power of the work's premiere: "There was such an incredible ovation for the piece, and that's always what I'm interested in – projecting the piece ... It was just extraordinary and really quite emotional, so that performance always stands out in my mind."[34] For MacMillan, *Veni, Veni Emmanuel* was a retrospective reflection on his Catholic beliefs; for Glennie it functioned as an anticipatory leap of faith into the future of solo multi-percussion. For both, it has shaped their journeys of personal and professional evolution. In a recent study of MacMillan's works, Cooke suggests that the popularity of *Veni, Veni Emmanuel* relates directly to this symbiotic relationship between composer and premiere performer: "Whether the work's popularity stems from its easily accessible form, its use of a well-known Christmas melody, or the fact that the work is associated with the glamorous and idiosyncratic percussionist Evelyn Glennie is difficult to ascertain – perhaps it is due in part to all three."[35]

The impetus to understand what makes Glennie special is embedded in Cooke's use of the term "idiosyncratic", less pertinent for the premiere performance when the world perceived her as the first and only solo multi-percussionist (unique by default), but much more important in an age where the profession has many proponents. Why does Glennie still possess the appeal to fill a concert hall? During the Léonie Sonning Music Prize the answer was rendered in the conflation of multiple fascinations: virtuosity,

---

[34] Lauren Vogel Weiss (2002) Evelyn Glennie, *Percussive Notes*, 40 (2), p. 15.

[35] Phillip A. Cooke (2019) *The Music of James MacMillan.* Woodbridge: The Boydell Press, p. 69.

drama, physicality, intent, charisma, visual appeal, the feeling of spontaneity, and above all the tangible awareness that this experience will never again occur no matter how many times the concerto is performed. Glennie thinks primarily of the listener when she plays and is honest about the pressures of making a meaningful connection in an environment where the smallest change can have significant consequences. The mood of the performer, the nature of the audience, the acoustics of the space, the instruments used, and the fluid nature of interpretation all determine the trajectory. Whilst *Veni, Veni Emmanuel* is familiar, its identity and impact changes with every performance. Despite the expectation that each well-rehearsed percussion entry will be accurate, there remains a sense of energy in the relationship forged in uniting the soloist with a new conductor, orchestra and audience. Listening for the heartbeat motifs which recur throughout the work, hearing the ways in which each percussion station is brought to life, and watching with breath suspended in advance of the final movement to the tubular bells feels both familiar and new. There was a sense of magic when the orchestral performers assumed the role of percussionists, and this frisson was retained as Glennie waited with arms aloft long after the final cascade of bells ended. Again, the space between action and reception is where the potency of live performance exists. The drama and skill of the complex virtuosic moments on marimba and the large drum configuration were striking, but the final gesture was the most memorable. One doesn't get to feel the full extent of a sound, of its complete journey, in other solo performance disciplines; when the final note is sounded, there is a breath, but this tends to segue quickly into applause. The solo percussionist uses the body to communicate directly with the listener; the performance does not end until the full resonance of the sound is exhausted.

Whilst less established in Glennie's canon, *Dreamachine* (2014) is a more accessible concerto for those less familiar with the discipline. It is a dazzling and wilfully eccentric work that embraces and demonstrates the diversity of multi-percussion to compelling effect. Each of the four movements presents a different facet of the percussionist's art, creating immersive soundscapes that conjure visual narratives based on the programmatic allusions of their title. To date, Glennie remains the only performer of the concerto; she is therefore intrinsically connected to realizing Daugherty's vision of a dreamachine. The term, when used in this contraction of two words, refers to a light box intended to induce a sense of wellbeing or euphoria without recourse to drugs or stimulants. It is the result of a collaboration between William Burroughs (a writer and visual artist), David Woodard (a writer and conductor) and Brion Gysin (multimedia artist and inventor), with the first prototype constructed in 1959. When viewed with eyes closed, the rhythmic recurrence of the flashing light creates imagery in the mind of the spectator. It is an aspirational concept wherein the subconscious serves as a form of healing and therapy.

Though Daugherty does not cite the original dreamachine in his programme notes, the intention to conjure positive sensory responses is nonetheless embedded in the concerto. Live music is an aural dreamachine in this context, supported by the visual stimulus of each movement title. The score also provides the performer (or researcher) with specific images as an enticing prelude to the music which follows. The first draws inspiration from Da Vinci's sketch of wooden wings (c.1488), subsequently mirrored in the timbres of the scoring: "Playing the marimba (also made of wood), the percussion soloist performs music that I have created to hover, flutter and rise in the imagination."[36] The second movement pertains to a cartoon by Rube Goldberg (1928), of a prototype "Locate Lost Collar Button" machine made from various household items; the multi-percussionist assumes the role of inventor in this movement with experiments on a range of small auxiliary instruments, "creating a chain reaction like one of Goldberg's carefully designed machines".[37] Fritz Kahn's *Electric Eel* (1952) is the visual reference for the third movement, wherein the eerie resonance of the vibraphone becomes the aural equivalent of Kahn's image. The final movement, titled "Vulcan's Forge", is anticipated with two pictures, one of Leonard Nimoy as Spock (1966) and a painting of Vulcan, weapon-maker for the gods, as imagined by Andrea Mantegna (1497). A heroic finale, Daugherty scores for snare drum, a reference to the military endeavours of both Spock and Vulcan.

Whilst there are four percussion stations, the scoring is more concerned with timbral contrast than with expansive configurations. The soloist plays only one instrument in three of the four movements (1: marimba, 3: vibraphone and 4: snare drum). "Da Vinci's Wings" opens with the fluttering of sustained marimba rolls, followed in bar 4 by a fitful ascending chordal figuration which remains a unifying structure throughout the movement (see Ex. 14).

The marimba cadenza segues to an orchestral soundscape which maintains emphasis on the wooden wings of Da Vinci, beginning with vibrations emanating from lower woodwind (bass clarinet, bassoon, contrabassoon) and *pizzicato* and *sul ponticello* strings. Whilst the solo percussion line is unquestionably difficult, it is clearly enjoyable to play, with attainable

---

[36] Michael Daugherty (2014) *Programme Notes* (online). Available from: https://www.fabermusic.com/music/dreamachine (accessed 7 June 2023).

[37] Ibid.

Ex. 14: Marimba opening of *"Da Vinci's Wings"* from *Dreamachine* (Michael Daugherty).

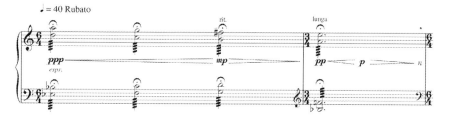

interval stretches in each hand, repeated rhythmic patterns, lengthy rolls exploiting wide dynamic ranges, emphatic glissandi and adequate rest time to change sticks later in the movement. The marimba becomes the sonic wings which float and drift on the winds of the orchestra; it is a compelling rhythmic and melodic force.

The second movement is filled with brief cadenzas for a range of hand-held auxiliary instruments. As detailed in Goldberg's sketch, the melody of "Home, Sweet Home" is first sounded on solo oboe, immediately inferring a relaxed and playful mood. In the DR Koncerthuset, this was the moment when Glennie definitively connected with the audience. There were no barriers to engagement; spectators laughed and murmured responses as each successive instrument was explored in short improvisations on vibraslap, ratchet, tambourine, triangle, flexatones and maraca. Theatricality superseded musical complexity; the soloist was at play, but there was a sense of purpose with each gesture, a genuine effort to bring sounds to life as both auditory and visual phenomena. Any feeling of distance between virtuoso and audience was removed; everyone could access and interpret what was happening on their own terms. There was an invitation extended to acquiesce to the strangeness of the moment, in which time felt altered – more intense yet more fluid. It was a period to reflect on the fact that the solo multi-percussionist can stand centre-stage with the simplest of tools and still captivate the listener; it was validation. The "Home, Sweet Home" melody returns at bar 92, joined by sleigh bells. In bar 100, the movement ended with a single loud whip strike. The audience applauded, as was the case for every part of *Dreamachine*, eschewing concert-hall conventions in an instinctive response to each soundscape.

"Electric Eel" exploits the unique beauty of the vibraphone, opening with a series of sextuplet chords hovering over a motor set on its lowest speed. This movement demands considerable skill, but the emphasis is on foregrounding the potential of the instrument in a haunting and atmospheric dialogue between soloist and orchestra.

"Vulcan's Forge" is an immediate contrast, opening with an extended snare drum cadenza; Glennie's improvisations grew from rudiments (including rolls, flams and paradiddles) which transformed into explorations of timbral nuance and dynamic range. As the orchestra enter, the soloist must adhere to the specifications of a score detailing placement of rim shots, strikes on various parts of the skin, double paradiddles and ever-changing accent patterns. In this balance between precision and freedom, Daugherty merges the military origins of the snare drum with its more experimental contemporary remit. Kick drum is added to the solo line from bar 58, with a focus on intense semiquaver figurations. Both instruments feature in a longer cadenza at bar 101, during which time the introductory material is further transformed using hands, fingers and a number of stick types to explore each part of the snare drum. A loud *tutti* conclusion drew the concerto to an emphatic close, followed by several curtain calls for the soloist.

It is difficult to describe the feelings that solo multi-percussion elicits in live performance, since there are so many responses operating on emotional, cognitive and visceral levels. Any expectations, assumptions or conventions are rendered wonderfully redundant; art music is both popular and purposeful, complex and accessible, familiar yet new; it is drama and spectacle in alignment with musical integrity. The two concertos, presenting distinct perspectives on the compositional process and the role of the soloist, offered a potentially transformative experience for the listener. This was certainly music, but it was also much more than that, an instinctive force that is intrinsic to the human experience. To see a virtuosic iteration of this primal and shared aspect of our being felt like an intersection where past, present and future co-exist.

Following *Dreamachine*, Glennie was formally awarded the Léonie Sonning Music Prize in a commendation speech given by Uffe Savery (the second member of *Safri Duo*). This was appropriately grand in its remit, acknowledging Glennie's innovations as a performer and her larger efforts to promote active listening. Briefly referencing the diagnosis of profound deafness, Savery narrated Glennie's career path, including her admission to the Royal Academy of Music and the early challenges of sourcing and purchasing instruments. He ended with a warm summary of her contribution to the future of solo multi-percussion: "Your musicality, imagination, creativity, curiosity, courage and not to mention your personality, got you through all these challenges, and you turned them all into strengths ... You created a blue ocean of possibilities." Interrupted for applause multiple times, Savery's commendation was focused on the achievements of one individual.

Glennie's acceptance speech instead looked outwards; her words were concerned with gratitude and acknowledgement of the fact that her career has depended upon collaboration and support. This she related to the subsequent effort to connect the community of music with society in more general terms, applying the intensity of listening as a performer to larger initiatives promoting better communication. Glennie began with thanks to Savery and Friis, recognizing the efforts of *Safri Duo* to create new possibilities for contemporary percussion, adding "We are all part of the chain." She spoke with clarity and a warm sense of humour, immediately gaining audience support with an observation on the awards experience: "I have to say that I thought that if any kind of tribute would happen towards myself it would perhaps be after I had died, but the fact that I can participate and enjoy this occasion is quite lovely and encouraging."

Glennie recalled her earliest collaborators, from teachers, mentors and family through to industry professionals who have played significant roles in the evolution of multi-percussion. The Evelyn Glennie Collection retains many of the letters exchanged in these initial networks; they include an impassioned request from Sandra Buchan (peripatetic teacher of the deaf) to Ann Rachlin in 1981. Her advocacy on Glennie's behalf led to a lifelong connection with the Rachlins, and with the Beethoven Fund for Deaf Children. In a series of letters exchanged between Glennie and the Rachlins in 1982, it was clear that the intention to pursue the career of solo multi-percussionist was not difficult only because of its rarity; it was a costly and labour-intensive profession. Finding (and paying) for repertoire, accessing instruments and finding suitable rehearsal spaces were pragmatic issues facing a young Glennie; Savery alluded to these challenges in his commendation. Glennie's acceptance speech recalls a life of determination, engagement and interaction; her subsequent success has depended on unwavering self-belief. In the summer of 1982, before her studies at the Royal Academy of Music began, Glennie ended a letter to Ann and Ezra Rachlin with this sense of conviction: "I can't express how much I really appreciate what you are all doing and I know what you are doing is right."[38] Support from Ann and Ezra Rachlin led Glennie to James Blades, a mentor who immediately accepted and encouraged Glennie's intention to work as a soloist.

Glennie progressed to thanking the composers who have also played a part in advancing futures for multi-percussion, acknowledging the fact that Másson (who has written several commissions) was in attendance. The final section was focused on social listening; Glennie mentioned The Evelyn Glennie Foundation as the next stage of her career, part of the ever-evolving network of support that continues to expand: "It's an absolute privilege to be involved in a profession which involves connections with every possible demographic on a global scale." Glennie's words were ambitious; she positioned percussion and sound creation as open-ended and democratic musical frameworks which embrace curiosity, inclusion and experimentation. These transferable skills create new possibilities to centralize the musician as a pivotal part of society. The speech was a concise yet impressive summary of the contributions that Glennie has made to the evolution of solo multi-percussion, and also evinced her pride in the fact that sound creation and expert listening have become part of the vocabulary of contemporary music and the cultural zeitgeist. The art of percussion has always looked outwards; it is the role of the percussionist to do the same.

---

[38] Evelyn Glennie, letter to Ezra and Ann Rachlin, 13 July 1982, kindly provided by The Evelyn Glennie Collection.

Legacy: A Series of New Beginnings 227

"Whichever instrument is in front of me is really my favourite instrument. But if I had to be stranded on a desert island with one instrument, it would be the snare drum."[39] The Léonie Sonning Music Prize ended with a challenge to the listener, foregrounding only the snare drum as the solo instrument in a work which must command attention using the fundamental tools of the percussionist: stick and skin. Másson's *Konzertstück for Snare Drum and Orchestra* is a ten-minute exposition of snare drum techniques with the orchestra performing an accompanying role. Anyone can certainly strike a drum; not everyone can bring it to life, creating a virtuosic narrative using the tools of timbre, rhythm, and gesture. This is the heart of multi-percussion: stick meeting surface, patterns unfolding, vibration, resonance and a sense of presence and immediacy that is inescapable. The snare drum is where percussion started for Glennie. At her first lesson with Ron Forbes at the age of twelve, this instrument initiated all of the experimentation, training and performance which followed:

> He sent me home with a snare drum, but no stand and no sticks. I started tapping it and pinching it and scraping it, and the next week he asked me how I'd got on. I said I didn't know. He said: "Now create the sound of a storm. Now create the sound of a whisper." Suddenly I had this picture I had to put into sound. This opened up my world. It was the best lesson I ever had. From then on it was just constant exploration.[40]

Glennie's first snare drum, first pair of snare drum sticks and first practice pad remain part of The Evelyn Glennie Collection (see Fig. 15), now joined by many later purchases, prototypes and signature editions.

The snare drum is an instrument capable of clamorous, ear-splitting power and whispering nuance. It is enjoyable to play, with the various rudimentary combinations, ostinato rhythms, timbral shifts and dynamic gradations typical of solo repertoire resulting in an almost hypnotic state of concentration. The challenge is in ensuring that the mesmerizing sensations experienced by the player are translated to the listener. Even at its most delicate, the snare drum does not produce sounds which are beautiful or emotive in any conventional sense. Likewise, its capacity for power and volume tends to exhaust the ear if extended over a prolonged period. As

---

[39] Evelyn Glennie (2019) *What is Your Favourite Instrument?* (video online), 2 April 2019. Available from: https://www.youtube.com/watch?v=1bEoqLpap68 (accessed 9 June 2023).

[40] Evelyn Glennie in Nick Morrison (2009) *My Best Teacher* (online), 10 April 2009. Available from: https://www.tes.com/magazine/archive/my-best-teacher-evelyn-glennie (accessed 9 June 2023).

Fig. 15: Glennie's first snare drum.

a solo or concerto instrument the snare drum poses a considerable challenge; its success is dependent upon the combination of careful scoring and interpretative skill.

Icelandic composer Másson has focused on embracing the ambiguities of percussion writing since the 1970s, resulting in an extensive and frequently performed range of solo, ensemble and orchestral works. Though the *Konzertstück* precedes Glennie's commissioning efforts (which date from 1985), its role in her early professional development segued to a number of subsequent collaborations: *Frum* (1995) for solo snare drum is now a familiar audition and competition piece; Másson's *Percussion Concerto* (2000) demands a fifty-seven instrument configuration for the soloist; the double percussion concerto *Crossings* (2002) culminates in a cadenza for Scottish Highland and piccolo snare drums; the most recent *Fo(u)r Mallets* (2015), for the *Fifty for Fifty* series, can be played with or without instruments. Glennie first performed the *Konzertstück* in July 1986, at a time when her programming was still largely dependent on transcriptions, vivacious ragtime encores and a limited number of established solo works such as Mayuzumi's *Concertino for Xylophone and Piano* (1965) and John Beck's *Sonata for Timpani* (1969). Whilst her success in commissioning new works provided freedom from these early standards, the *Konzertstück* has remained a presence for almost forty years. It has become an unlikely crowd-pleaser, in effect a study of core snare drum rudiments moulded into a compelling exploration of timbre, dynamics and rhythm.

There was an immediate visual power in seeing a small female at a single drum pitted against the weight of the orchestra. The audience understood the pretext, and were familiar with the instrument, but in the early stages of the *Konzertstück* there was some degree of uncertainty as to how the work would evolve. Glennie took considerable liberties in interpreting the score, extending cadenzas into almost relentless barrages of sound. The intensity and insistence of the solo line eventually compelled the listener to submit to the overtones, patterns and resonance which emerged. It became impossible to concentrate on anything other than the snare drum; it filled the space to an extent not generally achieved by tuned instruments. This work was about listening with an open mind; it articulated the musical voice of auxiliary instruments; it was a celebration of rhythm. For Glennie, it was an entirely appropriate way to end, for now, at the beginning.

Concluding Thoughts

Glennie's legacy will be preserved as documents, scores, recordings, images and artefacts. She has provided sufficient creative stimulus for many subsequent generations of percussionists; the profession is now understood and recognized as integral to the foundations of new music. But the legacy of any performer is not one which can be represented through physical resources. Glennie's early successes in particular are not crystallized or captured for posterity; they are transient experiences that cannot be recreated or fully known. Her idiosyncratic performance style is witnessed most keenly in movements and works which are not precisely notated, and Glennie leaves only annotations concerning the mood and atmosphere of such moments.

There is a beauty in accepting this, in acknowledging that virtuosity in solo multi-percussion is subjective, personal and ephemeral. The most difficult notated repertoire will be played by subsequent performers, but Glennie has always been most persuasive in the music which presents as deceptively simple, in the pages where little is written, in the places where instinctive creativity happens in the moment of performance. What is certain is that Glennie has taught the world to listen to solo percussion – to the boundless timbral and expressive potential of the medium and to its value in numerous musical genres and interdisciplinary contexts. She has also advocated for listening in new ways – refuting the perceived dichotomy between deafness and music, encouraging engagement with the endless creative landscape of improvisation, and demonstrating the productive outcomes of collaborative artistic interaction. Glennie has given the musician a voice in the broader contexts of social inclusion, gender equality and disability rights as a deaf female role model. In reciprocity, Glennie has listened too – to the changing landscape of new music, to shifting aesthetic priorities, to pedagogical and cultural trends, and to current discourse on diversity and inclusion. In a philosophical sense, Glennie listened to the world and responded by extending her role of sound creator to activism, advocacy and philanthropy. A legacy of listening, however, proves equally resistant to framing through words and artefacts.

On a final visit to The Evelyn Glennie Collection to review resources, the question which has informed and directed this book remained: what makes Glennie special? She may not be the first solo multi-percussionist in history, but she is the first to have made this a full-time career. She is the first to have sustained this career over the course of five decades. She has accomplished a huge number of firsts over the course of her professional life, including many Proms events, but also extending into collaborations and interdisciplinary projects which were perhaps never even considered as possible roles for the multi-percussionist. She has forged new paths and creative directions as a contemporary performer and entrepreneur. She has become a resonant presence in the cultural zeitgeist and, with that, has brought the world of multi-percussion to the general public. She is a sound creator whose curiosity and passion for making music, and experimenting with instruments is genuine, heartfelt and wondrously childlike. There is no artifice here, no divide between public persona and personal identity; there is no concern with the trappings of success, fame or ego. There is just a vocation, a genuine desire to teach the world to listen. The music industry is a turbulent and unforgiving domain. This was certainly made more challenging given the fact that Glennie had to innovate and network in the early stages of her career within an undeniably male-dominated environment; there is more still to be overcome in this respect. To have a female figurehead for an emerging discipline remains seminal and hugely significant for the next generation of creative minds and entrepreneurs. In terms of integrating Glennie's deafness into appraisal of what makes her special, a source of fascination in the early decades, it seems right to adhere to her own views on the subject. When Glennie performs and creates, deafness is not relevant; listening is the focal point. This is a process which, for Glennie, is multi-sensory and embodied, but in fact this is the case for everyone regardless of their levels of auditory perception. All histories are incomplete; regardless of their rigour, they will always be imbued with some degree of subjectivity. It is impossible to address all of the repertoire, performances, collaborations, interactions and experiments which are part of Glennie's legacy. But it is important that this process begins. The art of solo multi-percussion deserves its place in history; so too do the performers who shaped it.

Conclusion

"To Teach the World to Listen"

Percussion transcends boundaries, an omnipresent medium which connects genres, cultures, disciplines and communities. It is the heartbeat of contemporary musical innovation. Whilst this book is a study of one performer, it is ultimately an ode to a discipline which has patiently made its way to the foreground of the cultural consciousness. The multi-percussionist is the conduit between past and present, old and new, convention and rebellion, sound and music, art and life. Transitioning from (and yet still embracing) descriptors such as noisy, simplistic and colouristic to terms including revolutionary, virtuosic and experimental, the trajectory of solo percussion continues to diversify and expand. The journey of solo percussion – pioneered and validated by Glennie – will never be complete.

The vignettes presented in this book offer some sense of what it means to be a solo multi-percussionist, sound creator and expert listener, inviting the reader to explore the scores, repertoire and instruments which make this discipline the most diverse musical medium in contemporary music. They situate the role of the musician as one which extends beyond the boundaries of the concert hall. The spirit of curiosity which makes multi-percussion an exciting and limitless medium can be applied in multiple contexts; when people are willing to experiment, to be open-minded, to reject convention, to rebuke cultural conditioning, progress happens both in musical and social terms. Glennie is a leading figure in a discipline which dates to the beginning of civilization, and which will continue to progress and metamorphose long after her career ends. Her innovations have reshaped the direction of contemporary music, reframed our understanding of the relationship between deafness and listening, positioned a female role model at the centre of cultural innovation, and reconceptualized the social responsibility of the artist. Dealing with a living research subject, still active in their domain, is not without its difficulties. Glennie continues to diversify, to increase her philanthropic commitments, to advance as an entrepreneur, and ultimately to pursue new horizons for solo percussion performance. This perhaps offers the most logical rationale as to why

Glennie has not been studied in detail to date: her work as an artist is not yet complete. In alignment with the work of The Evelyn Glennie Collection, an intersection of past, present and future, this publication must function as both a reflective process and an anticipation of what is yet to come.

Three intersecting themes have shaped the narrative of Glennie's diverse professional remit: creativity, collaboration and diversification. Creativity alludes to an ongoing sense of curiosity and passion for seeking out new challenges and opportunities; Glennie's career is perhaps best viewed as a series of new beginnings – an exploration of the experimental and wide-ranging potentialities of sound creation both within and beyond the domain of music performance. Collaboration reaffirms the fact that music is human-centred. Musical experiences are innately social, even for solo performers; they will always be dependent upon the triumvirate of creator, performer and listener. In many instances, the multi-tasking multi-percussionist must be all three, but ultimately the intention is to disseminate and share this intense experience with others; the sounds and sights of percussion invite interaction. Music-making, engagement and participation are parts of an interactive and dynamic communal ecosystem; creativity is thus dependent upon collaboration. Similarly, collaborative endeavour embraces change and diversification, which references the unfolding and often unpredictable path of solo percussion performance. Diversification denotes a desire to wilfully elude classification or standardization, which also applies to Glennie's work as an entrepreneur, advocate and activist.

Co-existing with these three connective themes there are two central ideas which pervade all aspects of the research: listening and interrogating the ideological constructs which determine that which is deemed other. Fundamentally, Glennie's career has focused on the centrality of listening, originating as a desire to promote the potentialities of solo percussion performance and sound creation, and expanding to address the larger issue of social deafness. Otherness permeates the research in relation to the historical positioning of percussion as the primitive, exotic, multi-cultural other of art music. It is also discernible in the concept of the percussionist as the other of performance, working with unfixed instrumental media and operating in a domain beholden to no single culture, epoch or musical genre. Glennie, as a female performer working in a traditionally male instrumental discipline, has challenged the othering of women as percussionists, creators, leaders, and entrepreneurs. As a deaf musician, Glennie also refutes the ideology of the disabled other in a discipline which for so long had determined that auditory perception was a prerequisite for musical engagement.

The introduction followed the structure of *Good Vibrations*, an early autobiography which openly discussed the formative stages of Glennie's career, noting the diagnosis of profound deafness but subsuming this into a more holistic account of the experiences and people who shaped her professional development. Chapter 1 addressed the evolution of multi-percussion, tracing its gradual assimilation into the vocabulary of art music and eventual emancipation as a solo discipline; the prominent role of the performer as co-creator was foregrounded. Chapter 2 appraised Glennie's maturation as a performer, wherein the identity of virtuoso extended into sound creation, improvisation and collaboration. Percussion became a language which could communicate across disciplines, and Glennie a role model whose work resonated beyond her primary professional identity. Chapter 3 engaged with the issue of gender, considering Glennie's significance as a female pioneer in several respects. The power of the virtuoso was channelled into empowerment for women in business and the creative industries; Glennie did not need to claim a feminist identity to achieve this. Chapter 4 was about inclusion and activism, wherein the voice of the musician was heard beyond the concert hall. Music is a cultural commodity, but it is also a social imperative, a right which should be available to all. Inclusion pertained most obviously to disability rights and gender, but this is only the beginning of the ways in which music can offer commentary on issues of social justice and serve as impetus for change. Chapter 5 was concerned with legacy, a narrative which must remain unfinished given the fact that Glennie continues to perform and diversify. Her mission to teach the world to listen may well only be in its infancy, even as she approaches her sixth decade as a professional solo percussionist.

In several instances, reference has been made to the importance of the spaces in between – the divides between percussionists and their peers, the process of bringing score directives to life, the performances that are not captured as recordings, the collaborations that happen as natural parts of the creative process, the inner dialogue of the musician. It is equally relevant to mention this in the concluding section, as words alone cannot harness the power, beauty and eccentricity of multi-percussion. Glennie invites us to listen; I ask you to do the same. This repertoire and these performances are not niche; they are not the purview of the percussion world. They are reflections of the sounds and experiences which surround and envelop us all. Final thoughts on legacy reach a number of conclusions: Glennie has changed the world of music; the terms sound creator and expert listener feel right and accurate descriptors, but they should not be applied only to Glennie. Glennie's most important contribution has been in showing us that we can all be sound creators and we can all be expert listeners.

Appendix 1:
Concerto Commissions

Evelyn Glennie concerto commissions for tuned, auxiliary and multi-percussion configurations. Includes all scores published and/or catalogued by The Evelyn Glennie Collection to date.

Year	Composer	Title	Percussion instrumentation	Duration (if known)
1985	Kenneth Dempster	*Concerto Palindromos*	Marimba, vibraphone	
1985	Alan Ridout	Concertino for Percussion	Vibraphone, glockenspiel, xylophone, cymbals, snare drum, tenor drum, bass drum	
1987	John McLeod	Percussion Concerto	Timpani, snare drum, cymbal, marimba, 5 temple blocks, 5 tom-toms, 3 cowbells, mark tree, 3 Chinese cymbals, vibraphone, crotales, 3 gongs	26'
1990	Richard Rodney Bennett	Percussion Concerto	Marimba, 10 "skins" (bongos, timbales, tom-toms etc.), 3 wood blocks, 5 temple blocks, 3 triangles, 4 suspended cymbals, hi-hat, bell tree, glass chimes, agogo bells, tambourine, side drum, bass drum with foot pedal	24'
1991	Dominic Muldowney	*Figure in a Landscape*	Marimba, xylorimba, 4 suspended cymbals, Japanese bell, 5 tom-toms, bongos, 2 congas, vibraphone, 4 small drums, pedal bass drum, 4–8 boobam (an ancestor of the octoban), 4 wood blocks	20'
1992	David Gow	Marimba Concerto	Marimba	

Appendix 1: Concerto Commissions   235

Year	Composer	Title	Percussion instrumentation	Duration (if known)
1992	James MacMillan	*Veni, Veni Emmanuel*	2 tam-tams, 2 snare drums, 2 congas, 6 tom-toms, 2 timbales, pedal bass drum, 6 Chinese gongs, 6 temple blocks, log drum, 2 wood blocks, 2 cowbells, marimba (5-octave), mark tree, large cymbal, sizzle cymbal, tubular bells	26'
1992	Rodney Newton	*Variations for Percussion*	Xylophone, glockenspiel, vibraphone, mark chimes, bell tree, wood block, cowbell, snare drum, 3 tom-toms, suspended cymbal, 3 timpani, triangle, bongos, cabasa, tam-tam	13'
1992	Terry Trower	*To Freedom*	Marimba	22'
1993	Rory Boyle	Marimba Concerto	Marimba	20'
1994	Howard Skempton	Concerto for Hurdy Gurdy and Percussion	Snare drum, xylophone, congas, guiro, marimba	19'
1994	Thea Musgrave	*Journey Through a Japanese Landscape*	Marimba, tam-tam, 4 wind chimes (bamboo, wood, metal, glass)	23'
1995	Derek Bourgeois	Concerto for Percussion and Brass Band	Snare drum, marimba	20'
1995	Andrew Keeling	*Nekyia*	Vibraphone, marimba, medium and low tam-tams, drum kit, 2 cowbells, 2 cymbal discs, 2 bongos, tubular bells, crotales	20'
1995	Geoffrey Burgon	*City Adventures*	3 suspended cymbals (small, medium, large), clashed cymbals, large bass drum, tam-tam, maracas, snare drum, tambourine, tubular bell (d')	20'
1995	Dave C. Heath	*African Sunrise/Manhattan Rave*	Vibraphone, marimba, "trash"/industrial percussion	20'

Year	Composer	Title	Percussion instrumentation	Duration (if known)
1996	Stewart Wallace	*Gorilla in a Cage*	Bell cymbal, splash cymbal, Chinese splash cymbal, handmade cymbal, handmade cymbal with sizzles, large crash cymbal, 9 temple blocks, 4 timbales, 2 agogo bells, medium cowbell, OM chimes (9), 6 bass chimes, kick drum, 5 tom-toms, snare drum, Batonka	25'
1997	Piers Hellawell	*Drum of the Nājd* (Double Concerto for Percussion and Recorder)	Small drum, marimba	22'
1997	Jonathan Harvey	*Percussion Concerto*	Marimba, vibraphone, 2 Balinese gamelan keyboards, 8 temple blocks, 6 wood blocks, mark tree	25'
1998	Roberto Sierra	*Con Madera, Metal y Cuero*	Glockenspiel, xylophone, vibraphone, marimba, crotales, mark tree, tambourine, maracas, guiro, bongos, congas, 5 suspended cymbals, 2 cencerros, steel drum, 5 temple blocks, 3 timbales, 6 tom-toms, pedal bass drum	28'
1998	Paul Hart	*Cathcart Concertina for Percussion*	Marimba, 4 gongs, vibraphone, xylophone, 4 bicycle bells	15'
1998	Christopher Rouse	*Der Gerette Alberich*	4 wood blocks, 4 log drums, 4 tom-toms, 2 bongos, 2 timbales, snare drum, steel drum, marimba, 2 guiros, kick drum, drum kit	25'
1998	Michael Daugherty	*UFO*	Waterphone, mechanical siren, xylophone, ice cymbal, crasher, slasher, brake drum, spring (or other "trash" instruments), earth plate, cymbal disc, Chinese gong, vibraphone, 3 cymbals, mark tree, non-pitched "alien" instruments (for movement 4), 5 tom-toms, 8 octobans, bongos, drum kit, alien cymbal, 3 small cymbals, various metal objects, 3 temple blocks, 3 Latin cowbells	40'

Appendix 1: Concerto Commissions   237

Year	Composer	Title	Percussion instrumentation	Duration (if known)
1998	Gerard Brophy	*Trance ... Dakar*	Shaker (African basket rattle, Brazilian ganza or egg shaker), tambourine, 2 bongos, 3 congas, 2 crash cymbals, 2 cowbells, djembe, marimba	20'
1998	Adam Gord	*Elements*	7 octobans, xylophone, bongos, congas, bass drum, cowbells, tom-toms, temple blocks, marimba, vibraphone, cymbals, thunder sheet, tambourine, crotales, chimes	28'
1998	Minoru Miki	*Requiem 99*	Marimba	23'
1999	Chen Yi	Percussion Concerto	Vibraphone, xylophone, marimba, mark tree, bowl chime, Chinese cymbal, 6 Peking gongs, medium gong, large gong, tam-tam, Japanese high wood block, 5 temple blocks, 5 Chinese tom-toms, dagu (Chinese bass drum)	20'
1999	Frangis Ali-Sade	*Silk Road*	Bass drum, vibraphone, marimba, glass chimes, Chinese gong, gosha-nagra, tenor drum (tamborino)	20'
1999	Gareth Farr	*Hikoi*	4 marching drums, suspended cymbal, Chinese cymbal, hi roto-tom, Simtak, exhaust pipes, cowbells, temple blocks, marimba, 2 small bells, 3 metal plates, large tom-tom, large bass drum, 5 roto-toms, small tam-tam, 4 tom-toms, hi-hat, kick drum, high timbale, splash cymbal	30'
1999	David Bedford	Percussion Concerto	Simtak, glockenspiel, cowbells, temple block, log drum, octobans, tom-toms, gong, Batonka	20'
2000	Tjunde Jegede	*Savannah*	Marimba	15'

Year	Composer	Title	Percussion instrumentation	Duration (if known)
2000	Nebojša Jovan Živković	*Concerto of the Mad Queen*	2 12" China cymbals (slightly different in pitch), 2 Chinese opera gongs, 4 cymbals (arranged high to low), 1 tam-tam, thunder sheet, rainstick, 2 metal tubes with a split and a hole for "wah wah" sounds, wooden split drum, bass drum with pedal, 5 tom-toms, 5 wood blocks, 1 octave of crotales, 7 Japanese drums (Uchiwa-Daikos), 5 earth plates, vibraphone	16'
2000	Mark Anthony Turnage	*Fractured Lines* (Double Concerto for Two Percussionists)	Crotales, marimba, ride cymbal, bell cymbal, 2 Chinese gongs, 6 cowbells, metal sheet, brake drum, scaffolding, metal bar, 3 snare drums, 7 tom-toms, 2 bass drums, 3 pedal bass drums, 10 wood blocks	16'–20'
2000	Áskell Másson	Percussion Concerto	Marimba, 2 wood blocks, 5 temple blocks, 4 slit drums, snare drum, sizzle cymbal, piccolo snare drum, 5 suspended hand bells (c, e, g, a), vibraphone, crotales (2 octaves), 3 suspended cymbals, 3 resting bells, tubular bells, glockenspiel, 9 Asian gongs, medium tam-tam, small tam-tam, 4 octobans, 4 tom-toms, 28' timpani, China cymbal, 4 bongos, bass drum with pedal, Peking gong	38'
2001	Margaret Brouwer	*Aurolucent Circles*	3 Tibetan opera gongs, cowbell, crotales, glockenspiel, mark tree, tam-tam, vibraphone, marimba, bell with handle, mark tree, suspended cymbal, tam-tam, tubular bells, temple blocks, triangle, wood block, 6 fairly light hollow-sounding drums, small low resonant drum, small bass drum	27'
2001	John Psathas	*View from Olympus* (Double Concerto for Percussion and Piano)	Vibraphone, marimba, Simtak, dulcimer, bass steel drums, wind chimes (2 or 3 sets), bell tree, mark tree, triangle, finger cymbals, 4 octobans, 4 tom-toms, 3 paddle drums, cymbals – trash, splash, medium crash, china crash, plus a cluster of smallest possible splash cymbals, hi-hat	20'

Appendix 1: Concerto Commissions

Year	Composer	Title	Percussion instrumentation	Duration (if known)
2001	Joan Tower	*Strike Zones*	Vibraphone, glockenspiel, timbales, tom-tom, tenor drum, bass drum, marimba, 4 temple blocks, very small wood block, small maracas (resting on pillow), 3 suspended cymbals (high, medium, low), Chinese gong, hi-hat, glockenspiel, xylophone, crotale, snare drum, mounted castanets	22'
2001	George Tsontakis	*Micrologia*	8 drums, tuned gong, 2 suspended cymbals (high and low), crowbar, tam-tam, snare drum, chimes, bass drum, crotales, incense bell, timbales, voice, "junk" metal, steel drums/tuned metal drums	25'
2001	Richard Causton	Concerto for Solo Percussion and Gamelan	Xylophone, 8 log drums, 3 temple blocks, 4 wood blocks (different pitches), 5 suspended cymbals, cuica, medium tam-tam, very large tam-tam, waterphone (with bow)	20'
2002	George Newson	*Both Arms*	Marimba, suspended bell, 4 tom-toms, cowbells, Chinese bells, sizzle cymbal, timbales, snare drum, suspended cymbals, school bell, tuned pans, octobans, congas, bongos, bass drum, suspended bell, jingles, rain tree	20'
2002	Jason Eckhardt	*Reul na Coile*	2 triangles (small, medium), hi-hat (with pedal), 3 suspended cymbals (small, medium, large), 2 suspended sizzle cymbals (medium, large), 2 handheld cymbals, anvil, metal sheet (very large), tam-tam (very large), Nipple gong (very large), claves, castanet (small, mounted), wood block (large), washboard (amplified if necessary), chocolo, maraca, Indian bells, bamboo chimes, glass chimes, guiro, whistle (North American police style), tambourine (with jingles, no membrane head), bongo (small), 3 timbales (very small, small, medium), 3 tom-toms (small, medium, very large: wide registral range between medium and very large), snare drum, bass drum	17'

Year	Composer	Title	Percussion instrumentation	Duration (if known)
2002	David Horne	*Ignition*	Tom-toms, crotales and vibraphone (only played with bow), marimba, a selection of drums	25'
2002	Christian Jost	*Cosmodromion*	Large water basin (offstage), vibraphone, marimba, tubular bells, Batonka, bass drum, 2 basins, 2 temple blocks, 8 octobans, electronic drum kit, 3 earth plates	25'
2002	Erkki-Sven Tüür	*Magma*	Glockenspiel, vibraphone, bongos, drum kit, marimba, congas	30'
2002	Áskell Másson	*Crossings* (Double Concerto for Two Percussionists)	Percussion 1: ocean drum, 5 tuned Asian gongs (e, f#, g#, a, b), amplified Udu drum, vibraphone, glockenspiel, flexatone, tubular bells, whirltube, 3 octobans, 2 tom-toms, Scottish Highland snare drum Percussion 2: large rain tree, 7 bell plates (g#, b, c#, d, d#, e, f), amplified Udu drum, vibraphone, crotales (2 octaves), whirltube, 2 bongos, 3 roto-toms, piccolo snare drum. Large bass drum laid flat in the centre for both players to use.	22'
2003	Steven Stucky	*Spirit Voices*	Tam-tam, 3 cymbals, 2 suspended cymbals (with bow), 2 bongos, 3 gongs, 3 wood blocks, 4 log drums, 5 Peking opera gongs, 3 tom-toms, 2 agogo bells, 2 brake drums, 3 cowbells, large automobile suspension spring coil, glockenspiel, vibraphone, marimba, chime, crotale	25'
2003	Eddie McGuire	*Prazdnik*	Vibraphone, marimba, xylophone, tubular chimes	12'
2004	Bright Sheng	*Colours of Crimson*	Marimba	20'
2004	Sally Beamish	*Trance o Nicht*	Marimba, voice, temple blocks, bells, bowed cymbals, tam-tam	20'

Appendix 1: Concerto Commissions   241

Year	Composer	Title	Percussion instrumentation	Duration (if known)
2004	David Lang	*Loud Love Songs*	7 graduated tambourines, 1 bell or bell-like object, with the pitch D♭, preferably played with a thimble, "woodthing" – 3 tiny woodblocks, or other pieces of wood, attached together, played with thimbles	18'
2004	Ned Rorem	Concerto for Mallet Instruments	Vibraphone, glockenspiel, marimba	25'
2005	Marijn Simons	*Concerto for an Odd Couple* (Double Concerto for Percussion and Violin)	Marimba	23'
2005	Kevin Puts	Percussion Concerto	Vibraphone, marimba, glockenspiel, crotales, tubular bells	26'
2005	Matthew Hindson	Percussion Concerto	Cymbals, tam-tam, vibraphone, drums	23'
2006	Ney Rosauro	Concerto for Vibraphone and Orchestra	Vibraphone	19'
2006	Thea Musgrave	*Two's Company* (Double Concerto for Percussion and Oboe)	Tam-tam, tubular bells, Chinese bell tree, mark tree, vibraphone, cymbals (high, medium, low), 5 congas, 5 tom-toms, 5 bongos, bass drum, snare drum, 5 temple blocks, 2 wood blocks, marimba	21'
2006	Jacob ter Veldhuis	*Barracuda Concerto*	Marimba, hi-hat and bass drum (triggered by one pedal), temple block, 2 small tom-toms, crash cymbal, vibraslap	14'
2007	Christos Hatzis	*Tongues of Fire*	Bass drum, drum kit, marimba, bender gongs, whistle, vibraphone, cloud gongs	40'

Year	Composer	Title	Percussion instrumentation	Duration (if known)
2008	John Corigliano	*Conjurer*	Xylophone, marimba, wood block, claves, log drum etc (arranged from high to low), tubular bells, tam-tams, suspended cymbals, vibraphone, "talking" drum, kick drum, timpani (used in the style of a talking drum) (Cadenza 1: wood, cadenza 2: metal, cadenza 3: skin)	35'
2009	Sean Beeson and Adam Lochstampfor	*Prometheus Rapture*	Snare drum	15'
2009	Marta Ptaszyńska	*Drum of Orfeo*	Marimba, vibraphone, crotales, drums, cymbals, gongs, triangle and non-Western instruments: hand drums, bodhráns, Japanese odaiko drum, Peking opera gong, Thai gongs, Japanese temple bells, agogo steel pan, sarna bells	30'
2009	Yiu-Kwong Chung	Concerto for Solo Percussion and Chinese Traditional Orchestra	Two snare drums, marimba, eleven drums of various sizes	28'
2009	Norbert Palej	Concerto for Percussion and Wind Ensemble	Glockenspiel, xylophone, vibraphone, marimba, 3 suspended cymbals (small, medium, large), bass drum (large), tam-tam (large)	30'
2009	Marlos Nobre	Concerto for Percussion No. 2	4 tom-toms/timbales, xylophone, marimba, piccolo snare drum, glockenspiel, 5 temple blocks, tam-tam, vibraphone	11'
2010	Eric Ewazen	*Songs to the Banks of Ayr*	Crotales, marimba, glockenspiel, vibraphone, xylophone, tom-toms, snare drum, cymbals	20'
2010	James Barrett	*Toilers of the Elements*	Vibraphone, marimba, tam-tams, waterphones, Hopi drum	20'

Year	Composer	Title	Percussion instrumentation	Duration (if known)
2010	Vincent Ho	*The Shaman*	3 different "stations" Station 1: 5 octave marimba, vibraphone (with something to hold the pedal down), 4 suspended cymbals, 1 set of wind chimes Station 2: prepared timpani (3 temple bowls with their bottoms duct-taped to the timpani head), 3 suspended cymbals, 2–5 additional metal instruments of performer's choice Station 3: bass drum, 10 drums in ascending order, optional set of suspended cymbals (for use in cadenza)	33'
2011	Joseph Phibbs	*Bar Veloce*	Xylophone, glockenspiel, crotales (to be bowed and struck), halo, pair of agogo bells, 2 pairs of Latin-style cowbells, waterphone, medium Chinese gong (used in Peking opera), two suspended cymbals (medium and small), hi-hat cymbal, snare drum, mounted tambourine, pair of high claves, whip, pair of log drums (low and medium-low), pair of slappers, pair of congas, pair of bongos, several pairs of shakers, vibraslap, two wood blocks (small and very small), medium-low timpani. Improvised instruments: wooden toy train whistle, two cereal packets with a half-full bag in each, leather belt, bar bell, 75ml spirit bottle, medium cocktail shaker (1/2 filled), pint-sized glass tumbler, small tin saucepan, metal dustbin lid	15'
2011	Jean-Luc Darbellay	*Cosmos*	Snare drum, temple blocks, xylophone, glockenspiel, marimba	30'

Year	Composer	Title	Percussion instrumentation	Duration (if known)
2012	Vincent Ho	From Darkness to Light – A Spiritual Journey	3 different "stations" Station 1 may be comprised of any instruments of the performer's choice; this is for an improvisatory section. Voice may also be used. Some suggestions from the composer include waterphones, tam-tams, thunder sheets, temple bowls, gongs Station 2: bass drum, 10 drums in ascending order (any combination of tom-toms, conga, bongos, or drums of choice) Station 3: vibraphone, marimba, waterphone, a collection of suspended cymbals (min. 5), at least 1 tam-tam	30'
2012	Olga Hans	Entelecheia – Sinfonia Concertante for Percussion, Cello and Orchestra	2 crotales, guiro, 2 wood blocks, 5 temple blocks, log drum, 4 cowbells, Chinese cymbal, 3 suspended cymbals, tam-tam, vibraphone, wind chimes, triangle, snare drum, 2 bongos, 3 tom-toms, bass drum, marimba	24'
2012	Mark Bowden	Heartland	Maracas (as resonant as possible), marimba, 5 temple blocks, large bass drum, pair of bongos, pair of congas, pair of tumbas (deeper pitched than congas), Aluphone, 4 tuned gongs (E3, D4, A4, B4), glockenspiel (with pedal), large brake drum, large metal pipe, two temple bowls (medium and large), pair of cowbells (small and large), pair of suspended cymbals (medium and large), Chinese cymbal, splash cymbal	23'
2012	Michael Oesterle	Kaluza Klein	Vibraphone	15'
2012	Peter Wallin	Space III – Beyond the Pleiades	Aluphone	45'

Year	Composer	Title	Percussion instrumentation	Duration (if known)
2013	Anders Koppel	Concerto for Aluphone, Marimba and Orchestra	Aluphone, marimba	30'
2013	Randolph Peters	*Musicophilia*	Triple superball friction mallet for inside piano, Tibetan prayer bowl for inside piano, rattly things, pots and pans, junk metal, large bass drum, large tam-tam, 3 tom-toms, 2 roto-toms, snare drum, 2 suspended cymbals, vibraphone, marimba, 6 cloud gongs, bow for vibraphone, bass waterphone, 2 wood blocks	20'
2014	Sean O'Boyle	*Portraits of Immortal Love*	Bass drum, Chinese bell tree, crotales, 3 triangles, wind chimes, marimba, mark tree, piccolo snare drum, vibraphone, shell wind chimes, tubular bells, waterphone	26'
2014	Fabian Müller	*Clatterclank*	Snare drum (and string orchestra)	7'
2014	Fabian Müller	Concerto for Vibraphone and Orchestra	Vibraphone	27'
2014	Michael Daugherty	*Dreamachine – Concerto for Percussion and Orchestra*	Marimba, vibraphone, snare drum, small selection of handheld instruments	30'
2014	Jill Jarman	*Mindstream* (Double Concerto for Percussion and Violin)	Marimba, vibraphone	
2016	Christian Lindberg	*Liverpool Lullabies* (Double Concerto for Percussion and Trombone)	Temple blocks, glockenspiel, xylophone, vibraphone	11'

Year	Composer	Title	Percussion instrumentation	Duration (if known)
2017	Clarice Assad	*Ad Infinitum*	32″ orchestral bass drum, 3 roto-toms (8″, 10″, 12″), 3 double-headed tom-toms (12″, 14″, 16″), 4 Tama octobans, 1 pair of congas, 1 pair of timbales, 1 pair bongos, 32″ timpani, 14″ Sabian bright clash cymbal, selection of wind chimes, vibraphone, xylophone, high Chinese tom-tom, doumbek, large djembe, piccolo snare drum, large traditional Chinese cymbal, Evelyn's own choice of temple bowls, music boxes and toy instruments	28′
2019	Kamran Ince	*Cikirikcilar Hill*	Bass drum, log drums, crotales, flexatone, tenor drum, 2 pebbles, snare drum, whistle, darbuka, vibraphone, sizzle cymbal, ratchet, tam-tam, siren	32′

Appendix 2:
Solo Commissions

Evelyn Glennie solo commissions (with or without accompaniment). List excludes *Fifty for Fifty* series. Includes all scores published and/or catalogued by The Evelyn Glennie Collection to date.

Year	Composer	Title	Instrumentation (where available)	Duration (if known)
1985	John Mayer	*Damaru* (solo + piano)	Gong, bass drum, vibraphone, marimba, 5 concert tom-toms, glockenspiel, bell tree, xylophone	
1986	Malcolm Singer	*Rags to Riches* (solo + piano)	4 tom-toms, 4 temple blocks, 4 cowbells, suspended cymbal, xylophone, marimba, vibraphone, glockenspiel, mark tree	12'
1987	Edward Shipley	*Old Battlefields* (percussion + trumpet)	Marimba, metal chimes, bamboo chimes, tom-tom	11'
1987	Ray Russell	*Steeple Chase*	Marimba, 3 timpani, boobams, shaker, triangle, bass drum, drum kit, congas	5'
1988	Ronald Stevenson	*The Harlot's House* (solo + accordion)	Triangle, cymbals, snare drum, maracas, bongos, crotales, tubular bells, xylophone, marimba, vibraphone, bass drum, gong	25'
1988	John McLeod	*The Song of Dionysius* (solo + piano)	Piano (played at beginning by solo percussionist), gong, 2 stones, claves, marimba, 4 cowbells, temple blocks, 4 tom-toms, suspended cymbal, wind chimes	15'
1988	Michael Boo	*Psalms for Marimba*	Marimba	

248 *Evelyn Glennie: Sound Creator*

Year	Composer	Title	Instrumentation (where available)	Duration (if known)
1990	Robert Steadman	*Solo for Timpani*	Timpani	
1990	Robert Steadman	*Ikon*	Chinese cup bells	4'
1991	Edward Ross	*Prelude and Dragonfly Dance* (solo + percussion ensemble)	Marimba	8'
1991	Christopher Brown	*La Legende de l'Etoile* (percussion + organ)	3 timpani, 3 tom-toms, 2 bongos, bass drum, 5 gongs, tam-tam, tubular bells, crotales, triangle, bell tree, 2 cowbells, 2 suspended cymbals, wind chimes, claves, 2 wood blocks, glockenspiel, vibraphone, xylophone, marimba	23'30"
1991	Michael Boo	*Prayer in a Time of War*	Marimba	
1991	Jeffrey Sharkey	*Toccata* (percussion + piano)	Marimba	
1992	Goff Richards	*Zimba Zamba* (solo + piano/brass band)	Marimba	
1992	John Dankworth	*Prelude, Blues and Godiva* (solo + piano)	Marimba, vibraphone, narration (spoken by solo percussionist)	8'
1992	Michael Boo	*Three Short Lollipops*	Tuned percussion	
1993	John Psathas	*Drum Dances* (solo + piano)	Drum kit, glockenspiel	10'
1994	Robert Godman	*Eye assume you knew two ...* (solo + tape)	Multi-percussion and tape	14'
1995	Piers Hellawell	*Takla Makan*	Marimba	

Year	Composer	Title	Instrumentation (where available)	Duration (if known)
1995	Barbara Thompson	*Rhythms of the Gods* (percussion, saxophone, piano)	Marimba, suspended cymbals, vibraphone, 4 tom-toms, snare drum	20'
1995	Áskell Másson	*Frum*	4 bongos, 4 octobans, 4 tom-toms, bass drum	7'
1995	David Horne	*Reaching Out*	2 sets of bongos, 4 tom-toms, 2 timbales, bass drum, 2 suspended triangles, 2 suspended cymbals, 5 temple blocks, 3 wood blocks, tam-tam, bell tree	10'
1996	John Psathas	*Happy Tachyons* (solo + piano)	Marimba, vibraphone	8'
1996	Django Bates	*My Dream Kitchen*	Kitchen utensils: tuned plates and bowls, cooking timers, cheese grater, roasting tins, 1 rolling pin, 1 pedal bin, 20 palette knives	15'
1997	Iannis Xenakis	*O-Mega* (solo + chamber orchestra)	Bongos	4'
1997	Dave C. Heath	*Darkness to Light* (solo + piano)	Waterphone, drum kit, wind chimes, vibraphone	11'
1997	Ian Finkel	*Jealous of Pianists* (percussion, guitar, bass, drums)	Marimba	
1997	Ian Finkel	*The Gypsy Xylophonist* (solo + piano/brass band)	Xylophone	
1997	Vinko Globokar	*Pensee Ecartelee*	1 bass drum, 1 jazz bass drum with pedal, 1 wooden African log drum, 1 suspended tam-tam, 1 charleston, 1 metal sheet, 2 anvils (different sizes)	11'

Year	Composer	Title	Instrumentation (where available)	Duration (if known)
1997	Michael Gordon	*XY*	5 tuned drums	15′
1997	Steve Martland	*Street Songs* (percussion + vocal ensemble)	Marimba	25′
1997	Peter Klatzow	*Return of the Moon* (percussion + vocal ensemble)	Marimba	16′
1998	Henning Sommerro	*Vesterled* (percussion + Celtic ensemble)	Marimba, crash cymbal, ride cymbal, 3 bongos, tom-tom, wood block, gong, snare drum	
1998	Motofumi Yamaguchi	*Marimba and Taiko* (duet)	Marimba	
1998	Haflidi Hallgrímsson	*Ears Stretch – A Sensitive Sail* (solo + string quartet)	Suspended cymbal, tam-tam, steel drum, glockenspiel, tom-toms, bass drum, tubular bells, crotales, snare drum, marimba, sizzle cymbal, cowbells	
1998	Frédéric Macarez	*Des Pieds et des Mains*	4 timpani	7′
1998	Christopher Rouse	*Mime*	Snare drum	2′
1999	Roberto Sierra	*Los Destellos de la Resonancia* (solo + piano)	5 suspended cymbals, crotales, 5 floor cymbals	5′
1999	Stewart Wallace	*The Cheese and the Worms* (solo + piano)	Bongos, congas, vibraphone and bagpipes	12′
1999	Nebojša Jovan Živković	*The Castle of the Mad King*	China cymbal, suspended cymbal, opera gongs, tam-tam, thunder sheet, rainstick, metal tubes, split drum, bass drum, crotales (1 octave), Japanese drums, earth plates, wind chimes	17′
1999	Gareth Farr	*Taiko Tango*	Taiko	

Year	Composer	Title	Instrumentation (where available)	Duration (if known)
1999	Dave C. Heath	*Dawn of a New Age* (percussion, saxophone, piano)	Wind chimes, small bells, mark trees, tam-tam, vibraphone, drum kit	12'
2000	Stephen Montague	*Black'n'Blues* (solo + piano)	Marimba	10'
2000	Ruud Wiener	*Capriccio Virtuoso*	Marimba	1'30"
2000	Karl Jenkins	*Metallum* (percussion + hand bells)	Vibraphone, glockenspiel, suspended cymbal, tubular bells, tam-tam, bell tree, triangle, 3–5 small gongs	4'
2000	Sir Harrison Birtwistle	*The Axe Manual* (percussion + piano)	Marimba, vibraphone, hi-hat, 3 low drums, log drum, 2 congas, 2 bongos, cowbell, 4 wood blocks, 5 temple blocks	23'
2000	Robert Carl	*Written on Wood*	3 different "stations" Station 1: 2 mounted wood blocks, 2 mounted claves, rack of 5 wood blocks, rack of 5 temple blocks Station 2: anklung (1 octave), rack of 4 temple blocks, xylophone, portable wood block Station 3: 3 slit log drums, marimba Pianist also plays various percussion instruments: 2 sandpaper blocks, 2 castanets, 2 maracas, guiro, bamboo wind chimes, 2 aboriginal sticks, vibraslap, wood block, crackmar	9'
2001	Jeffrey Hoover	*Fourth World* (solo + piano)	Bongos, congas, talking drum, surdo, gong	10'30"
2001	Stewart Wallace	*Irving in Indonesia* (solo + piano)	Indonesian gongs	5'
2001	Christopher Rouse	*Àmhran* (percussion + bagpipes)	Tambour Provençale	

Year	Composer	Title	Instrumentation (where available)	Duration (if known)
2001	David Bedford	*To Ullapool and Beyond*	Vibraphone	
2001	Elena Kats-Chernin	*Vitalia's Steps* (percussion + piano)	Crotales, marimba, vibraphone, metal wind chimes, 2 suspended cymbals, 4 temple blocks, 5 cowbells, piccolo snare drum, tenor drum, claves	10′
2001	Nebojša Jovan Živković	*Quasi Una Sonata* (solo + piano)	Vibraphone, 1-octave almglocken, 3 Chinese temple bowls, 2 plastic blocks and 2 "crashers" above them, 1 "zillbell", 5 cymbals, 5 flats (or tom-toms), bass flat with pedal (or 18″ bass drum)	15′
2001	Nebojša Jovan Živković	*Born to Beat Wild* (percussion + trumpet)	Large drum	8′
2001	Joe Cutler	*Koroviev's Tricks* (percussion + piano)	Lithophone, crotales, ice bell (with rivets), 5 gongs, 22″ Chinese cymbal, 12″ splash cymbal, 2 suspended cymbals, 2 long thin metal pipes suspended from frame, metal pipe, metal block (or cowbell), 10 wood blocks, snare drum, 4 bongos, 3 congas, bass drum	10′
2002	Alistair King	*The Games we Play* (percussion + piano)	Marimba	
2002	Randall Woolf	*Missing*	Marimba, vibraphone	
2003	Steve Heitzig	*Free!*	Bass drum, 2 bell plates, chimes, 2 cowbells, glockenspiel, 7 llama hooves, small metal cage door, 2 metal pipes, metro police whistle, pedal bass drum, 3 sarna bell ropes, snare drum, 2 stones, tam-tam, temple blocks, tom-toms, thunder sheet (percussion, piano – who also plays with metal handcuffs, pencil and a sweetgrass bundle and tape)	15′

Year	Composer	Title	Instrumentation (where available)	Duration (if known)
2004	Jonathan Girling	*Long Lost Son* (percussion + choir)	Waterphone, various chimes, 5 double mark trees, 7 Uchiwa-Daikos, congas, tom-toms, 2 bass drums, whistle, cabasa, wrist bells, 6 cowbells, tam-tam, crotales, vibraphone, marimba, timbales, 4 spring drums, cymbals, 7 car exhaust pipes, 4 temple blocks	
2004	Karl Jenkins	*La Folia* (percussion + orchestra)	Marimba	15′
2004	Joseph Turrin	*Zarabanda* (percussion + wind band)	Xylophone, marimba	5′
2006	Jacob ter Veldhuis	*Barracuda Solo*	Marimba, hi-hat, bass drum, temple block, 2 small tom-toms, crash cymbal	9′
2006	Dorothy Hindman	*Tapping the Furnace*	Sprechstimme, snare drum, tom-toms, a selection of metal (cymbals, coins)	14′
2009	Christos Hatzis	*Mirage?* (solo + orchestra)	Vibraphone, cloud gongs	12′
2010	Yiu-Kwong Chung	*Emperor Qin* (2 percussionists + orchestra)	Marimba, glockenspiel, 4 tom-toms, 3 bass drums, 2 bongos, metal sheet, 2 roto-toms, 1 suspended cymbal, 2 China cymbals	13′
2011	Julia Wolfe	*Iron Maiden*	Hi-hat	12′
2011	David Lang	*Stuttered Chant* (percussion + cello)	Cello (as percussion instrument)	4′
2012	Phillip Sheppard	*Engine Block* (percussion + piano)	An improvised "xylophone" made from wrenches and spanners	

Year	Composer	Title	Instrumentation (where available)	Duration (if known)
2013	Luigi Morleo	*Art No War* (9 percussionists + orchestra)	Timpani, 2 vibraphones, 3 marimbas, drum kit, odaiko drum, bongos, congas, bass drum	
2015	James Keane	*Piece for Dance*	Bass drum, 5 tom-toms, cymbals, thunder sheet, marimba	
2015	Fabian Müller	*Extempore* (percussion + double bass)	Vibraphone	
2015	Bertram Wee	*Dithyrambs*	Aluphone	6′
2016	Luna Pearl Wolf	*Entanglement* (percussion + cello)	Cello (as percussion instrument)	10′
2016	Joan Tower	*SMALL*	For "small" percussion instruments	7′
2016	Jill Jarman	*Sounds of Science*	Details in Chapter 1	21′
2016	Francesco Antonioni	*Venus*	Marimba, waterphone, tam-tam	20′
2016	Derek Charke	*Tree Rings* (percussion + violin)	Marimba	
2017	Allan Bell	*Littoral/Liminal*	1 crash cymbal	
2017	Omar Daniel	*STELCO* (percussion + piano)	Vibraphone, 2 bells, 4 pieces of industrial metal, suspended cymbal	8′
2017	Jacques Cohen	*Firefly* (percussion + strings)	Xylophone	8′
2020	Stephen Goss	*The Lake of Time* (percussion + theorbo)	Marimba	9′
2021	Jill Jarman	*The Language of Bells*	Range of handheld bells, vibraphone, marimba, Aluphone	

Year	Composer	Title	Instrumentation (where available)	Duration (if known)
2022	Vincent Ho	*Nostalgia* (percussion + piano)	Vibraphone	5'
2022	Dorothy Chang	*Fragility* (percussion + cello)	Glockenspiel, marimba	15'
2022	Eugene Astapov	*Tiny Shattered Pieces* (percussion + electric violin)	Marimba, 5 triangles, 1 tubular bell, 5 wood blocks, 2 crotales, 1 tom-tom	12'
2022	Harry Stafylakis	*Incinerate* (percussion, violin, cello, piano)	Drum kit, vibraphone, marimba	17'
2022	Aitor Etxebarria	*Gernika 85* (percussion, choir, orchestra)	Timpani, snare drum, tubular bells, vibraphone, marimba	
2022	Ailís Ní Ríain	*Revelling and Reckoning*	Waterphone, 2 octobans, snare drum, 2 cymbals, Chinese anvils, Noah bells, cowbells, range of small metal instruments	15'
2022	Jill Jarman	*Across the Divide* (percussion + double bass)	Frame drum, gong, marimba, suspended cymbal, wood block, jam block, hi-hat, tambourine, snare drum, bass drum	

Bibliography

Additional Instruments (1898) *The Musical Times and Singing Class Circular,* 39 (662)

Alzheimer's Society (2023*) How Many People Have Dementia in the UK?* (online). Available from: https://www.alzheimers.org.uk/blog/how-many-people-have-dementia-uk

Anderson, M. (2001) Royal Albert Proms (3): Selected Premieres, *Tempo*, New Series No. 215

Ashley, T. (1997) Arts Review Classical: NSO Washington, Royal Festival Hall, London, *Guardian*, 20 October 1997

Barra, E., M. Fitts Ward, L.M. Anderson, A.M. Brown (2022) *Women in the Mix Study.* Recording Academy, Arizona State University, Berklee Institute for Creative Entrepreneurship

Bennett, R.R. (1990) *Percussion Concerto.* London: Novello and Co. (World)

Berlioz, H. (1844) *A Treatise on Modern Instrumentation and Orchestration,* trans. Mary Cowden Clarke. London: Novello

Biressi, A. (2013) The London 2012 Olympic Games Opening Ceremony: History Answers Back, *Journal of Popular Television*, 1 (1)

Björk (1996) *Björk on the Aftershock of Hate Mail and Love Affairs* (online). Available from: http://www.bjork.fr/Blah-Blah-Blah-1996

Borroff, E. (1975) Women Composers: Reminiscence and History, *College Music Symposium*, 15

Bowden, M. (2012) *Heartland: Description* (online). Available from: www.markbowden.net/music/heartland.html

Bowen, C. (1998) Shock of the New, *Scotland on Sunday*, 4 October 1998, section 16

Brennan, I. (2023) *Evelyn Glennie: "Sound can be the most subtle thing, but the body does need to slow down in order to connect with it."* (online). Available from: https://tapeop.com/interviews/154/evelyn-glennie/

Broom, C. (2018) Dame Evelyn Glennie Teams Up With Jazz Group Trio HLK at Petworth Festival, *The News*, Portsmouth (online), 26 July 2018. Available from: https://www.portsmouth.co.uk/whats-on/gigs-and-music/dame-evelyn-glennie-teams-up-with-jazz-group-trio-hlk-at-petworth-festival-1-8580199

Cage, J. (1937) *The Future of Music: Credo* (online). Available from: https://www.liberationofsound.org/words/the-future-of-music-credo/

———. (1960) *27'10.554" For a Percussionist.* New York: Henmar Press Inc./C.F Peters Corporation

———. (1961) *Silence.* Middleton: Wesleyan

Cairns, D. (1989) Performers Who Play with Fire, Record Choice, *The Sunday Times*, 30 July 1989

Childs, D. (2015) The Dame of Percussion. *Brass Band World* (online). Available from: https://www.brassbandworld.co.uk/features/705/the-dame-of-percussion

Chung, Y.-K. (2018) Programme Notes in *Percussion Concerto No. 3 for Solo Percussion and Orchestra.* New York: Universal Edition

Cline, D. (2016) *The Graph Music of Morton Feldman.* Cambridge: Cambridge University Press

Cooke, P.A. (2019) *The Music of James MacMillan.* Woodbridge: The Boydell Press

Corigliano, J. (2007) *Conjurer: Concerto for Percussionist and String Orchestra (with optional brass),* New York: Schirmer

Cundell, S. (2023) Variety is the Spice of Life … (online), 6 April 2023. Available from: https://www.evelyn.co.uk/variety-is-the-spice-of-life/

Curtis, L. (2018) *A View From Germany: Classical Music is So Sexist* (online). Available from: https://wophil.org/a-view-from-germany-classical-music-is-so-sexist/?doing_wp_cron=1561375680.6319100856781005859375

Dame Evelyn Glennie Speaks with Disability Talk (2017), online. Available from: https://disabilitytalk.co.uk/2017/09/28/dame-evelyn-glennie-speaks-disabilitytalk/

Daugherty, M. (1999) *UFO.* London: Boosey and Hawkes

———. (2014) *Programme Notes* (online). Available from: https://www.faber-music.com/music/dreamachine

Deaflympics: History (online). Available from: https://www.deaflympics.com/icsd/history

Doubleday, V. (1999) The Frame Drum in the Middle East: Women, Musical Instruments and Power, *Ethnomusicology*, 43 (1)

———. (2008) Sounds of Power: An Overview of Musical Instruments and Gender, *Ethnomusicology Forum*, 17 (1)

Duerden, N. (2012) How We Met: Marc Brew and Dame Evelyn Glennie, *Independent* (online), 22 August 2012. Available from: https://www.independent.co.uk/news/people/profiles/how-we-met-marc-brew-dame-evelyn-glennie-8073470.html

Duffie, B. (1994) *Percussionist Evelyn Glennie: A Conversation with Bruce Duffie* (online). Available from: http://www.bruceduffie.com/glennie.html

EKU Health and Safety PDF (online). Available from: https://www.eku.edu/musicprogram/wp-content/uploads/sites/59/2023/09/ekuhealthandsafety.pdf

Ellis, J. (2009) Evelyh [*sic*] Glennie. *Metro* (online), 27 October 2009. Available from: https://metro.co.uk/2009/10/27/evelyh-glennie-241150/

Evelyn Glennie Receives the Léonie Sonning Music Prize 2023 (online). Available from: https://www.sonningmusik.dk/evelyn-glennie/?lang=en

Evelyn Glennie review (2001) *Guardian* (online), 15 March 2001. Available from: https://www.theguardian.com/culture/2001/mar/15/artsfeatures4

The Evelyn Glennie Foundation: Charity Overview (2023), online. Available from: https://register-of-charities.charitycommission.gov.uk/charity-search/-/charity-details/5193276/full-print

The Everyday Sexism Project (2012), online. Available from: https://everyday-sexism.com/?s=music

Fellows, E. (2008) Dame Evelyn Glennie: Percussion's "First" Lady, *The American Music Teacher*, 57 (6)

Ferreira, M. (2022) *A symphonic work with testimonies of the victims will pay tribute to Gernika on the 85th anniversary of the bombing* (online), 20 April 2022. Available from: https://www.eldiario.es/euskadi/obra-sin-fonica-testimonios-victimas-homenajeara-gernika-85-aniversario-bombardeo_1_8924065.html

Fidler, F.G. (1921) *A Handbook of Orchestration*. London: Kegan Paul, Trench, Trubner and Co.

Fisher, P. (1992) A Woman on the Move: Paul Fisher Meets Evelyn Glennie, the World's Only Full-Time Female Solo Percussionist, *Independent* (London), 7th August 1992

Frith, F. *About Fred* [online]. Available from: http://www.fredfrith.com/ueber-mich/

Galton, F. (1892) *Hereditary Genius: An Inquiry Into Its Laws and Consequences.* London: Macmillan

Gammon, V. (1999) Cultural Politics of the English National Curriculum for Music, 1991–1992, *Journal of Educational Administration and History*, 31 (2)

Gay, R. (2014), *Bad Feminist*, New York: Harper Collins

Gibbs, C.H. and D. Gooley, eds. (2006), *Franz Liszt and His World.* Princeton: Princeton University Press

Ginn, K. (2002) The Stubborn Virtuoso, *Daily Mail*, 19 June 2002

Glennie, E. (1990) *Good Vibrations: My Autobiography.* London: Hutchinson

———. (2002) *Oxygen* (online). Available from: http://www.bjork.fr/Evelyn-Glennie,2716

———. (2003; revised 2015) *Hearing Essay* (online). Available from: https://www.evelyn.co.uk/hearing-essay/

———. (2004) Letter: Save Music at Exeter, *Guardian*, 10 December 2004

———. (2012) *Shadow Behind the Iron Sounds* (online blog), 18 April 2012. Available from: https://www.evelyn.co.uk/shadow-behind-the-iron-sounds/

———. (2018) Music Interview: Dame Evelyn Glennie, *Yorkshire Post* (online), 2 November 2018. Available from: https://www.yorkshirepost.co.uk/arts-and-culture/music-interview-dame-evelyn-glennie-i-knew-i-would-be-out-my-comfort-zone-thats-always-good-thing-any-musician-experience-230770

———. (2018) Percussionist Evelyn Glennie: Listen – Immersive Sound Opens Up Amazing Theatrical Possibilities, *The Stage* (online), 19 October 2015.

Available from: https://www.thestage.co.uk/opinion/percussionist-evelyn-glennie-listen--immersive-sound-opens-up-amazing-theatrical-possibilities

———. (2019) *I'm a Grammy Award Winning Musician and I'm Deaf* (online), 28 May 2019. Available from: https://www.evelyn.co.uk/im-a-grammy-award-winning-musician-and-im-deaf/

———. (n.d.) Waterphone (online). Originally available from https://waterphone.com. At the time of publication, this website is in the process of being updated.

———. (n.d.) *Dame Evelyn Glennie: Virtuoso Solo & Multi-Percussionist* (online). Available from: https://www.percworks.co.uk/dameevelynglennie

Great Scot or Great Human Being: It Doesn't Matter as Long as They're Giving Back to the Next Generation Says Evelyn Glennie (2003) *Sunday Mail* (Glasgow), 22 June 2003

Groeneveld, E. (2009) "Be a Feminist or Just Dress Like One": *BUST*, Fashion and Feminism as Lifestyle, *Journal of Gender Studies*, 18 (2)

Gunton, E. (2021) Drumming Up Future Talent: Dame Evelyn Glennie, *Music Teacher* (online), 1 July 2021. Available from: https://www.musicteachermagazine.co.uk/features/article/drumming-up-future-talent-dame-evelyn-glennie

Henken, J. (1991) Percussionist Plays from Her Heart: Hearing Loss Hasn't Slowed Evelyn Glennie, *Los Angeles Times* (online), 13 September 1991. Available from: http://articles.latimes.com/1991-09-13/entertainment/ca-2291_1_hearing-loss

Higgins, C. (2000) Drum Machine, *Guardian* (online), 18 July 2000. Available from: https://www.theguardian.com/culture/2000/jul/18/artsfeatures.proms2000

Holmes, J. (2017) Expert Listening Beyond the Limits of Hearing: Music and Deafness, *Journal of the American Musicological Society*, 70 (1)

Howe, B. (2010) Paul Wittgenstein and the Performance of Disability, *The Journal of Musicology*, 27 (2)

Info for Composers (online). Available from: https://aluphone.dk/info-for-composers/

Jackson, C. (2021) *Classical Music's Enduring Relationship with Fashion* (online), 25 January 2021 (originally published in *BBC Music Magazine* June 2020). Available from: https://www.classical-music.com/features/articles/classical-musics-enduring-relationship-with-fashion/

James Blades Collection (online). Available from: https://www.ram.ac.uk/museum/collections-index/performers

Jarman, J. (2016) *Sounds of Science: Telling Our Story Through Music* (online), 23 June 2016. Available from: https://www.evelyn.co.uk/sounds-science-telling-story-music/

Jeal, E. (2003) BBCSO/Tortelier: Royal Albert Hall, *Guardian* (online), 21 August 2003. Available from: https://www.theguardian.com/music/2003/aug/21/classicalmusicandopera.proms2003

——. (2007) Prom 63: BBCSO/Belohlavek, Royal Albert Hall, London, *Guardian*, review section, 3 September 2007

Kennicott, P. (2000), Percussionist Evelyn Glennie's Otherworldly Rhythms, *Washington Post* (online), 6 October 2000. Available from: https://www.washingtonpost.com/archive/lifestyle/2000/10/06/percussion-ist-evelyn-glennies-otherworldly-rhythms/e076d1e2-3227-4d02-9f0d-7353987559f4/?utm_term=.194946cd4bf5

Kimberley, N. (2000) Classical – Even More Bangs for your Buck in David Bedford's New Percussion Concerto, *Independent*, 3 March 2000

Kite, R. (2007) *Keiko Abe: A Virtuosic Life.* Leesburg: GP Percussion

Klein, H. (1964) Music: Avant-Garde Festival Closes, *New York Times,* 4 September 1964

Koskoff, E. (2014) *A Feminist Ethnomusicology: Writings on Music and Gender.* Urbana: University of Illinois Press

Lacey, H. (1994) How We Met: James Blades and Evelyn Glennie, *Independent* (online), 21 May 1994. Available from: http://www.independent.co.uk.arts-en-tertainment/how-we-met-james-blades-and-evelyn-glennie-1437629.html

The Language of Bells (2021), online. Available from: https://www.evelyn.co.uk/evet/the-language-of-bells/

Lewis, K. and Gustavo Adler, eds. (2014) *The Modern Percussion Revolution: Journeys of the Progressive Artist.* London: Routledge

MacLeod, F. (2009) Glennie Calls for Every Scots Child to be Given "Lifeline" Education in Music, *The Scotsman,* 23 December 2009

MacMillan, J. and R. McGregor (2010) James MacMillan: A Conversation and Commentary, *The Musical Times,* 151 (1912)

Maddocks, F. (2013) Marin Alsop, Conductor of Last Night of the Proms, on Sexism in Classical Music, *Guardian* (online), 6 September 2013. Available from: https://www.theguardian.com/music/2013/sep/06/marin-alsop-proms-classical-sexist

Manderson, D. (2010) Fission and Fusion: From Improvisation to Formalism in Law and Music, *Critical Studies in Improvisation,* 6 (1)

Marc Brew (online). Available from: https://www.disabilityartsinternational.org/artists/profiles/marc-brew/

Maria Rud biography (online). Available from: https://www.mariarudart.com/about

Marsh, C. (2011) "The Pride of Noise": Drums and Their Repercussions in Early Modern England, *Early Music,* 39 (2)

Martin Grubinger Biography (2019/20), online. Available from: https://www.harrisonparrott.com/artists/martin-grubinger

Martinson, J. and J. Adetunji (2012) Generation of Women Hit by "Toxic Combination of Ageism and Sexism", *Guardian* (online), 29 September

2012. Available from: https://www.theguardian.com/world/2012/sep/29/generation-women-toxic-ageism-sexism

Masłowska, A. (2013) *Polish music, especially composition, is doing very well: Interview with Marta Ptaszyńska* (online), 24 June 2013. Available from: https://meakultura.pl/artykul/polska-muzyka-a-zwlaszcza-kompozycja-ma-sie-doskonale-wywiad-z-marta-ptaszynska-598/

Mattingly, R. (1996) Nexus. *Percussive Notes*, August 1996

McClary, S. (1993) Reshaping a Discipline: Musicology and Feminism in the 1990s, *Feminist Studies*, 19 (2)

Mental Health Foundation (2015) *Dementia, Rights, and the Social Model of Disability: A New Direction for Policy and Practice?* (online). Available from: http://www.innovationsindementia.org.uk/wp-content/uploads/2018/01/dementia-rights-policy-discussion.pdf

Middlehurst, L. (1996) Hearing Again Would be a Real Handicap. *Daily Mail*, 20 January 1996

Milhaud, D. (1930) Work Introduction, from *Concerto Pour Batterie et Petit Orchestre*. Vienna: Universal Edition

Moir, J. (1993) Women: Good Vibrations, Public Lives: Evelyn Glennie, Catapulted into the Media Spotlight by her Protest Resignation from the Arts Council Last Week, *Guardian*, 8 December 1993

Moore, E. (1997) My Inspiration: Evelyn Glennie and Her Favourite Teacher Spill the Beans About Each Other, *Guardian*, Education Supplement, 2 December 1997

Morrison, J. (2002) Education: Classical Stars Rail at Musical "Illiteracy", *Independent on Sunday*, 1 December 2002

Morrison, N. (2009) *My Best Teacher* (online), 10 April 2009. Available from: https://www.tes.com/magazine/archive/my-best-teacher-evelyn-glennie

Naxos (2005) *Programme notes for Virtuoso Timpani Concertos* (online). Available from: Virtuoso Timpani Concertos NAXOS 8.557610 [RH]: Classical CD Reviews- October 2005 MusicWeb-International

Nepilova, H. (2021) Evelyn Glennie: How Do You Listen Through Technology?, *The Financial Times* (online), 7 January 2021. Available from: https://www.ft.com/content/0678c546-2683-4db8-9b49-e2073d28db0e

Nickalls, S. (2013) The Animotion Show, St Giles' Cathedral Edinburgh – Review, *The Financial Times* (online), 19 December 2013. Available from: https://www.ft.com/content/d987e920-6806-11e3-8ada-00144feabdco

Norris, M. and M. Block (2005) *NPR: All Things Considered: Thomas Riedelsheimer Discusses Stretching the Senses in 'Touch the Sound'* (online), 30 September 2005. Available from: https://www.npr.org/2005/09/30/4931402/stretching-the-senses-in-touch-the-sound

Oates, J.C. (1966) The Ambiguity of Troilus and Cressida, *Shakespeare Quarterly*, 17 (2)

Oestreich, J.R. (2001) Call Her a Musician, Pure and Simple, *New York Times*, section 2, 30 September 2001

262   *Bibliography*

One Day Band (2019), online. Available from: http://www.trestlerec.com/one-daybands.html

Paige, R. (1952) Why Not Women in Orchestras?, *Etude*, 70

Pasternak, S. (2013) Evelyn Glennie on the Olympics Opening Ceremony, *TomTom Magazine* (online). Available from: https://tomtommag.com/2013/02/evelyn-glennie-on-the-olympics-opening-ceremony/

Peisner, D. (2013) *Deaf Jams: The Surprising, Conflicted, Thriving World of Hearing-Impaired Rappers* (online), 29 October 2013. Available from: https://www.spin.com/2013/10/deaf-jams-hearing-impaired-rappers/

Petrie, C. (2023) World-Renowned Musician Adds Voice to Calls to Save Big Noise Torry (online), 27 February 2023. Available from: https://www.pressandjournal.co.uk/fp/education/5443255/dame-evelyn-glennie-big-noise-torry/?fbclid=IwAR2I_j9GFs2WGS8b9YRRWgxmNG-YFHxcK-miICFoANjJvG-maaWpUPHCBU3Y

Pillow, I. (1997) Hard Heart, Soft Stroke, *Independent* (online), 24 July 1997. Available from: http://www.independent.co.uk/arts-entertainment/msuic/hard-heart-soft-stroke-1252392.html

Pitman, J. (1996) Banging About in the Kitchen: Profile, Evelyn Glennie, *The Times*, 4 May 1996

Potter, K. (2003) Prom 41: Chen Yi/Evelyn Glennie, Royal Albert Hall, London/Radio 3, *Independent*, 27 August 2003

Produnov, I. (1998) The Castle of the Mad King, *Percussive Notes*, 35 (5)

PRS Foundation (2013) *Guest of the Month April 2013: Dame Evelyn Glennie* (online). Available from: http://prsfoundation.com/about-us/guest-of-the-month/guests-of-the-month-2013/april-2013-dame-evelyn-glennie/

Ptaszyńska, M. and B. Duffie (1988 and 1997) *Composer/Percussionist Marta Ptaszynska: Two Conversations with Bruce Duffie* (online). Available from: http://www.bruceduffie.com/ptaszynska.html

Ptaszyńska, M. (2009) *Drum of Orfeo: Concerto for Percussion and Orchestra.* Kraków: PWM Editions

Pyke, N. (2004) Top Musicians Attack Master Plan for Schools, *Independent on Sunday*, 4 July 2004

Quignard, P. (2016) Second Treatise: "It So Happens That Ears Have No Eyelids" from *The Hatred of Music*. Translated from French by Matthew Amos and Fredrik Rönnbäck. New Haven: Yale University Press

Reisler, J. (2014) *Voices of the Oral Deaf: Fourteen Role Models Speak Out.* London: Mc Farland and Company

Riot Grrrl Manifesto (1991), online. Available from: https://www.historyisaweapon.com/defcon1/riotgrrrlmanifesto.html

Roberts, A. (2022) *The Evelyn Glennie Collection – Picture This!* (online), 8 June 2022. Available from: https://www.evelyn.co.uk/the-evelyn-glennie-collection-picture-this/

Romano, W. (2014) Steven Schick: Interview, *Modern Drummer Magazine* (online), May 2014. Available from: https://www.moderndrummer.com/article/may-2014-steven-schick/

Ross, A. (2006) American Sublime, *The New Yorker*, 19 June 2006. Available from: www.therestisnoise.com/2006/06/morton_feldman_.html

Sabaneev, L. and S.W Pring (1928) The Destinies of Music, *The Musical Times*, 69 (1024)

Sawyer, R.K. (2006) Group Creativity: Musical Performance and Collaboration, *Psychology of Music*, 34

Schutz, M. and F. Manning (2012) Looking Beyond the Score: The Musical Role of Percussionists' Ancillary Gestures, *Music Theory*, 18 (1), online. Available from: http://www.mtosmt.org/issues/mto.12.18.1/mto.12.18.1.schutz_manning.php

Service, T. (2010) Taking the Knocks: The Chequered History of the Percussion Concerto, *Guardian* (online), 1 October 2010. Available from: https://www.theguardian.com/music/tomserviceblog/2010/oct/01/percussion-concerto-o-duo

Seymour, C. (2017) *Evelyn Glennie on Scintillating Form in Michael Daugherty's Percussion Concerto* (online), 18 June 2017. Available from: http://seenandheard-international.com/2016/06/evelyn-glennie-on-scintillating-form-in-michael-daughertys-percussion-concerto/

Simonton, D.K. (1994) *Greatness.* New York: Guilford Press

Small, C. (1998) *Musicking: The Meanings of Performing and Listening.* Connecticut: Wesleyan University Press

Smart, A. (2013) Female Trombonist Fought Battle Against Orchestra Sexism, *Times Colonist* (Vancouver), online, 17 September 2013. Available from: https://www.timescolonist.com/entertainment/music/female-trombonist-fought-battle-against-orchestra-sexism-1.628198

Smith, A. (2014) *Women Drummers: A History from Rock and Jazz to Blues and Country.* Lanham: Rowman and Littlefield

Smith, K. (2018) Dame Evelyn Glennie Shares Her Early Years, *Scottish Field*, 5 October 2018 (online). Available from: https://www.scottishfield.co.uk/culture/music/dame-evelyn-glennie-shares-her-early-years/

Sommers, P. (1994) A Different Drummer, *Washington Post*, 5 March 1994

Sounds of Science Translates the Story of Engineering into a Musical Masterpiece (online). Available from: http://www.imeche.org/news/news-article/the-sounds-of-science-translates-the-story-of-engineering-into-a-musical-masterpiece

Steve Weiss Music (n.d.) *Zivkovic-Concerto #1 for Perc. And Orch. (Concerto of the Mad Queen)* – Product Information (online). Available from: https://www.steveweissmusic.com/product/26025/multi-percussion-accompaniment#full-description

Stewart Howes, F. (1942) *Full Orchestra.* London: Secker and Warburg

Stokes. W. (2022) *Spitfire Audio teams up with legendary percussionist Dame Evelyn Glennie to create Resonate* (online), 9 June 2022. Available from: https://musictech.com/uncategorised/spitfire-audio-percussionist-evelyn-glennie-resonate/ (accessed 1 March 2023)

Stone, A. (2015) Deaf Rapper Sean Forbes Makes Himself Joyfully Heard on the Hip-Hop Scene, *Washington Post* (online), 25 January 2015. Available from: https://www.washingtonpost.com/entertainment/music/deaf-rapper-sean-forbes-makes-himself-joyfully-heard-on-the-hip-hop-scene/2015/01/25/15943fdc-a0f4-11e4-9f89-561284a573f8_story.html

Straus, J.N. (2011) *Extraordinary Measures: Disability in Music.* Oxford: Oxford University Press

These Terrible Album Covers Will Make you Laugh and Then Violently Cringe (online). Available from: https://www.classicfm.com/discover-music/latest/worst-classical-album-covers-ever/derek-bell-plays-with-himself/

Thompson, C. (2022) *The Evelyn Glennie Collection – Gathering Momentum* (online), 29 March 2022. Available from: https://www.evelyn.co.uk/the-evelyn-glennie-collection-gathering-momentum/

Titon, J.T. (2013) The Nature of Ecomusicology, *Música e Cultura: revista da ABET*, 8 (1)

Trillo Clough, R. (1961) *Futurism: The Story of a Modern Art Movement – A New Appraisal.* New York: Polyglot Press

Trotter, H. (2010) Virtuosity Reverberates in Percussive Artistry, *Buffalo News* (online), 19 April 2010. Available from: https://buffalonews.com/2010/04/19/virtuosity-reverberates-in-percussive-artistry/

Tumelty, M. (1992) Dazzle Factor. Evelyn Glennie, RSAMD, Glasgow, *The Herald*, 18 November 1992

Varty, A. (2013) Evelyn Glennie gets Unhinged with Musicophilia, *The Georgia Straight* (online), 24 September 2013. Available from: https://www.straight.com/arts/428916/evelyn-glennie-gets-unhinged-musicophilia

Vogel Weiss, L. (1993) *PAS Hall of Fame: Keiko Abe* (online). Available from: https://www.pas.org/about/hall-of-fame/keiko-abe#:~:text=The%20first%20woman%20ever%20inducted%20into%20the%20PAS,with%20the%20confident%20way%20she%20approaches%20the%20marimba

———. (2008) Evelyn Glennie, *Percussive Notes*, 46 (4)

Walker, L. (2001) Hit Me with Your Rhythm Schtick, *Independent*, 10 March 2001

Walters, C.A. (2003) *Music Development and Hearing Impairment: A Case Study of Evelyn Glennie*, MA thesis, University of Cape Town

Welter, B. (1966) The Cult of True Womanhood: 1820–1860, *American Quarterly* 18 (2), part 1

White, C.L. (1971) The Rite Timpani Player, *Percussionist*, 8 (4)

Whitworth, D. (2015) From the "Nobel Prize" of Music to Her Own Prom, *The Times*, 6 August 2015

Winters, K. (1960) Perspectives: The Paris Music Season 1959–60, *Canadian Music Journal*, 4 (4)

Young, J.O. (2010) Art and the Educated Audience, *The Journal of Aesthetic Education*, 44 (3)

Zimmerman, W. (1985) *Morton Feldman Essays.* Kerpen: Beginner Press

Videography and Audio Resources

Artful Narratives Media (2022) *Dame Evelyn Glennie Talks Percussion, Profound Deafness, and Learning How to Listen* (video online), 3 October 2022. Available from: https://www.youtube.com/watch?v=gfrz_MUOln4

BBC See Hear *When Evelyn Met Sean* (video online). Available from: https://www.facebook.com/bbcseehear/videos/1139039246148146/

Birnbaum, D. (2021) *Teach the World to Listen* (podcast online), 16 August 2021. Available from: https://podcast.davebirnbaum.com/teach-the-world-to-listen

The Cleveland Orchestra (2021) *John Corigliano: Crafting Conjurer* (video online), 6 May 2021. Available from: https://www.youtube.com/watch?v=92uPUONtanY

Corigliano, J. (2014) *Seminar and conversation with Michael Stern*, Nelson-Atkins Museum of Art (Kansas, Missouri), 30 January 2014 (video online). Available from: https://www.youtube.com/watch?v=X46Pgz8dHrM

Corigliano, J. and M. Damoulakis (2021) *John Corigliano and Mark Damoulakis: Improvisation in Conjurer* (video online), 16 June 2021. Posted by the Cleveland Orchestra. Available from: https://www.youtube.com/watch?v=-17fRLBo3IfY (accessed 21 March 2023).

Edeline Lee at AW19 at London Fashion Week (2019), video online. Available from: https://www.youtube.com/watch?v=UTMxA7G_6p0

Glennie, E. (2011) *Evelyn Glennie Shadow Behind the Iron Sun Show with Fred Frith & Trilok Gurtu Eindhoven 2006* (video online). Available from: https://www.youtube.com/watch?v=RviHoQQ2SNs

———. (2012) A rare interesting documentary 1988 Grammy winner recording of Bartok's sonata (videos online). Available from: https://www.youtube.com/watch?v=A6fyDv-Q3v4, https://www.youtube.com/watch?v=qjorUBaLc2c, and https://www.youtube.com/watch?v=A6MQHFe8loo

———. (2012) *Evelyn Glennie performs UFO by Michael Daugherty with the Kent County Youth Orch - 09/2000* (video online). Available from: https://www.youtube.com/watch?v=GyRlozJxDio

———. (2012) *Evelyn Glennie Documentary on the Making of the Album "Shadow Behind the Iron Sun"* (video online). Available from: https://www.youtube.com/watch?v=xGuUX1NEock

———. (2013) *Evelyn Glennie at Moers Jazz Festival, Germany – May 2013* (video online). Available from: https://www.youtube.com/watch?v=JkPXuPwaUCM

———. (2019) *World Elephant Day 2019: Behind the Scenes* (video online). Available from: https://www.evelyn.co.uk/world-elephant-day-2019-behind-the-scenes/

———. (2019) *What is Your Favourite Instrument?* (2019), video online, 2 April 2019. Available from: https://www.youtube.com/watch?v=1bEoqLpap68

———. (2020) *The Evelyn Glennie Collection – Volunteers* (video online), 28 July 2020. Available from: https://www.youtube.com/watch?v=9OMAzQFqiIo

———. (2021) *Evelyn Glennie at the EA Festival* (video online), 26 August 2021. Available from: https://www.youtube.com/watch?v=cnx9eyS9E28&t=1766s

Glester, A. (2017) *Love and Science: LISA's Gravitational Waves, Dame Evelyn Glennie and Hannah Peel* (podcast), 26 June 2017. Available from: https://loveandscience.podbean.com/e/lisas-gravitational-waves-dame-evelyn-glennie-and-hannah-peel/

LMEA Music (2021) *Healing Power of Music, An Interview with Dame Evelyn Glennie* (video online). Available from: https://www.youtube.com/watch?v=RRFYmnRNNn8&t=1553s

Musical U: Evelyn Glennie in Christopher Sutton (2019) *The Musicality Podcast: How to Truly Listen, with Evelyn Glennie* (video online), 26 February 2019. Available from: https://www.youtube.com/watch?v=HrgXUEF1Fjo

Olympic (2012) *The Complete London 2012 Opening Ceremony* (video online). Available from: https://www.youtube.com/watch?v=4Asoe4de-rI

Onward to Europe, Integrating the East and West (2012), DVD. Taiwan: Taipei Chinese Orchestra

Polar Music Prize (2015) *2015 Laureate Evelyn Glennie: Announcement Video* (online). Available from: https://www.polarmusicprize.org/laureates/evelyn-glennie

Polar Music Prize (2015) *Polar Music Prize Laureate Dame Evelyn Glennie Meets Her First Percussion Tutor Ron Forbes* (video online), 13 June 2015. Available from: https://www.youtube.com/watch?v=1ZNcMMx_J2I&t=52s

Radio New Zealand Interview with Evelyn Glennie: Composer of the Week (2015), *Evelyn Glennie – Percussion Champion* (online), 19 July 2015. Available from: http://www.radionz.co.nz/concert/programmes/composeroftheweek/audio/201762818/evelyn-glennie-percussion-champion

Riedelsheimer, T. (2004) *Touch the Sound: A Sound Journey with Evelyn Glennie* (DVD) Docurama

Ryabova, N. (2018) *Love is Listening: Dementia Without Loneliness* (DVD) Memory Bridge

Talks at Google (2023) *Evelyn Glennie "Listen World"* (video online), 8 December 2023. Available from: https://www.youtube.com/watch?v=MV1kuZSNCF4&t=67s

TED (2003; published 2007) *How to Truly Listen: Evelyn Glennie* (video online). Available from: https://www.youtube.com/watch?v=IU3V6zNER4g

Trestle Records (2019) *ODB 17 – Evelyn Glennie/Roly Porter Interview* (video online). Available from: https://www.youtube.com/watch?v=KblVihczuQg

Trio HLK (2019) *Trio HLK and Evelyn Glennie* (video online). Available from: https://www.youtube.com/watch?v=wTeb6OtsLQ4

VHS Bits (2019) *1988 Evelyn Glennie Interview – BBC1 "The Garden Party"* (video online), 11 November 2019. Available from: https://www.youtube.com/watch?v=7E3_BXgPdas

Index

Abe, Keiko, 8, 24, 25, 68, 69, 108, 149
Activism, 11, 78, 148, 172, 187, 229, 233
    disability, 147, 153, 159, 167
    education, 171, 173
    environmental, 183, 185
    feminist, 103
    social, 207
Ageism, 143, 176, 192
Alsop, Marin, 121, 134
Aluphone, 31, 34, 140, 170, 209
    Animotion, 82
    Concerto for Aluphone and Orchestra, 35
    Deaf and Loud Symphonic Experience, 168
    Glennie Concert, 35, 181, 182
    Sounds of Science, 51
    The Language of Bells, 189
    Troilus and Cressida, 198, 201, 202, 209
Ancillary, 19, 22
Animotion, 78–84, 87, *see also* Rud, Maria
Annotations, 217, 229
    Darkness to Light, 48, 49
    Drum of Orfeo, 131
    My Dream Kitchen, 113, 114
    Sounds of Science, 53
    The Jig, 90
    The Language of Bells, 190
    UFO, 42
    Veni, Veni Emmanuel, 40
Assad, Clarice, 26
Audio Network, 98
Avant-Garde, 1, 13, 30, 87, 88, 148

Barimbulum, 35, 59, 82, 200

Baroque, 12, 25, 28, 64, 104, 105, 127
Bartók, Béla, *Sonata for Two Pianos and Percussion,* 8–10
Bates, Django: *My Dream Kitchen,* 46, 111–115
Batonka, 31–33, *see also* Embliss, Will
BBC, 6, 103, 146, 167, 182
    Proms, 2, 25, 37, 134, 170
    Young Musician of the Year, 169, 170
Beamish, Sally, 204
    Whisper, 56
Beard, Mary, 136, 139, *see also Women in Power*
Becker, Bob, 66, *see also* Nexus
Bedford, David, 33
Beethoven, Ludwig Van, 146, 154
Beethoven Fund for Deaf Children, 155, 160, 226, *see also* Rachlin, Ann and Ezra
Bell, Allan, 46, 55
Björk, 69, 209
Blades, James, 7, 30, 116, 226
Boyle, Danny, 179–180, *see also* Olympics Opening Ceremony
Brauer, Michael, 62, 71, 72, *see also Shadow Behind the Iron Sun*
Brew, Marc, 84–85, *see also Fusional Fragments*
Britten, Benjamin, 7, 8, 30
Business, 10, 73, 107, 109, 140–143, 145, 233
    businesswoman, 133, 140

Cadenza, 18, 63, 64, 65, 220
    Concerto for Solo Percussion and Chinese Traditional Orchestra, 151

270 Index

Conjurer, 123, 124
Crossings, 228
Dreamachine, 222, 224
Drum of Orfeo, 131
Heartland, 35
Konzertstück (Másson), 228
Percussion Concerto (Bedford), 33
The Song of Dionysius, 24
Veni, Veni Emmanuel, 39
Cage, John, 4, 17, 20, 30, 149
  27'10.554", 15
  Credo in Us, 210
Canon, 65, 67 172
  gender, 101, 103, 104
  percussion, 31, 66, 118, 203, 207,
    219, 221
Caskel, Christoph, 2, 16, 18
Causton, Richard, 149
Choreography, 19, 21, 23, 34, 38, 42,
  84, 86, 180
Chung, Yiu-Kwong, *Concerto for
  Solo Percussion and Chinese
  Traditional Orchestra,* 149–152
Classical, 1, 12, 28, 64, 67, 105, 106,
    130, 166, 173, 208
  gender, 134, 135
  Grammy Awards, 122
  Shadow Behind the Iron Sun, 73
  Trio HLK, 70, 87–88
Collaboration, 7, 11, 54, 59, 75, 98, 127,
    128, 136, 139, 175, 221, 232, 233
  Audio Network, 98
  Bartók, 10
  Brew, 87
  Björk, 69, 209
  Etxebarria, 205
  Forbes, 160, 166
  Frith, 75
  Glennie, 9, 12, 25, 31, 35, 45, 61, 62,
    78, 85, 100, 147, 192, 211, 225, 230
  Jarman, 50, 188
  MacMillan, 40
  Másson, 228
  Milhaud, 14

Olympics, 179
online, 186
Roly Porter, 93–97
Royal Shakespeare Company, 196,
  203
Rud, 79–82
Spitfire Audio, 99
The Evelyn Glennie Collection,
  212, 213, 214
Trio HLK, 90, 93
Živković, 116, 119
Corigliano, John, *Conjurer,* 119–127,
  131
Corkhill, David, 9, 10
Coutelier, Theo, 14
COVID-19, 90, 95, 98, 144, 171, 207,
  214, 217
The Language of Bells, 185–191
Cults Percussion Ensemble, 3–5, *see
  also* Forbes, Ron
Currie, Colin, 34, 40, 122, 170, 207

Dance, 61, 78, 84
  Animotion, 81, 87
  Fusional Fragments, 84–85, 87
  L'Histoire du Soldat, 13
  Olympics, 180, 182
  Roly Porter (EDM), 94
  Shadow Behind the Iron Sun, 72
  Troilus and Cressida, 203
  zortziko, 206
Daugherty, Michael, 54
  Dreamachine, 27, 218, 221–224
  UFO, 41–45
*Deaf and Loud Symphonic
  Experience,* 166–169
Deaflympics, 149–152
Dempster, Kenneth, 25
Disability, 2, 85, 101, 135, 154, 156, 166,
  176
  activism, 147, 167
  claiming of, 147, 153, 159, 160, 163,
    165, 169
  rights, 192, 229, 233

Royal Academy of Music, 5
studies, 153, 158, 159
Diversification, 47, 103, 219, 232
and career, 75, 78, 143, 148, 175
Shadow Behind the Iron Sun, 70
Trio HLK, 87
Doran Greg, 196–197, *see also* Royal
Shakespeare Company and
Troilus and Cressida
Drum kit, 46, 107, 183, 210, 182
Animotion, 81
Darkness to Light, 48–49
L'Histoire du Soldat, 13
Shadow Behind the Iron Sun, 72
Trio HLK, 90

Ecomusicology, 182
Electronic dance music, 61, 94
Embliss, Will, 31–32, *see also* Batonka
Empowerment, 159, 233
gender, 102, 103, 111, 136, 139–140,
144
d/Deaf, 160, 163, 169
Entrepreneur, 7, 61, 102
Glennie as, 98, 133, 139–144, 195,
230–232
Etxebarria, Aitor, *Gernika 85,*
203–207
Eurocentric, 28, 105, 148
Evelyn Glennie Collection, The, 30,
31, 35, 40, 43, 85, 112, 136, 159,
193, 205, 208, 212–217, 226, 227,
230, 232
Evelyn Glennie Foundation, The, 144,
146, 175, 193, 216, 226
Evelyn Glennie Podcast, The, 139, 143
Evelyn Glennie's Hitlist, 49
Exclusion, 5, 87, 135, 153, 156, 175, 176
Expert listener, 11, 231, 233
Glennie as, 2, 76, 139, 163,
165–166, 169
Love is Listening, 177–178

Farr, Gareth, 33, 56

Feldman Morton, *The King of
Denmark,* 15–17
Feminism, 102–103, 136
Feminist, 102, 103, 109, 110–111, 128,
144, 233
Glennie as, 101, 103
musicology, 103–104
Women in Power, 134–136
Fifty for Fifty, 55–58, 152, 228
Forbes, Ron, 3–4, 68, 211, 227, *see
also* Cults Percussion Ensemble
Forbes, Sean, 166–169, *see also
Deaf and Loud Symphonic
Experience*
Frith, Fred, 74–77, *see also Touch the
Sound*
Fusional Fragments, 84–87
Futurism, 30

Glennie, Evelyn
and costume, 21–23, 41, 82, 113,
115, 135–136, 196–197, 212, 217
and d/Deafness, 3, 22, 87, 147,
150, 153–158, 176, 180, 209, 225,
229–233
as brand, 10, 46, 73, 107, 133, 135,
141, 142
as composer, 61, 78, 85, 98, 143,
196–197
as d/Deaf musician, 2, 6, 22, 72,
76, 103, 110, 135, 145, 192, 194,
211
as philanthropist, 61, 62, 147, 166
awards, 5, 10, 122, 123, 193–194,
207–208, 210, 212, 225
childhood, 3, 161, 170, 177, 204, 213
Good Vibrations, 3, 4, 10, 154, 156,
160–164, 170, 233
on d/Deafness, 5, 85, 146, 153, 156,
158, 159, 160–169, 171
on improvisation, 8, 49, 69, 70–73,
75, 78, 80, 83, 100
on recording, 21, 70, 88, 98, 133,
165, 194

272 *Index*

Grammy, 9, 42, 121, 122–123, 208
Graphic notation, 15–18, 116
Grubinger, Martin, 34, 122
Gualda, Sylvio, 2, 18

Hamilton Green, George, 65–66
Harrold, Richard, 87–92, 208, *see also*
  Trio HLK
Hearing Essay, 160–164
Heath, Dave C., 54, 81–82
  African Sunrise/Manhattan Rave,
    26, 170
  Darkness to Light, 47–50
HELP Musicians, 186
Ho, Vincent, 52, 54, 57, 133
Horne, David, 46, 48

Improvisation, *see* Glennie, Evelyn
Interdisciplinary, 50, 59, 61, 64, 78, 87,
    139, 182, 188, 195, 211, 229, 230
  disability studies, 153, 159
  Troilus and Cressida, 196
Intersectionality, 2, 102–103, 135

Janissary, 28–29, 104
Japanese, 8, 150
  performers, 67, 149
  instruments, 91, 117, 129, 130
Jarman, Jill, 54, 93
  Sounds of Science, 50–53, 94
  The Language of Bells, 187–191
Jazz, 8, 13, 46, 50, 61, 62, 66, 168, 210
  Darkness to Light, 48–49
  Moers Jazz Festival, 77
  My Dream Kitchen, 113
  Trio HLK, 87–89
Jewellery, 61, 142, 217

Kensington Town Hall, 2
Koppell, Anders, *Concerto for*
  Aluphone and Orchestra, 35

Lang, David, 57
Leadership, 111, 115, 127, 133, 139

Lee, Edeline, 136, 139, 140, *see also*
  Women in Power
Léonie Sonning Music Prize, 218–227
Listening, 46, 56, 69, 96, 159, 164–165,
    186, 192, 195, 212, 221, 229–232
  active, 60
  Deaf and Loud Symphonic
    Experience, 166–169
  ethical, 147
  Evelyn Glennie Foundation, 144,
    146, 175, 226
  Glennie on, 139, 160, 162–164,
    200, 225
  Love is Listening, 176–178
  processes, 21, 22, 96, 147, 155–159,
    161, 176
  through the body, 72, 76
  World Elephant Day, 183–185
Liszt, Franz, 29, 147, 194
Lloyd, Christopher, 50–51, 53, *see also*
  Sounds of Science
Lloyd Webber, Julian, 172–173
Love is Listening, 176–178

MacMillan, James, *Veni, Veni*
  Emmanuel, 25, 37–41, 170, 218,
    220
Mahler, Gustav, 29
Marc Brew Company, 84–86, *see also*
  Fusional Fragments
Masculine, 118, 127
  percussion as, 103–106
  stereotypes, 107, 117, 119, 141
Másson, Áskell, 116, 226, 228
  Fo(u)r Mallets, 56
  Konzertstück, 218, 219, 227
  Prim, 81, 170
McLeod, John, *Song of Dionysius,*
    24–25, 47–48
  Percussion Concerto, 25
Milhaud, Darius, *Concerto for*
  Percussion and Small
  Orchestra, 14
Moers Jazz Festival, 77

Monrad, Søren, 218, 219

Neuhaus, Max, 2, 17, 18
Nexus Percussion Ensemble, 66–67, 68, 149
Noise, 26, 33, 65, 72, 119, 148, 219
  Big Noise Project, 174
  emancipation of, 13, 30, 94
  percussion as, 1, 63
Non-Western, 13, 26, 36, 66, 148–149
Notation, 16, 57, 88, 113, 119, 120, 141, 217
  graphic, 15, 116

Olympics, 33, 139, 150, 152
  Opening Ceremony, 5, 35, 84, 179–182
O/Modernt, 93
One Day Band, 93, 96, *see also* Porter, Roly
Othering, 2, 102, 135, 147, 150, 162, 232

Partch, Harry, 31
Perahia, Murray, 9–10, *see also* Bartók, Béla
Percussion ensemble, 3–4, 15, 219, *see also* Cults and Nexus
Percussive Arts Society, 8, 30, 34, 207
Performance art, 18, 19, 41, 82, 113
  artist, 21, 78
Phibbs, Joseph, 26
Physicality, 22, 38, 41, 84, 119, 127, 141, 221
Playing Around the Office, 33, 35, 58–59, 95
Polar Music Prize, 159, 209–212, 217, 218
Porter, Roly, 93–97, *see also* One Day Band
Price, Dave, 197–202, *see also* Troilus and Cressida
Price, Paul, 4, 24–25
Primal, 1, 19, 84, 225
Psathas, John, 46, 48

Ptaszyńska, Marta, 116
  Drum of Orfeo, 127–134

Rachlin, Ann and Ezra, 155, 226
Recording, 56, 141, 144, 149
  albums, 5, 34, 44, 72, 88, 90, 94–97, 126, 198, 208
  artist, 69, 71, 216
  Glennie on, 70, 98, 133
  videos, 9
Reich, Steve, 40, 149
Riedelsheimer, Thomas, 5, 75–77, 163, *see also Touch the Sound*
Romantic, 1, 12, 18, 28–29, 62, 64, 67, 105–106, 148
Rouse, Christopher, 170
Royal Academy of Music, 9, 26, 30, 219, 226
  admission to, 5–6, 18, 162, 171, 210, 225
Royal College of Music, 5, 8, 170
Royal Shakespeare Company, 35, 36, 196–197, *see also Troilus and Cressida*
Rud, Maria, 79–84, *see also* Animotion
Russolo, Luigi, 30, *see also* Futurism

Safri Duo, 218, 225
Savery, Uffe, 225–226
Schick, Steven, 46, 170
Schulkowsky, Robyn, 36
Sexism, 145
  and ageism, 143
  casual, 101, 103, 106–107
Shadow Behind the Iron Sun, 34, 62, 70–75, 77, 87, 133
Sheppard, Philip, 80, 81, 85, 94
Simtak, 31, 33–34, 70, 71
Sistema, 174
Solti, George, 9–10, *see also* Bartók, Béla
Sound creator, 4, 11, 56, 100, 120, 188, 231, 233

Glennie as, 2, 7, 44, 45, 50, 58, 60, 70, 78, 99, 101, 115, 132, 147, 192, 195, 211, 217, 229, 230
Glennie on, 69, 160
Spitfire Audio, 99
Stereotypes, 100
  ageist, 143
  disability, 150, 153, 154, 159, 162
  gender, 102, 104, 106, 107, 111, 115, 119, 135
  percussion, 20, 148
Stockhausen, Karlheinz, *Zyklus*, 15, 17
Storyteller, 13, 23, 50, 219
Stravinsky, Igor, 84, 136, 218
  L'Histoire du Soldat, 13–14
Synaesthesia, 82, 128–129

Teach the World to Listen, 101, 146, 147, 184, 193, 230, 233
TED Talk, 5, 147, 160, 162–163, 171
Tenney, James, *Having Never Written a Note for Percussion*, 82
Theatricality, 19, 21, 44, 46, 85, 130, 133, 167, 224
The Sugar Factory, 77, 87
Thompson, Caroline, 159, 212–214, 216, 217
Touch the Sound, 5, 75–77, 81, 88, 160, 163–164
Tower, Joan, 47
Transcription, 24, 80
Trio HLK, 87–93, 187, 208
Troilus and Cressida, 35, 196–203
TROMP Percussion Festival, 74
Turnage, Mark Anthony, 27

Underworld (band), 182

Varèse, Edgard, *Ionisation*, 4
Verde, Michael, 176, *see also Love is Listening*
Virtuosity, 18, 19, 25, 42, 44, 68, 69, 74, 78, 195, 229
Glennie and, 21, 26, 120, 156, 211, 220
Glennie on, 42, 43

Wagner, Richard, 83
Wallace, Stewart, 33, 204
Waterphone, 23, 98
  Animotion, 82
  Darkness to Light, 48
  Evelyn Glennie Hyperstellar Waterphone, 36
  Fusional Fragments, 85–86
  One Day Band, 94–98
  Trio HLK, 91
  Troilus and Cressida, 201
Western Art Music, 4, 12, 13, 25, 28, 29, 83, 102, 105, 107, 127, 150, 152
  canon, 101, 104, 172
  history, 2, 18, 45, 64, 148, 194
Wigmore Hall, 74
Wolfe, Julia, 46, 55
World Elephant Day, 182–185

Xenakis, Iannis, 15, 16, 18, 170

Yi, Chen, 56, 152

Živković, Nebojša Jovan, 116–119